Hybrid Rule and State Formation

Neoliberalism has been the reigning ideology of our era. For the past four decades, almost every real-world event of any consequence has been traced to the supposedly omnipresent influence of neoliberalism. Instead, this book argues that state power across the world has actually grown in scope and reach.

The authors in this volume contest the view that the past four decades have been marked by the diminution of the state in the face of neoliberalism. They argue instead that we are witnessing a new phase of state formation, which revolves around hybrid rule—that is, a more expansive form of state formation that works through privatization and seeks pacification and depoliticization as instrumental to enhancing state power. Contributors argue that the process of hybridization, and hybrid rule point towards a convergence on a more authoritarian capitalist regime type, possibly, but not necessarily, more closely aligned with the Beijing model—one towards which even the United States, with its penchant for surveillance and discipline, appears to be moving.

This volume sheds new light on evolving public-private relations, and the changing nature of power and political authority in the 21st century and will be of interest to students and scholars of IPE, international relations and political theory.

Shelley L. Hurt is Associate Professor at the California Polytechnic State University, San Luis Obispo, USA.

Ronnie D. Lipschutz is Professor of Politics and Provost of College Eight at the University of California, Santa Cruz, USA.

RIPE Series in Global Political Economy

Series Editors: Jacqueline Best (University of Ottawa, Canada), Ian Bruff (Manchester University, UK), Paul Langley (Durham University, UK) and Anna Leander (Copenhagen Business School, Denmark)

Formerly edited by Leonard Seabrooke (Copenhagen Business School, Denmark), Randall Germain (Carleton University, Canada), Rorden Wilkinson (University of Manchester, UK), Otto Holman (University of Amsterdam), Marianne Marchand (Universidad de las Américas-Puebla), Henk Overbeek (Free University, Amsterdam) and Marianne Franklin (Goldsmiths, University of London, UK)

The RIPE series editorial board are:

Mathias Albert (Bielefeld University, Germany), Mark Beeson (University of Birmingham, UK), A. Claire Cutler (University of Victoria, Canada), Marianne Franklin (Goldsmiths, University of London, UK), Randall Germain (Carleton University, Canada) Stephen Gill (York University, Canada), Jeffrey Hart (Indiana University, USA), Eric Helleiner (Trent University, Canada), Otto Holman (University of Amsterdam, the Netherlands), Marianne H. Marchand (Universidad de las Américas-Puebla, Mexico), Craig N. Murphy (Wellesley College, USA), Robert O'Brien (McMaster University, Canada), Henk Overbeek (Vrije Universiteit, the Netherlands), Anthony Payne (University of Sheffield, UK), V. Spike Peterson (University of Arizona, USA) and Rorden Wilkinson (University of Sussex, UK).

This series, published in association with the Review of International Political Economy, provides a forum for current and interdisciplinary debates in international political economy. The series aims to advance understanding of the key issues in the global political economy, and to present innovative analyses of emerging topics. The titles in the series focus on three broad themes:

- the structures, processes and actors of contemporary global transformations
- the changing forms taken by governance, at scales from the local and everyday to the global and systemic
- the inseparability of economic from political, social and cultural questions, including resistance, dissent and social movements.

The RIPE Series in Global Political Economy aims to address the needs of students and teachers. Titles include:

Transnational Classes and International Relations
Kees van der Pijl

Globalization and Governance
Edited by Aseem Prakash and Jeffrey A. Hart

Nation-States and Money
The past, present and future of national currencies
Edited by Emily Gilbert and Eric Helleiner

Gender and Global Restructuring
Sightings, sites and resistances
Edited by Marianne H. Marchand and Anne Sisson Runyan

The Global Political Economy of Intellectual Property Rights
The new enclosures?
Christopher May

Global Political Economy
Contemporary theories
Edited by Ronen Palan

Ideologies of Globalization
Contending visions of a new world order
Mark Rupert

The Clash within Civilisations
Coming to terms with cultural conflicts
Dieter Senghaas

Capitalist Restructuring, Globalisation and the Third Way
Lessons from the Swedish model
J. Magnus Ryner

Transnational Capitalism and the Struggle over European Integration
Bastiaan van Apeldoorn

World Financial Orders
An historical international political economy
Paul Langley

Global Unions?
Theory and strategies of organized labour in the global political economy
Edited by Jeffrey Harrod and Robert O'Brien

Political Economy of a Plural World
Critical reflections on power, morals and civilizations
Robert Cox with Michael Schechter

The Changing Politics of Finance in Korea and Thailand
From deregulation to debacle
Xiaoke Zhang

Anti-Immigrantism in Western Democracies
Statecraft, desire and the politics of exclusion
Roxanne Lynn Doty

The Political Economy of European Employment
European integration and the transnationalization of the (un)employment question
Edited by Henk Overbeek

A Critical Rewriting of Global Political Economy
Integrating reproductive, productive and virtual economies
V. Spike Peterson

International Trade and Developing Countries
Bargaining coalitions in the GATT & WTO
Amrita Narlikar

Rethinking Global Political Economy
Emerging issues, unfolding odysseys
Edited by Mary Ann Tétreault, Robert A. Denemark, Kenneth P. Thomas and Kurt Burch

Global Institutions and Development
Framing the world?
Edited by Morten Bøås and Desmond McNeill

Contesting Globalization
Space and place in the world economy
André C. Drainville

The Southern Cone Model
The political economy of regional capitalist development in Latin America
Nicola Phillips

The Idea of Global Civil Society
Politics and ethics of a globalizing era
Edited by Randall D. Germain and Michael Kenny

Global Institutions, Marginalization, and Development
Craig N. Murphy

Governing Financial Globalization
International political economy and multi-level governance
Edited by Andrew Baker, David Hudson and Richard Woodward

Critical Theories, International Relations and 'the Anti-Globalisation Movement'
The politics of global resistance
Edited by Catherine Eschle and Bice Maiguashca

Resisting Intellectual Property
Debora J. Halbert

Globalization, Governmentality, and Global Politics
Regulation for the rest of us?
Ronnie D. Lipschutz, with James K. Rowe

Neoliberal Hegemony
A global critique
Edited by Dieter Plehwe, Bernhard Walpen and Gisela Neunhöffer

Images of Gramsci
Connections and contentions in political theory and international relations
Edited by Andreas Bieler and Adam David Morton

Global Standards of Market Civilization
Edited by Brett Bowden and Leonard Seabrooke

Beyond Globalization
Capitalism, territoriality and the international relations of modernity
Hannes Lacher

Global Public Policy
Business and the countervailing
powers of civil society
Edited by Karsten Ronit

**The Transnational Politics of
Corporate Governance Regulation**
*Edited by Henk Overbeek, Bastiaan
van Apeldoorn and Andreas Nölke*

**Critical Perspectives on
Global Governance**
Rights and regulation in
governing regimes
Jean Grugel and Nicola Piper

**National Currencies
and Globalization**
Endangered specie?
Paul Bowles

**Conflicts in Environmental
Regulation and the
Internationalization of the State**
Contested terrains
*Ulrich Brand, Christoph Görg,
Joachim Hirsch and Markus Wissen*

Beyond States and Markets
The challenges of
social reproduction
*Edited by Isabella Bakker and
Rachel Silvey*

**Governing International
Labour Migration**
Current issues, challenges
and dilemmas
*Edited by Christina Gabriel and
Hélène Pellerin*

The Industrial Vagina
The political economy of the global
sex trade
Sheila Jeffreys

**The Child in International
Political Economy**
A place at the table
Alison M.S. Watson

Capital as Power
A study of order and creorder
*Jonathan Nitzan and
Shimshon Bichler*

**Global Citizenship and the Legacy
of Empire**
Marketing development
April Biccum

**The Global Political Economy of
Intellectual Property Rights,
Second Edition**
The new enclosures
Christopher May

**Corporate Power and Ownership in
Contemporary Capitalism**
The politics of resistance
and domination
Susanne Soederberg

Savage Economics
Wealth, poverty and the temporal
walls of capitalism
*David L. Blaney and
Naeem Inayatullah*

Cultural Political Economy
*Edited by Jacqueline Best and
Matthew Paterson*

**Development, Sexual Rights and
Global Governance**
Resisting global power
Amy Lind

Cosmopolitanism and Global Financial Reform
A pragmatic approach to the Tobin Tax
James Brassett

Gender and Global Restructuring
Second Edition
Sightings, sites and resistances
Edited by Marianne H. Marchand and Anne Sisson Runyan

Variegated Neoliberalism
EU varieties of capitalism and international political economy
Huw Macartney

The Politics of European Competition Regulation
A critical political economy perspective
Hubert Buch-Hansen and Angela Wigger

The Political Economy of Global Remittances
Gender and governmentality
Rahel Kunz

A Critical History of the Economy
On the birth of the national and international economies
Ryan Walter

The International Political Economy of Transition
Neoliberal hegemony and Eastern Central Europe's transformation
Stuart Shields

The Global Political Economy of Trade Protectionism and Liberalization
Trade reform and economic adjustment in textiles and clothing
Tony Heron

Transnational Financial Associations and the Governance of Global Finance
Assembling wealth and power
Heather McKeen-Edwards and Tony Porter

The Capitalist Mode of Power
Critical engagements with the power theory of value
Edited by Tim Di Muzio

The Making of Modern Finance
Liberal governance and the gold standard
Samuel Knafo

The State of Copyright
The complex relationships of cultural creation in a globalized world
Debora J. Halbert

Transnational Financial Regulation after the Crisis
Edited by Tony Porter

The Political Economy of Global Capitalism and Crisis
Bill Dunn

Global Capitalism
Selected essays
Hugo Radice

Debtfare States and the Poverty Industry
Money, discipline and the surplus population
Susanne Soederberg

Currency Challenge
The euro, the dollar and the global financial
Miguel Otero-Iglesias

Fringe Finance
Crossing and contesting the borders of global capital
Rob Aitken

Asymmetric Crisis in Europe and Possible Futures
Critical political economy and post-Keynesian perspectives
Edited by Johannes Jäger and Elisabeth Springler

Hybrid Rule and State Formation
Public–private power in the 21st century
Edited by Shelley L. Hurt and Ronnie D. Lipschutz

Hybrid Rule and State Formation
Public–private power in the 21st century

**Edited by
Shelley L. Hurt and Ronnie D. Lipschutz**

LONDON AND NEW YORK

First published 2016
by Routledge
2 Park Square, Milton Park, Abingdon, Oxon OX14 4RN

and by Routledge
711 Third Avenue, New York, NY 10017

Routledge is an imprint of the Taylor & Francis Group, an informa business

© 2016 selection and editorial material, Shelley L. Hurt and Ronnie D. Lipschutz; individual chapters, the contributors

The right of Shelley L. Hurt and Ronnie D. Lipschutz to be identified as author of the editorial material, and of the individual authors as authors of their contributions, has been asserted by them in accordance with sections 77 and 78 of the Copyright, Designs and Patents Act 1988.

All rights reserved. No part of this book may be reprinted or reproduced or utilised in any form or by any electronic, mechanical, or other means, now known or hereafter invented, including photocopying and recording, or in any information storage or retrieval system, without permission in writing from the publishers.

Trademark notice: Product or corporate names may be trademarks or registered trademarks, and are used only for identification and explanation without intent to infringe.

British Library Cataloguing in Publication Data
A catalogue record for this book is available from the British Library

Library of Congress Cataloging in Publication Data
Hybrid rule and state formation : public-private power in the 21st century / edited by Shelley L. Hurt and Ronnie D. Lipschutz.
    pages cm. – (RIPE series in global political economy)
   1. Public-private sector cooperation–Political aspects. 2. State, The. 3. Political science–Economic aspects. I. Hurt, Shelley L. II. Lipschutz, Ronnie D.
    HD3871.H83 2016
    322'.3–dc23
                 2015008222

ISBN: 978-1-138-79911-0 (hbk)
ISBN: 978-1-315-75126-9 (ebk)

Typeset in Times New Roman
by Taylor & Francis Books

Printed and bound in Great Britain by
TJ International Ltd, Padstow, Cornwall

For Aristide R. Zolberg. Who taught legions of students about the meaning of state formation in history and theory.

Contents

List of figures	xv
Preface	xvi
Acknowledgement	xix
List of contributors	xx
Introduction: Hybrid rule and state formation SHELLEY L. HURT AND RONNIE D. LIPSCHUTZ	1

PART I
Analytics 11

1 Bringing politics back in 13
SHELLEY L. HURT AND RONNIE D. LIPSCHUTZ

2 Roving elites and sedentary subjects: The hybridized origins of the state 39
IVER B. NEUMANN AND OLE JACOB SENDING

3 Neoliberal bureaucracy as an expression of hybrid rule 59
BÉATRICE HIBOU

4 Post-Fordist hybridization: A historical-materialist approach to two modes of state transformation 79
ULRICH BRAND

PART II
Empirics 99

5 What's at stake in the privatization debate?: Enclosing the public domain through hybrid rule 101
SHELLEY L. HURT

xiv *Contents*

6 Sovereign wealth funds and varieties of hybridization   123
   HERMAN M. SCHWARTZ

7 Seen and unseen: Hybrid rule in international security   143
   ANNA LEANDER

8 World war infinity: Security through economy, economy
   through security   160
   RONNIE D. LIPSCHUTZ

9 Biology as opportunity: Hybrid rule from a molecular point
   of view   175
   REBECCA J. HESTER

PART III
Reflections   193

10 Hybrid rule and state formation: Some preliminary thoughts,
   arguments and research items   195
   SHELLEY L. HURT AND RONNIE D. LIPSCHUTZ

   Bibliography   203
   Index   234

List of figures

1.1 Funding for R&D 21
1.2 The economics and politics of science 22

Preface

This volume emerges from the bowels of the National Archives and Records Administration in College Park, MD when I began conducting dissertation research in the Nixon Presidential Materials Staff in 2004. I traveled frequently to the National Archives while living in residence in Charlottesville, Virginia on a fellowship with the Miller Center of Public Affairs between 2003 and 2004. I also had the pleasure that year of asking Ronnie to serve as my "Dream Mentor" as part of the Miller Center's fellowship program. During that year of archival exploration, I read thousands of pages of documents on the Nixon administration's ambitious efforts to remake the domestic political economy at home and relaunch U.S. foreign policy abroad. In particular, the archival records show Nixon administration officials rethinking the deployment of state power to outwit domestic adversaries and international competitors through the application and popularization of "reprivatization" policies. Foremost among the administration plans for promoting "reprivatization" was not only jumpstarting the sagging economy but also centralizing political authority and decision making in the midst of profound social unrest and new Cold War challenges. Reprivatization then served political goals more than economic ones.

The implications of using the private sector to enhance rather than diminish American state power became clearer as my research focused on the high stakes of Nixon's 1969 decision to convert the nation's Biological Warfare Program into the Biological Research Program. While this episode is rarely studied and little understood among political scientists and historians alike, it became apparent as I buried myself in the materials that the conversion process represented a critical juncture in American political history with profound implications for world politics. Most interestingly, President Nixon and administration officials conceived of the private sector as an extension of U.S. state power as they carefully negotiated a way to carry out the conversion process during détente and arms control negotiations. Among the innovative strategies for accomplishing this goal, the administration launched a series of ambitious industrial policies that would ensure reprivatization became a new governing credo. To draw attention to these plans, Nixon officials held a series of high-profile events in 1971 and 1972, such as the White House Conference on the Industrial World Ahead: A Look at Business in 1990. Therein, a senior unofficial advisor to the Nixon White House, Dr. Simon Ramo, vice chairman of the board and chairman of the executive committee of TRW, Inc., who later received the Medal of Freedom from President Reagan in 1983, delivered a speech where he previewed a new era: "Our hybrid economy, part free enterprise and part governmentally controlled, will take on a new form constituting a virtual Social-Industrial Complex by 1990, this developing government-business teaming greatly influenced by resource and technology matters." Our inspiration, so to speak, comes from this prescient speech and fertile historical moment when the American state shifted gears, setting the country on both an altered political economy and national security path toward one defined by hybrid rule.

My investigative journey led to an invitation to present my research findings on "An Underground Arms Race: Biodefense Policy in Historical and Contemporary Perspective" at the Center for Global, International & Regional Studies, UC Santa Cruz in 2005 and then to present my research findings on a panel at the International Studies Association (ISA) Convention in Hawaii in 2006. The next year I received the Carl Beck Award from the ISA for a paper entitled, "Patent Law, Biodefense, and the National Security State, 1945–1972." Therein, I presented one of my most surprising and controversial research findings, namely that the "private sector serves as a shield of the national security state" more often that scholars recognize or Americans admit. The potential significance of this realization and its relationship to a hybrid future, where public accountability and democratic deliberation are severely circumscribed, led Ronnie to suggest we pursue the topic in more depth. Little did we know at the time that controversies surrounding Blackwater, the National Security Agency's partnering with AT&T, and the Edward Snowden revelations, to name just a few, would spotlight the American state's updating and retrofitting the military-industrial complex for a new age.

The journey to complete this book spans five long years from the time we held our first workshop in New York City at the Annual International Studies Association conference with generous support from a Venture Capital Grants in the spring of 2009 to our finalizing the project this year. We've benefited tremendously from the initiative of our colleagues who assisted with raising funds for us to debate our ideas in person in Sydney, Australia, and Paris, France. We also came together during ISA conference proceedings in New Orleans and Montreal. Through it all, the participants and contributors to this volume have taken the ideas seriously and engaged in lively and stimulating debates. Those spirited debates infused the development of this project after we were privileged to receive the participation of "A-list" scholars from around the world and from a variety of theoretical and methodological perspectives. The stature of the senior contributors to the volume meant the stakes were high. Nevertheless, together we cultivated a respect for intellectual diversity while recognizing that ideas matter because they shape perceptions of reality and influence political action. We hope this book provides an xviii *Preface*

opening to challenge long-held assumptions from a variety of viewpoints in order to shed light on this critical issue in world politics while broadening and deepening this on-going debate.

We are grateful for the incisive comments we received from three anonymous referees who contributed significantly to the final manuscript. We also want to thank the RIPE Series editors, at Routledge, such as Jacqueline Best and Nicola Parkin, with special thanks to Peter Harris, who assisted us kindly with every step of the process. We are also grateful to all of the many participants who generously attended our many roundtables and panels at the Annual International Studies Association conferences over the past five years and who helped us to sharpen our focus. Most notably, Ronan Polan deserves special thanks for pushing us to foreground the issue of state formation in our larger analysis about hybrid rule and global convergence.

Shelley L. Hurt
April 2015

Acknowledgement

This project and book have been supported by a number of funding sources, including the Workshop Grants Program of the International Studies Association through a Venture Capital Grant, the France-Berkeley Fund at the University of California, Berkeley, the Academy of the Social Sciences in Australia, and the School of Social and Political Sciences and the Institute for the Social Sciences at the University of Sydney. The editors and contributors wish to thank Béatrice Hibou and Linda Weiss for their generous assistance in securing financial support for the multiple meetings the contributors held over the past five years. The editors wish to thank all of the contributors for their dedication to the project and for their patience in seeing the book to completion.

List of contributors

Ulrich Brand is Professor of International Politics and Head of the Institute of Political Science at the University of Vienna, Vienna.

Rebecca J. Hester is Assistant Professor of Social Medicine and Director of the Social Medicine Track in the Institute for the Medical Humanities at the University of Texas, Medical Branch, Galveston, Texas.

Beatrice Hibou is Director of Research at the French National Centre for Scientific Research, Science-Po, Paris.

Shelley L. Hurt is Associate Professor of Political Science in the Department of Political Science at the California Polytechnic State University, San Luis Obispo, California.

Anna Leander is Professor with Special Responsibilities in the Department of Management, Politics, and Philosophy at the Copenhagen Business School, Copenhagen.

Ronnie D. Lipschutz is Professor of Politics and Provost of College Eight at the University of California, Santa Cruz, California.

Iver B. Neumann is the Montague Burton Professor at the London School of Economics, London.

Herman M. Schwartz is Professor of Politics in the Department of Politics at the University of Virginia, Charlottesville, Virginia.

Ole Jacob Sending is the Research Director at the Norwegian Institute of International Affairs, Department of International Politics, Oslo.

Introduction
Hybrid rule and state formation

Shelley L. Hurt and Ronnie D. Lipschutz

One of the greatest political surprises after the tumultuous first decade of the 21st century is the enduring policy prescription of privatization. Despite the 2008 financial crisis and the serious scandals surrounding private security contractors, such as the company formerly known as Blackwater in Iraq, privatization remains a favored policy ideal across the political spectrum for all that ails contemporary capitalist economies and the liberal democratic systems that undergird them.[1] Such robust adherence to a major tenet of market fundamentalism calls out for explanation because in practice this policy ideal has counterintuitively led to substantial growth in state power, rather than its diminution, as is commonly believed.

In this book we examine this puzzle by revisiting the historical causes that led to privatization as a preferred policy ideal. We seek to understand the political forces that initiated privatization as public policy in order to rearrange the puzzle pieces, and thus create a new image, and hence, a new narrative about the growth and resilience of state power. We explain how and why these public sector forces sought novel ways of deploying the private sector to pursue national goals, shield elite activities, and enhance control of the social order. This book argues that pursuing an alternative narrative about the sources of privatization is an urgent matter; the implications of our arguments suggest that electoral representation and democracy are at stake.

The research question animating this investigation asks: Why has privatization come to be regarded as the preferred public policy prescription in domestic and international affairs? For three decades, social scientists have debated the rise of privatization as the main plank of a resurgent *laissez faire* doctrine, one attributed to President Reagan and Prime Minister Thatcher, both of whom broke from the Keynesian post-WWII paradigm of economic governance. The dominant explanation for the move toward privatization has been neoliberalism.[2] Whether proponents or detractors, such claims have come in three variants. The first is based on the ideology of equating market mechanisms with natural laws. Privatization then supposedly emerges as a result of the benefits it confers from strengthening the hand of the market over the state and freeing individuals from control by the latter. This version aligns with the so-called neoconservative movement. The second is based on the liberal economic principle that market mechanisms are more efficient than public ones in providing services and in ensuring cost savings. This version aligns with mainstream centrists who propose widespread efficiency gains from privatization. The third version of neoliberalism is based on the Marxian view that corporations control the public policymaking process and are systematically impoverishing the polity. This version can be represented by either instrumental or structural claims, but in both the practice of privatization represents capital gaining the upper hand over the state. In all three accounts, the state drops out of the equation or is at least diminished substantially as a power and a player.

Yet, as a number of chapters in this book illustrate, we are confronted increasingly with many real-world examples of privatization that have failed to provide the economic benefits or costs claimed by its adherents and detractors. Instead, the process produces a wholly different set of outcomes than those expected. Indeed, privatization's very mixed record suggests quite strongly that conventional explanations based on support or critique of neoliberalism shed little light on the nature of political power today or how it is being deployed.[3] A particularly provocative consequence of this process—documented in several chapters in this volume—is the way in which national security considerations move to the foreground in explaining a large fraction of instances of privatization, replacing the ideological and economic considerations enumerated above and helping to shield from public view our awareness of how security and economy work together.

In asking why privatization has come to pervade *public* life, the contributors to this volume seek to uncover political patterns and processes that are hidden or obscured from view. The proposition we advance here centers on the term *hybrid rule*. While seemingly faddish, inasmuch as the word "hybrid" has come to be associated with everything from cars to scientific discoveries, *hybrid rule* is a political concept that encompasses the implications of both privatization and so-called public-private partnerships in newfound ways. More specifically, we define *hybrid rule* as follows:

> Hybrid rule results from a set of practices deployed by political elites that rely on the private sector to shield national security activities by expanding state power while constraining democratic accountability. This hybrid rule strategy seeks to safeguard the state's legitimacy through valorization of the market as a primary mechanism in pursuit of myriad political objectives.

In contrast to studies of international regimes, for instance, which refer mostly to real-world, tangible institutions in space and time, *hybrid rule* is a process whereby public and private sectors, encompassing states, businesses and even civil society, converge in new and unanticipated ways (Krasner 1983). Most importantly, hybridization, the activity of implementing *hybrid rule*, describes the metamorphosis of the state as it contracts with and then deploys the private sector on behalf of the former's objectives. To put this activity another way, *hybrid rule* emerges as the state harnesses the private sector and generates a new pattern of state–capital or government–business relations that redefine our understanding of political authority and power as well as the boundaries between public and private within contemporary Western traditions and societies.[4] We hope that the specificity, yet breadth, of these definitional boundaries will spark a new research agenda into this alternative causal account of the rise and consequences of privatization.

We suggest that the chapters in this volume highlight an historical shift in state formation based on a newly emerging form of political organization in the 21st century, with far-reaching implications for the nature and exercise of political authority and power in the contemporary world. Suffice it to say, the account of historical change in state–capital relations offered here challenges the three variants of neoliberal-based frameworks that purport to explain the rise of privatization and the emergence of *hybrid rule*. Our contribution to the debate on privatization revolves around three organizing principles that loosely comprise our explanatory framework and buttress the concept (and practices) of *hybrid rule*. These principles center on first, periodization, a resetting of the conventional historical clock of the onset of privatization to the late 1960s to identify the causal origins of privatization; second, politics, an emphasis on the causal influence of the state and political elites on privatization with particular attention paid to political struggle over the issue of *political legitimacy*; and third, convergence, an argument that counters the commonly held post-Cold War assumption that the world is converging on a liberal capitalist regime type based on the American model, instead demonstrating that privatization and *hybrid rule* are circumscribing democratic values and practices. We suggest that this development points, instead, toward a convergence on a more authoritarian and managerial capitalist regime type, one toward which the United States risks becoming more closely aligned with the Beijing "model."

We do believe, with Marx and others, that the past does not wholly determine the future but that we are not entirely free of what has happened in the past. We do not believe, in line with those searching for law-like logics in human behaviors, that social organizations and human behaviors can be reliably explained and predicted. We do not eschew the importance of material factors, such as economy, technology and geopolitics, in accounting for state formation and development, but we also do not fall into idealism, either, putting the burden of change on ideas and imaginaries. We seek to understand what has happened, is happening, and might happen in and to our world. To this end, we have encouraged methodological pluralism and innovation from the contributors to the volume, in the hope of speaking across differences even as we address the same phenomena. The theories and arguments that dominate international relations and political economy remain important, but they are incomplete and not up to accounting for that world. Someone, we believe, has to do work on the margins.

Contributors to this volume

In the interest of motivating scholarly attention and debate, as well as cross-fertilization among American, comparative, and international politics, our approach to the puzzle of privatization is methodologically and intellectually pluralist. Contributors to the book utilize differing and sometimes contrasting ontologies, epistemologies and even methods, but all agree that hybrid rule, as we have described and explained it, is a new or distinct phenomenon. The volume embraces the shared theme of trying to understand the tendency of the public sector to grow even as it pursues privatization policies. It also shares the theme of exposing how these practices depoliticize democratic societies. By re-historicizing privatization at various starting points, the contributors offer a more complex understanding of its dynamics and of its consequences. They have also chosen to focus on different parts of the "elephant," so to speak, in order to elucidate the extent to which hybridization is taking place. The scale of their focus ranges from the molecular (in terms of biotechnology) to the body (in terms of its shaping) to the global (in terms of system and structure), facilitating illumination of the relationships between these notionally distinct levels. Such "analytical eclecticism" (Sil and Katzenstein 2010) offers, we believe, a way of communicating across languages and approaches in ways that permit greater specification of the real-world puzzle we want to solve—that after at least three decades of supposed privatization, the state has gotten significantly larger and more powerful in every measureable way—and how we might go about solving it. Not every reader will agree with either the arguments or conclusions offered here, but this study should be regarded as the launch of a new research agenda, rather than the concluding words on an old one.

The contributions to this volume are presented in three parts: Analytics, Empirics, and Reflections. "Analytics" offers four distinct theoretical excursions into the organization and motivations behind the phenomenon of hybrid rule. These different perspectives serve to entice scholars to research these developments from their unique vantage points. Together we hope and expect that the kaleidoscope of viewpoints sheds colorful bright lights on the seemingly opaque and complicated dynamics of hybrid rule. In the first chapter in this section, "Bringing Politics Back In," Shelley L. Hurt and Ronnie D. Lipschutz argue for a more detailed examination and account of the rise of privatization and hybrid rule to develop a set of *political* arguments and explanations for these phenomena. This examination provides the cornerstone for the volume's inspiration while not detracting from the equally valuable contributions and insights of the other three chapters in the "Analytics" section, which all aim to frame this new research agenda surrounding hybrid rule in particular ways. We do not doubt that many will disagree with and attack our propositions and arguments (indeed, we hope that is the case). Some will point to historical precedents for hybrid rule (e.g. royal patents and monopolies) and minor quibbles (e.g. the notional division between public and private). Others will prioritize the economic side of the equation. Anticipating such criticisms, we note in Chapter 1, with a few exceptions, we prefer that the focus on hybrid rule centers on the post-World War II period and, especially, the past 40 years in the American context. We concede that accumulation is important, but it is part of hybrid rule and not driven merely by capital and capitalism. And while the boundary between "public" and "private" has always been problematic, that history is not a major concern here.

Chapter One argues that hybrid rule's historical origins lay squarely in the legitimacy crisis of the 1960s when three concurrent developments caused U.S. political elites to turn to the private sector for cover once public authority became increasingly contested. This chapter by Hurt and Lipschutz put forth their explanation for why privatization policies became a priority for America's political elites during this tumultuous period in American history. The growing reliance on and valorization of the private sector provided political elites with an alibi, so to speak, in both domestic and international fora. Hence, the chapter explores the evolution of an elite counterattack, which the Nixon administration initiated and then unfolded throughout the 1970s, cementing a new privatization doctrine in policies and ideas that would persist and accelerate for decades to come. Consequently, Chapter One situates the rise of hybrid rule within the domain of political elites in a concrete time and space, suggesting that the dominant economic explanations for the rise of privatization fail to take political and national security considerations into account.

In Neumann and Sending's Chapter 2, they propose that hybridization can only exist in Western societies where the separation of the political and economic became an exercise of "boundary drawings" by the powerful. Hence, these authors stress along constructivist lines that "a relational understanding of the social" reflects the larger theoretical point that boundaries constitute entities in the first place and not the other way around. Their chapter highlights the weak Western understanding of the state in contrast with Russian state formation, which penetrated every crevice of society, deepening individuals' interaction with and understanding of the state in modern life. These authors' case study of the Russian experience enables them to take a longer historical view of the public–private divide that animates debates in the West but remains meaningless in much of the East. A core insight of this valuable chapter notes that state formation developed from normative to sedentary politics, reshaping political behavior and sensibilities toward passivity in contemporary times.

In Chapter 3, Hibou retains the historical timeline proposed in Chapter One while advancing a novel aspect of privatization that remains obscured from public view. Her chapter recognizes that hybrid rule is a political project whose goal is to restore or enhance state authority and sovereignty through the practice of private sector delegation; however, she explores the concept of "neoliberal bureaucratization" to show that hybrid rule operates through various societal intermediaries that are not directly related to the state.

Controversially and interestingly, Hibou argues that neoliberal bureaucratization results as much from non-political behavior and logic of action as from overt political deeds. Her primary focus in Chapter 3 centers on the production and dissemination of norms in the neoliberal era, particularly from the 1970s onward, wherein "a set of bureaucratic and legal rules" came to pervade everyday life in profound ways. She examines the International Standards Organization as a case study to "exemplif[y] a paradox" whereby "a process of normalization" of these bureaucratic norms and rules has overtaken developed and developing societies alike. The one area she differs with Hurt and Lipschutz's chapter stems from the "question of intentionality" since, according to her view, Max Weber's broader conceptualization of bureaucracy accounted for big business not just state apparatuses. Nevertheless, in criticizing the limits of the "new public management" literature, Hibou emphasizes "neoliberal bureaucracy is one of the strongest expressions of hybrid rule that characterizes the current political situation." Her chapter adds valuable insights into the embedded dimensions of hybridization.

The final chapter in the "Analytics" section, Chapter 4 by Brand, brings an historical materialist analytical frame to bear on the question of privatization by focusing on two dimensions of hybridization: 1) public–private and 2) national–international. This dynamic perspective provides Brand with the ability to examine the changes in state formation since the 1970s with a critical lens, albeit one that hones closely to Nicos Poulantzas and Antonio Gramsci for insights into the state as a contested social relation. In particular, Brand argues that "hybridization and hybrid rule also reflect shifts in power techniques and technologies," which takes on added significance in Lipschutz's Chapter 8 about the National Security Agency as well as others within the new purview of the national security state in the 21st century. These new state tools, according to Brand, illicit a new dimension in the post-Fordist era that signaled the onset of the "neoliberal imperial state project." Brand suggests that hybridization is a direct outgrowth and "consequence of social conflict," which reflects a "rescaling of politics" in the contemporary era. He cautions us to distinguish between singular hegemonic states and hegemonic constellations in our analysis of hybridization as governance.

In turning to the "Empirics" section of the volume, several authors scrutinize various empirical studies, broadly conceived, to examine the scope and breadth of hybrid rule's impact on politics and society. These empirical explorations include analyses about biotechnology, sovereign wealth funds, military contractors, and surveillance technologies to shed light on the manifestation of hybrid rule in real-world practice. The first chapter in this section, Chapter 5 by Hurt, draws upon newly declassified archival material from Presidents Nixon and Ford administrations to show how the historical origins of hybrid rule can be linked to the revolution in the biological sciences in the 1960s and 1970s. Hurt argues that the stakes of this scientific revolution had implications for Cold War tensions with the Soviet Union as well as with domestic anti-war constituents, such as students and scientists. The archival record demonstrates that Nixon and Ford administration officials were keenly aware of and concerned about public access to state secrets surrounding these science and technology developments, which prompted them to use the private sector in innovative ways. Hurt emphasizes that these initiatives in public–private relations point to the establishment of hybridization policies and practices that would evolve into hybrid rule in the present day.

Chapter 6 by Schwartz focuses on the recent re-emergence of sovereign wealth funds (SWFs) as a case study for exploring an aspect of hybrid rule and state formation. The chapter explores three distinct kinds of sovereign wealth funds to define and understand them in more depth. In challenging the conventional wisdom about SWFs, Schwartz argues that SWFs are more varied than most analyses suggest, which tends to "homogenize SWFs" rather than recognize their distinctiveness in various parts of the world. Importantly, Schwartz notes that SWFs have been around since 1953 but they existed beneath the radar, only recently re-emerging in the contemporary era. SWFs now have taken on three distinct forms: developmental, pension, and patrimonial. These three types demonstrate how secrecy and depoliticization are both expressions of power that SWFs exercise in whatever context they take root. Hence, from Norway to Singapore, SWFs display a few core characteristics that illustrate their relation to the contemporary "hybrid state." Schwartz emphasizes "privatization or the delegation of tasks to the private sector is a way for the state to regain autonomy and create a social base of support for itself." Chapter 6 provides an important set of insights into the practical, real-world machinations of SWFs in the 21st century.

Chapter 7 examines private security contractors as a clear empirical expression of hybrid rule or what Leander refers to as "hybridity." Leander looks at two prongs of this modern-day phenomena that are both essential aspects of influence on society. First, Leander explores how security can be seen and unseen in these public–private guises, obscuring its penetration of society as well as the fetishization surrounding it. Second, Leander reveals how the hybridity surrounding private security becomes its source of normalization, reinforcing its power within liberal capitalist states. These two intertwined prongs of hybridity have allowed military markets to become more pronounced in conflict activities of various kinds. In raising a fascinating and perceptive point about the consequences of these "apolitical hybrids" in political life, Leander argues that old "worries about the influence of a military-industrial complex seem irrelevant while the normality of the hybrid market is preserved." Thus, Leander stresses that these security markets, and the logic they portend, obscures their impact on politics and power by relying on a discourse of "technical and efficient solutions" to complex problems of war and peace. Chapter Seven offers an important corrective to the common views about private security contractors and their impact on state formation in the contemporary era.

In Chapter 8, Lipschutz investigates the complex meanings of advanced technological surveillance capabilities in the hands of telecommunications companies, which the National Security Agency and other entities of the vast American national security state contract with to shield many of its activities from democratic accountability and oversight. In what Lipschutz refers to as World War Infinity (WWInf), the contemporary "bio-opticon" "yoke[s] together" economy and security "in the service of hybrid rule." Lipschutz's chapter pays particular attention to the "digital or electronic pocket litter" that emerges from this sweeping surveillance dragnet of citizens as consumers who unwittingly produce extraordinary amounts of information on a daily basis. Lipschutz proposes that this dragnet of personal information represents an historical turning point whereupon the state declares a type of war on the populace because everyone is a suspect. The chapter provides searing insights of a "new form of property and a new property regime, one that is central to hybrid rule" that has emerged out of the "bio-opticon."

The final chapter in the "Empirics" section, Chapter 9, enables Hester to reframe the changing nature of the biological revolution's impact on society and economy. Hester challenges the dominant explanation of biotechnology's implications that rely on capitalist development and scientific progress to one that centers squarely on the American state. Hester argues that the biological sciences now provide the state to manage and regulate the human body at the molecular level where the private and public sectors work in tandem to subject the individual to a different, albeit similar, kind of surveillance than that experienced in Lipschutz's "new property regime." In reflecting back on the political lessons of the Tuskegee experiments, Hester suggests that contemporary developments within the biological sciences are increasingly obscured from public view because the grand narratives of molecular biology depoliticize these phenomena. The chapter offers a unique perspective of the far-reaching boundaries of hybrid rule and depoliticization.

The last section of the volume is called "Reflections" and contains Chapter 10, which offers possible suggestions for future research into the area of hybrid rule and state formation. It offers a set of insights into the shifting boundaries of citizen and state. The authors argue that the threats to political legitimacy that drove the emergence of hybrid rule remains central to understanding the changing nature of state authority and practice in the contemporary era. Hurt and Lipschutz also suggest that these changes might fundamentally alter relations between East and West, particularly between liberal capitalism and authoritarian capitalism. In highlighting the potential for convergence at the global level, the authors point toward hybrid rule's political significance for world politics, especially for the future of democratic governance.

Notes

1 The literature on the vast expansion of privatization activities in the wake of 9/11 is extensive, especially in the areas of Blackwater and related activities. (See, for instance, Stanger 2009; Singer 2007; Verkuil, 2007; Abrahamsen and Williams 2010; Hibou 2004; Scahill 2008.)

2 An enormous literature on neoliberalism exists. (See, e.g., Harvey 2007; Glyn 2007; Duggan 2004; Roland and Stiglitz 2008).
3 For instance, Braithwaite (2005) and Hibou (2004), just to mention a few, demonstrate these developments took place far beyond Americans shores. However, the book argues that the origins of this development began within the U.S. in the wake of the turbulent 1960s.
4 For a critique, see Wood 1995: 19–48.

Part I
Analytics

Part 1

Analytics

1 Bringing politics back in

Shelley L. Hurt and Ronnie D. Lipschutz

> Our hybrid economy, part free enterprise and part governmentally controlled, will take on a new form constituting a virtual Social-Industrial Complex by 1990, this developing government-business teaming greatly influenced by resource and technology matters.
>
> Dr. Simon Ramo, White House Conference on the *Industrial World Ahead,* 1972

At the turn of the 20th century, neoliberal ideology seemed ascendant, and an avalanche of articles and books predicted that the state would be swept away by globalization, technological change, and growing corporate power. Yet, the state and state power not only endured but expanded. How has the state endured and expanded its power even as it privatized many functions? We deploy the concept of hybrid rule to explain the state's resilience. Most analyses deploy a static, zero-sum understanding of state power and the state's relationship with private actors. In contrast, the hybrid rule approach presented in this chapter stresses on-going processes of state formation—not all of which strengthen state power—and shows how the state can use delegation to private actors of certain public functions to magnify its control over society and its ability to shape social outcomes.[1] The hybrid rule approach shows how neoliberalism cloaks the aggrandizement of state power that Simon Ramo predicted and promoted over four decades ago, well before neoliberalism existed as a label for a coherent philosophical outlook.

We argue that a clearer understanding of the causes and effects of privatization requires a much more nuanced approach to political power, to the power of the state and, in particular, to the power of the *American* state during the past forty-plus years. The conventional wisdom of neoliberalism as the dominant view in explaining privatization policies is misleading because it privileges economistic explanations above all else. By contrast, we see national security considerations as a core driver of privatization policy since the early 1970s. We do not claim that national security is the exclusive rationale for our explanation of privatization policies; however, we challenge the omission of national security in any serious study of privatization in American and world politics. The common thread running throughout the past four decades of privatization policies, and the outcome we call *hybrid rule*, centers on political elites' desires to *restore* state power and authority, and in particular, the power and authority of the *American* state in support of a distinct American social order at home and abroad. Privatization, or as we prefer to see it, delegation to the private sector, was a crucial element in efforts to restore state power in the face of political, economic, and societal challenges of the 1960s.

This chapter moves through three sections that lay out this core claim. The first section defines *hybrid rule* and the process of hybridization to argue that our alternative causal account provides researchers with an opportunity to bring politics back in when analyzing the causes and consequences of privatization policies within democratic society. The second section provides our causal account of change during the past four decades by revisiting the historical origins of privatization in the United States. The final section offers our approach to debates on the state by examining the intellectual inspirations that frame our analysis. In Chapter Ten of this volume, we call for a new research agenda in this area, arguing that the emergence of *hybrid rule* represents an inflection point in state formation with implications for global governance, democracy, and human betterment at stake.

Hybrid rule as a source of state strength: bringing politics back in

Hybrid rule opens a conceptual lens for understanding a political phenomenon that remains surprisingly understudied. To reiterate our definition:

> Hybrid rule results from a set of practices deployed by political elites that rely on the private sector to shield national security activities by expanding state power while constraining democratic accountability. This hybrid rule strategy seeks to safeguard the state's legitimacy through valorization of the market as a primary mechanism in pursuit of myriad political objectives.

We propose that a thoroughgoing investigation into these practices, alongside their attendant outcomes, is essential for constructing an alternative narrative about one of the most significant developments in world politics in the contemporary era. We expand upon these definitional boundaries by outlining our causal account of the rise of privatization policies in response to the legitimacy crisis of the 1960s below.

Legitimacy crisis as cause of hybrid rule's emergence

During the 1960s, a political legitimacy crisis emerged, one regarded as threatening the social order as well as the political elites who sought to preserve the status quo. This legitimacy crisis altered the perception of political elites about whether the American state, Western Europe, Japan and many other nations could exercise sufficient capacity to achieve national goals in a highly volatile and ever-shifting political, economic, and social climate. These profound challenges to the social order arising from the Cold War, Vietnam, and growing global economic competition generated a palpable fear among political elites that the executive branch might lose its ability to conduct national security affairs, a fear that motivated political elites to devise innovative paths for securing the prerogatives of the executive branch without stirring a restless and disgruntled public. Indeed, privatization policies began at this critical juncture to insulate national security issues from democratic accountability and oversight (see Hurt chapter). Hence, we argue that a major aspect of privatization policies has been overlooked and misunderstood—given a reliance on neoliberalism as the explanatory framework, which privileges economistic explanations—stemming from an historical emphasis on the accumulation crisis of the 1970s rather than the legitimation crisis of the 1960s. In turning toward a political explanatory framework to account for the rise of privatization policies, with our emphasis on the legitimation crisis, we bring politics back into this important topic of debate.

While the notion of a legitimacy crisis in the 1960s and 1970s is well known, we link our analysis to that made by Jürgen Habermas, especially his older works, such as *The Structural Transformation of the Public Sphere* (1962), *Toward a Rational Society* (1968), and *Legitimation Crisis* (1973), in which he noted the numerous disruptions beset by industrial capitalism's influence on modernity's shape and direction (Habermas 1995). Our reliance on the Habermasian formulation of a legitimacy crisis stems from his recognition of the systemic nature of this pivotal moment in the postwar era. In particular, we highlight his emphasis on the dark side of modernity's quest for rationalization, which can slip dangerously close toward forms of political domination,[2] a Weberian reference that addresses the shifting nature of authority once modernity comes of age. Habermas tried to understand the deep-rooted sources of the crisis, noting that elites sought to remake politics as they confronted the newly empowered middle classes, who arose in the economic prosperity boom following WWII. Significantly, these elites also confronted rebellious professionals especially the nation's scientists and academics that resisted continued participation in a war-prone system. With American and European youth joining the fight, political elites recognized the growing instability of the status quo.

Hence, Habermas argued, in this moment of political volatility, that the threat of perpetual contingency and uncertainty in advanced societies must be minimized to restore political authority: "The fundamental function of world-maintaining interpretive systems is the avoidance of chaos, that is, the overcoming of contingency. The legitimation of orders of authority and basic norms can be understood as a specialization of this 'meaning-giving' function" (Habermas 1975: 118). Consequently, we argue, political elites re-imagined the private sector's relationship to public authority anew by drawing upon the material and ideational dimensions of the private sector to deflect state responsibility away from democratic mechanisms of accountability and to insulate state power from charges of illegitimacy. This dialectical interplay of push and pull with the private sector offered political elites an opportunity to accomplish domestic and geopolitical goals with renewed vigor.

Our approach

In particular, our focus on the national security dimensions of privatization as a core feature and primary assumption of *hybrid rule* stands apart from the existing literature debates, including those that have come before. Within the international relations literature, a number of prominent scholars have engaged with questions about privatization and its implications at home and abroad (Stanger 2009; Abrahamsen and Williams 2010; Verkuil 2007). In particular, a number of scholars have noted the implications of privatization for democratic accountability and the fundamental role of political elites. As long ago as 1987, Paul Starr argued that privatization enhanced political power as much as it potentially constrained it:

> Privatization does not transform constraint into choice; it transfers decisions from one realm of choice—and constraint—to another. These two realms differ in their basic rules for disclosure of information: the public realm requires greater access; private firms have fewer obligations to conduct open proceedings or to make known the reasons for their decisions … . Privatization diminishes the sphere of public information, deliberation, and accountability-elements of democracy whose value is not reducible to efficiency. If we are to respect preferences, as conservatives urge that we do, we ought to respect preferences for democratic over market choice where they have been long and consistently demonstrated.
> (Starr 1987: 132)

Starr's insights about the pressing, yet overlooked, issue of democratic accountability, suggest an early recognition of the perils of economic rationales for privatization. Along similar lines, Harvey Feigenbaum and John Henig point out the curious avoidance in the literature of the political when evaluating privatization policies, noting, "privatization is an intensely political phenomenon and ought to be analyzed as such" (Starr 1988: 6–41; McAllister and Studlar 1989; Braithwaite 2005). They go on to criticize the literature for its limited focus, which "deemphasizes its consequences for political ideas and political institutions and instead presents it [i.e. privatization] as a pragmatic adaption of well-tested administrative techniques or a necessary exercise in economic adjustment to structural constraints" (Feigenbaum and Henig 1994: 186). We build upon these insights in highlighting the political and national security rationales for privatization policies while stressing the costs to democratic practices of oversight.

In furthering our understanding about the political perils of privatization, Béatrice Hibou proposed that privatization represented a "new modality for producing the political" and an indirect "method of government," cautioning scholars who study privatization's impact within developing countries to broaden their conceptualization of that phenomenon (Hibou 2004: 3, 4, 45). Arguing forcefully, Hibou shows that "Privatisation should not be interpreted as an advance of the liberal strategy ... . [In Africa and elsewhere] the private sector remains tied to state power." In breaking free from the zero-sum view of private vs. public power that dominates the literature, Hibou insists scholars pay attention to another possibility: "Privatisation corresponds not so much to a decline of the public to the advantage of the private as to a new combination of the public and private, and continued exercise of state power and of the political." Her insights go a long way toward illuminating the political dimension of privatization.

Others have noted the active role of political elites in the process. For instance, in their analysis of public and elite support for the efforts of the Thatcher government, Ian McAllister and Donley Studlar argue that "Privatization is a policy which did not emerge because of popular demands among voters; rather, privatization was a product of elites who saw it as one remedy for Britain's economic ills, *and as an electoral asset*" (emphasis added) (McAllister and Studlar 1989: 174). The critical question to be addressed, therefore, is not so much *who* appears to be "empowered" by privatization but, rather, what are the authoritative effects of empowerment through privatization? How does *hybrid rule*, through privatization, enable the state and its agencies to pursue policies and paths that support continued domination by political elites as well as secure political legitimacy for states and governments? Finally, how does privatization concentrate governmental authority in newfound ways through the state's penetration and harnessing of the private sector?

As we seek to make clear, *hybrid rule* is, first and foremost, a *political* project, one that serves the interests of both the state and its elites, who are concerned primarily about maintenance of an environment beyond democratic accountability and control. By deploying the private sector in myriad novel ways in the 21st century, states are able to generate a strengthened capacity to accomplish their goals while resisting much, if any, accountability to the electorate. Even when elections are contested, and even validated by outside observers, there are clear limits to democracy and the expansion of the electoral franchise. The political stakes of *hybrid rule* demonstrate the uncomfortable possibility of restoring something akin to the feudal sovereign's absolute right and authority to eavesdrop on, secretly apprehend and even assassinate persons deemed "dangerous," with qualification of that term being quite elastic (see Lipschutz, in this volume). More broadly, *hybrid rule* illustrates the exercise of *political power,* not only in a coercive or instrumental sense but also in the ways in which hybrid rule shapes institutions, practices and activities. Here, we draw on more nuanced understandings of power, as developed by a number of scholars over the past several decades, including Susan Strange, Michael Mann, Michel Foucault, Pierre Bourdieu, Kenneth Boulding, Steven Lukes, and others. In particular, power flows through various social and political channels and, as Foucault put it, serves to *constitute* particular relations among people for establishing "political authority and legitimacy" (sometimes these arrangements are called "hegemony" or "governmentality") (Foucault 2003: 229–245).

Resetting the clock: privatization's new timeline and the rise of hybrid rule

What are the actual historical origins of the privatization effort? Why did senior U.S. policymakers turn to the private sector during one of the most volatile periods in American history? And why do the answers to these questions matter? In our resetting of the clock to account for the rise of privatization in this chapter, we argue that this policy change first appeared more than forty years ago in response to the *legitimation crisis* that began during the 1960s, which the United States and its allies experienced quite dramatically. Across the political spectrum, worldwide protests and social movements gathered steam, culminating in the events of 1968, shaking the existing political order to its core. In response to social upheaval and turbulence, Richard Milhous Nixon was inaugurated in 1969 on a platform of peace abroad as well as law and order at home. In full recognition of the threats to the social order faced by a troubled monetary and capitalist system, a war seemingly without end, an enduring Cold War competition, and an unraveling of the existing cultural fabric, policymakers initiated a series of policies that would slowly, yet imperceptibly, acquire a life of their own.

The seriousness of these culminating and converging threats led Daniel P. Moynihan, counselor to the president for urban affairs, to write a lengthy and detailed memorandum to President Nixon on November 13, 1970 about the present crisis facing the country.[3] The first out of four "propositions" Moynihan discussed in this classified memo centered directly on the legitimacy crisis:

> 1 The primary problem of American society continues to be that of the eroding authority of the principal institutions of government and society.
>
> You will recall that in a long memorandum I sent you before the Inauguration I argued that the challenge to the legitimacy of our institutions and the processes associated with them was then the primacy issue facing the nation. It seems to me it has continued to be such, and that this situation is not likely to change. In one form or another—from calls for "law and order" on the Right to demand for revolutionary change on the Left—the central theme of American politics at this time is that our institutions are failing.

By the 1970s, policymakers responded to the legitimation crisis by moving numerous government responsibilities subject to public disclosure requirements into the private sector. In so doing, the domestic public as well as leaders and publics abroad were prevented from gaining access or knowledge about certain, potentially controversial, public policies. These policy shifts of governmental authority and oversight from the public to the private sector, rather than restricting state power, actually enhanced it.

These shifts came to be categorized by several different terms. The public administration literature trace the terminological genealogy of privatization and public–private partnerships to a new political organization type begun in the United States in the late 1960s, called "quangos," for "quasi-governmental entities." As Brian W. Hogwood, notes:

> In Britain the term quango is now normally taken to stand for quasi-autonomous national government organizations, but what does that mean? The origin was the term, invented in the USA at the end of the 1960s as a half joke—quasi-non-governmental organizations. It referred to organizations which were in no way officially part of government, such as not-for-profit corporations, but which were effectively used by government to deliver public policy. This was taken up by the participants in a British–US research programme, contracted to QNG, hence (due to Anthony Barker) quango.
>
> (Hogwood 1995: 207–225)

Similarly, Matthew V. Flinders and Martin J. Smith, editors of a recent volume on the emergence of quasi-government, pinpoint the late 1960s as the origin for these new institutional forms (Flinders and Smith 1999). Hence, by the time Nixon entered the White House in January 1969, some initiatives and ideas about erecting a new political organization type had already begun to emerge; however, the Nixon administration raised this state-led initiative to new heights.

In other words, privatization is not a practice that began during the Reagan Administration, as the conventional wisdom would have it, but rather, long before the onset of Reaganomics or Thatcherism, as a bipartisan effort to institute a different type of political order. The chronological periods presented in this section are heuristic devices; they do not represent hard and fast temporal boundaries and they overlap to some degree. They do highlight pivotal moments in the evolutionary path toward the *hybrid rule* era of contemporary times, signaling an historical inflection point in state formation. The first period provides an historical background of the influences leading up to this shift toward the private sector. The second period chronicles three interrelated developments that sparked the legitimation crisis in the late 1960s and early 1970s. Finally, the third period chronicles the elite counterattack of the 1970s, which planted the seeds of the *hybrid rule* era of the present day.

Historical origins of the legitimation crisis

Although the first stirrings of the legitimation crisis can be identified in the 1950s and early 1960s, with various civil rights activities in the South and the student demonstration against the 1960 hearings by the House Un-American

Activities Committee held in San Francisco, the full-blown version only emerged in the mid-1960s when Lyndon Johnson, elected president on a "peace platform" in 1964, began to send large numbers of troops to Indochina, an action that threatened numerous draft-age men, politicized many parents, and expanded the anti-war movement. The growing Civil Rights Movement, along with passage of the Voting Rights Act and the Great Society legislation, came under violent attack in the American South and elsewhere across the United States, leading to the alienation of white Southerners from the Democratic Party.

These social upheavals unfolded in a country raw with emotion and beset with suspicion after President John F. Kennedy's assassination. The domestic turbulence paralleled international troubles—Sputnik, the Cuban Missile Crisis, Berlin Wall Crisis, Cambodia Civil War, Gulf of Tonkin controversy—that appeared to challenge the U.S. and its allies, generating broad-ranging skepticism about government transparency and accountability. In response to this volatile mix, Congressional leaders and President Johnson decided to make a major gesture to the American public by passing the Freedom of Information Act of 1966. Significantly, Bill Moyers, then the president's press secretary, revealed later that Johnson initially resisted this Congressional gesture before being "dragged kicking and screaming" to his Texas ranch on July 4th in a discreet, non-public signing ceremony.[4] This landmark piece of legislation altered considerably the calculation of policymakers who were now—at least on paper—more accountable to the public for their decisions and actions. For instance, Henry Kissinger famously said in 1975 that "The illegal we do immediately; the unconstitutional takes a little longer. But since the FOIA, I'm afraid to say things like that."[5]

Persistent shockwaves roiled the country throughout the decade, but the apotheosis of the legitimacy crisis came with the traumatic (and potentially revolutionary) events of 1968 when urban riots and protest movements erupted in the United States and around the world, French president Charles de Gaulle resigned, Martin Luther King, Jr., Robert Kennedy, and Malcolm X were assassinated, the Tet Offensive appeared to undermine the American mission in Indochina, the Soviet Union invaded Czechoslovakia, and Wisconsin senator Eugene McCarthy challenged LBJ, who decided not to run for re-election.[6] These and other events led political elites to lose their firm footing as they scrambled for positions of strength in order to grapple with undercurrents of opposition and resistance. Initially, the responses of government officials and others were scattered and unsure but, in the United States, the Republican Party began racking up notable victories in the late 1960s that signaled conservative political elites were going to try and regain the upper hand. For instance, Ronald Reagan, then a highly visible spokesman for the Right, was elected governor of California in 1967—which reflected efforts to roll back the Great Society programs under the auspices of "shrinking the government." However, it is very important to note that "shrinking the government" sentiment represented progressive positions at the time, too, because many on the Left sought to weaken corporate monopolies through the elimination of state regulations that supported and subsidized them. For instance, Ralph Nader launched such attacks during the late 1960s, insisting that deregulation of big business represented a progressive cause.[7] Hence, political elites confronted a perilous predicament from across the political spectrum, leading to novel strategies to cope with the legitimacy crisis.

Our analysis of the legitimacy crisis focuses on three areas of conflict and contestation that gave rise to the initial unrest and were then followed by an elite counterattack, which included government officials, industry executives, and prominent scientists. The first involves the confrontation surrounding the burgeoning civil rights movement and the expanding welfare state. The second involves the controversies surrounding military and campus unrest throughout the country. And the third involves geopolitical competition with allies and adversaries as economic competition increased and the Cold War continued to grind on. These three areas serve to capture the core sources of the *legitimacy crisis* as policymakers and other elites saw it at the time. As Walter Dan Burnham noted in 1972, "In a larger, perhaps almost mystical sense, the struggle is for the American soul. On its outcome, in my view, literally hangs the future of human freedom in the United States" (Burnham 1975: 501). Indeed, both protagonists and antagonists viewed the unfolding drama of the 1960s as a world historical event—akin even to 1848 in Europe—with consequences then unknown.

Cultural turmoil: civil rights and the welfare state in transition

One of the premier sources of social unrest and resistance to change in the United States involved the burgeoning civil rights movement, with its

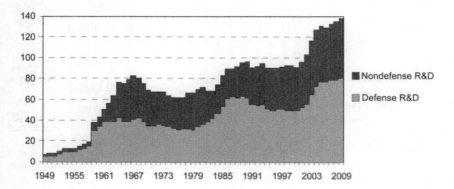

Figure 1.1 Funding for R&D
Notes: Constant dollar conversions based on GDP deflators. FY 2009 is the President's request. Some energy programs shifted ro General Science beginning in FY 1998.
Source: American Association for the Advancement of Science, based on OMB Historical Tables in *Budget of the United States Government FY 2009*.

Has spending for research and development been going UP or DOWN? The situation is more complex than it may first appear.

In inflation-adjusted dollars, the U.S. federal funding of basic science has **increased** by about $60 billion since 1953...

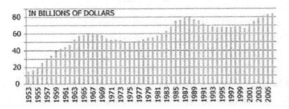

...however, when considered as a percentage of the Gross Domestic Product, federal funding has **decreased** since 1964.

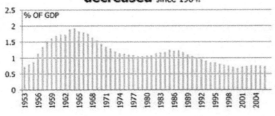

The year-to-year percent change of funding is seen to **yo-yo** erratically.

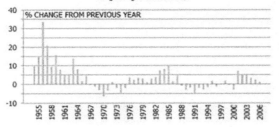

Based on this data, party control of the White House or Congress, the success of ongoing scientific projects and even the economy at large seem to have little influence on federal science funding.

Total proposed 2011 outlays: $3.84 trillion
Science spending represents only a tiny fraction of the total U.S. budget.

DEFENSE/MILITARY 18.81%
HEALTH AND HUMAN SERVICES 24.37%
ALL OTHER 19.01%
TREASURY 15.48%
SOCIAL SECURITY 20.59%

SCIENCE AGENCIES COMBINED 1.74%

NATIONAL INSTITUTES OF HEALTH
$32.09 billion

NATIONAL AERONAUTICS AND SPACE ADMINISTRATION
$17.68 billion

NATIONAL SCIENCE FOUNDATION
$6.79 billion

NATIONAL OCEANIC AND ATMOSPHERIC ADMINISTRATION
$5.56 billion

DEFENSE ADVANCED RESEARCH PROJECTS AGENCY
$3.10 billion

UNITED STATES GEOLOGICAL SURVEY
$1.14 billion

KARL TATE and STUART FOX, LiveScience.com

Figure 1.2 The economics and politics of science
Source: United States Office of Management and Budget, Defense Advanced Research Projects Agency, RAND Corporation.

significant legislative victories alongside those of an expanding welfare state. Together, these two issues forged an engine of socioeconomic and political change that appeared to challenge the existing order. In recognizing this volatile mix, intellectual and political elites began to engage in widespread rethinking of ways to address the fraying social fabric. One telling example illustrates the concerns policymakers and others had about how national myths of solidarity and mobility appeared to be coming undone. Hence, it is instructive to quote from some provocative "notes" prepared by the National Research Council (NRC) for White House use. On January 31, 1969, soon after President Nixon began his administration, Vincent P. Rock, executive secretary of the NRC, sent H. R. Haldeman, Chief of Staff, "Some Preliminary Thoughts On A Program Theme" entitled, "U.S. National Interest and the Myth of Equality."[8] These "notes" or "thoughts" amounted to an 18-page report, which covered in some detail the "vital moral myth" of equality in America. The report concerned itself with answering the question of "why" "the pervasive discrepancy between the standard of equality and the actuality of human existence [has led] in nearly every civilization known to history, [to ...] have ended in dissent and disorganization, revolution and war." After reviewing issues pertaining to sections titled, "Childhood and Youth," "Color," and "Urban Living," the report then discussed the changing relationship between the government and business under the title of the "Nation's Resources" wherein it states, "in the post-industrial era, the myth of equality gives rise to new demands upon both government and enterprise." To cite one of its passages at length:

> As the role of enterprise expands, that of government will need to change. It is possible that government may be able to divest itself of many of the service activities acquired in the welfare state period and return to its historic mission of maintaining order. However, coercion seems likely to become both less acceptable and more costly as a means of maintaining order. New knowledge is needed. The government may be more and more engaged in the subtle and complex task of integrating the activities of vast enterprises. The aim of this integration effort will be to achieve a stronger and more satisfying sense of community both at the local and national level.

Presumably the authors of this provocative NRC report meant corporations when referring to the need for "integrating the activities of vast enterprises." When submitting these "notes" to Haldeman, Rock suggested that the item on "'equality might provide a theme for a future State of the Union message." Indeed, somewhat ironically in retrospect, restoring legitimacy to the American political system became a primary objective of the Nixon administration.

Among Nixon's first policy pronouncements toward this end was the New Federalism initiative, which he announced during his first State of the Union Address in 1970, proclaiming, "After 190 years of power flowing from the people and local and State governments to Washington, DC, it will begin to flow from Washington back to the States and to the people of the United States" (Nixon 1970). While a large part of this new policy initiative focused on appealing to the so-called "Silent Majority" for political gain, it also introduced Community Block Grant Development and Revenue Sharing programs in what some referred to as "New Contracting" (Terrell 1979: 56–74, 59). These programs encouraged local reliance on the private sector for providing public services, tiptoeing into a new public policy domain in forging public–private linkages and hinting at the profound, large-scale institutional reforms to come. By claiming to disperse some of the federal power to the states, this new policy simultaneously ensured a firmer hand on the central levers of power in Washington. In other words, Nixon's objective with the New Federalism initiative aimed to restore *executive* power and authority inasmuch as the Block Grants minimized the role of Congress in allocating resources to localities for specific programs, thus allowing the president to take greater credit for that "largesse" (Perlstein 2008).

From the outset of his administration, Nixon sought to accomplish simultaneous goals in domestic and international affairs, embodying the contradictions between appearances and objectives. On the one hand, the "New Federalism" initiative and the Nixon Doctrine argued for devolving federal power to the states or to regional allies and powers; on the other hand, both initiatives sought to centralize power in novel ways within the executive branch in both domestic politics and international relations. This contradiction between appearances and objectives highlights one of the important aspects of the *hybrid rule* strategy that began to emerge at this time. It also helps us to understand the historical puzzle that emerged in the 1970s of the discrepancy between the mantra of privatization and deregulation and the fact that the state grew and centralized power at an accelerating rate at the same time. By rhetorically insisting on "burden sharing" and appealing to "states rights," for instance, American policymakers deflected attention from the actual centralization of power within the federal government.

Among the intellectual influences that reverberated within the Nixon White House was business guru Peter Drucker who coined the term "reprivatization" in a *Wall Street Journal* opinion piece in the summer of 1971.[9] Reprivatization sought to "return" public sector functions and services that had been absorbed by government since the late 19th century and the Progressive Era, but especially since WWII, back to the private sector without diminishing the centrality of the federal government as the ultimate arbiter within society. Importantly, the archival record shows that Drucker's ideas were enthusiastically circulated and extolled within the Nixon administration's inner circle.[10] In an earlier 1969 *Public Interest* article entitled "The Sickness of Government," Drucker proclaimed:

> The best we get from government in the welfare state is competent mediocrity. More often we do not even get that; we get incompetence such as

we would not tolerate in an insurance company ... . [T]he more we expand the welfare state, the less capable of even routine mediocrity does it seem to become.

(Drucker 1969: 7)

According to Drucker, "This growing disparity between apparent power and actual lack of control is perhaps the greatest crisis of government." What solution did he offer? Here, Drucker is worth quoting at length, for his goal was not elimination of the state but, rather, initiation of "decentralization" which would paradoxically make government, "the central, the top institution" in society:

The term [decentralization] is misleading. It implies a weakening of the central organ, the top management of a business. The true purpose of decentralization, however, is to make the center, the top management of business, strong and capable of performing the central, top-management task. The purpose is to make it possible for top management to concentrate on decision-making and direction, to slough off the "doing" to operating managements, each with its own mission and goals, and with its own sphere of action and autonomy.

(Ibid.: 17)

And he continued:

Reprivatization would give us a different society from any our *social* theories now assume. In these theories, government does not exist. It is outside of society. Under reprivatization, government would become the central social institution ... . The nongovernmental institutions—university, business, and hospital, for instance—would be seen as organs for the accomplishment of results. Government would be seen as society's resource for the determination of major objectives, and as the "conductor" of social diversity [emphasis in original].

Drucker's provocative and seemingly contradictory ideas resonated throughout large swathes of society, both Left and Right, as many tried to find firmer footing in turbulent times. His influential views contributed significantly to the political discrepancy between appearances versus objectives that emerged from the corridors of state power.

Military resistance and campus rebellion

Another aspect of the emerging *hybrid rule* strategy dealt with the legitimacy crisis within the armed services, and between civil society and the services, particularly as a result of the draft. In recognizing the unsustainability of the status quo, early in Nixon's first term, administration officials began considering alternatives to the draft. In fact, the archival record demonstrates the administration's preoccupation with widespread controversy over the "military-industrial complex." Members of the administration frequently circulated alarmed memoranda about television shows or public speeches depicting the supposedly nefarious aspects of the complex's "activities." In one typical memo, Alexander Butterfield, deputy assistant to the president, told Nixon about a recent public television program that "creamed the so-called 'military-industrial complex' for about an hour."[11] Butterfield provided the grim details, writing that "The segment concluded with MacNamara [sic] speaking on the 'Race of Reason' as opposed to arms, while film footage displayed gravestones, German soldiers, topless go-go dancers and crippled Vietnamese." In another memo, National Security Advisor Henry A. Kissinger informed the president about some recommendations Moynihan had prepared on the controversial topic. Kissinger suggested that Nixon might want to "think about a statement [...] putting the issue in its proper perspective. Perhaps a 'white paper' or 'fireside chat' setting out your views on national defense would provide an appropriate vehicle."[12] These internal memos provide just a glimpse into the challenges the administration confronted with this vexing aspect of the legitimacy crisis during its first few months in office. Not surprisingly, one of the most enduring legacies of the Nixon administration was ending the nation's draft. By transitioning the armed services to an all-volunteer military in 1973, the administration subdued the middle-class protests that were increasingly viewed as a threat to society and the nation state.

An essential aspect of this transition involved shifting the burden of policing and fighting in Vietnam from U.S. forces to the Army of the Republic of Vietnam (ARVN), which fulfilled part of the Nixon Doctrine's goals.[13] "Vietnamization" placed future responsibility for prosecuting the Vietnam War on ARVN, with equipment and air support provided by the United States, leaving only American "advisory" forces on the ground. Both the opening of China and the onset of détente with the Soviet Union in the early 1970s made it possible to limit communist support for North Vietnam and arrange an "honorable" exit from Indochina. Reducing American troop levels and military manpower requirements together with "contracting out" policing duties to regional allies made it possible to end the draft and rely instead on the "volunteer" military, which enervated an already weakened anti-war movement and pacified the general public. The Nixon Doctrine promised nothing, however, about reducing American adventurism abroad as international "burden sharing" also increased allies' dependency on U.S. security guarantees and military largesse.

An often-overlooked dimension of this aspect of the *legitimacy crisis* centered on the major upheaval within the nation's research universities and college campuses. While students were galvanized to action over the draft, their concerns did not stop there. American students mobilized over civil rights, women's liberation, environmental pollution, and numerous other social issues, seeking to throw off the metaphorical chains of the 1950s and earlier generations. While these issues greatly animated White House and Congressional politicians anxious over the country's future, a more serious issue concerned political elites, namely the growing anti-science and anti-technology mood tightening its grip over both students and scientists, jeopardizing the country's ability to retain its economic and military might (Mendelsohn 1993). This specific dimension of the *legitimacy crisis* struck at the heart of the country's leaders, who had spent the decades after WWII trumpeting the technological wizardry of American scientists and engineers. Once scientists began vocally protesting weapons research, executive and legislative leaders realized that something major had to change. By 1971, the problem seemed so acute that Nixon administration officials began drafting presidential speeches addressing the "Present Attack on Science & Technology."[14] While White House and Congressional leaders initially thought pep talks to the public might suffice, they soon realized that large-scale institutional and policy reforms were required to stem the tide of discontent among students and scientists. As will be discussed in the section below, policymakers enacted a sweeping change on the nation's campuses by replacing the post-WWII-era military–university partnership with an industry–university partnership.

New geopolitical and economic challenges

A final source of the legitimacy crisis stemmed from growing challenges to the supremacy America had enjoyed since WWII. This source in which the new privatization policies, or rather delegation to the private sector policies, had clear national security rationales dealt with a range of emerging geopolitical and economic challenges that tested political elites' capacity in newfound ways, including the rise of Europe and Japan as revitalized competitors in the global political economy. With the U.S. economy sagging under the weight of Vietnam War expenses and domestic outlays for an expanding welfare safety net, the battle for world market share picked up dramatically, leading policymakers to wonder whether the American state could retain a modicum of its post-WWII dominant position. Around the same time, an historical shift began to occur within the U.S. industrial base from what historian Charles Maier called an "Empire of Production" in the decades following WWII to an "Empire of Consumption" by the end of the decade (Maier 2006). Nixon's rather desperate, and audacious, step to dissolve the Bretton Woods system and delink the dollar's convertibility to gold represented a *Faustian bid,* as Peter Gowan describes it, to buttress American economic dominance (Gowan 1999). Senior government officials widely recognized at the time that these dramatic structural changes in the nation's economy posed a type of existential threat to the country's capacity to exercise so-called "leadership" in the world. With the Cold War stakes persisting unabated, the Nixon administration devised novel strategies for achieving strategic objectives.

The onset of détente negotiations with the Soviet Union, particularly in the area of arms control, provides an illustration of these strategies and illustrates the discrepancy between appearances versus objectives. While détente claimed to represent a cooling of geopolitical tensions and a new era of cooperation between rivals, in reality it simply served as a pretext for the U.S. and Soviet Union to accomplish their strategic goals short of war. For instance, in November 1969, President Nixon unilaterally renounced biological weapons, thereby converting the U.S. Biological Warfare Program into the Biological Research Program. This process enabled the U.S. and Soviet Union to sign the newly launched Biological Weapons Convention (BWC) in 1972 during the same year that détente took effect. As Shelley Hurt has shown elsewhere, the geopolitical stakes in the molecular biology revolution during this time prompted the Nixon administration to spin-off the country's vast biological warfare research into the private and university sectors, in effect replacing the notorious military-university partnership with an industry-university partnership (Hurt 2010; Hurt 2011: 31–56).

This institutional transformation provided American political elites with two clear advantages. First, it enabled administration officials an opportunity to quell the opposition of scientists and academics protesting Pentagon funding of university research by moving the National Science Foundation and other civilian agencies to the foreground of the nation's R&D effort. Second, a primary purpose of détente was to facilitate scientific exchanges between the two countries through the establishment of several science and technology cooperation agreements. Despite these newly established agreements, the administration accomplished an impressive geopolitical feat of maintaining restrictive disclosure practices of scientific information by moving some biological R&D from the military sector into the private sector even though the BWC of 1972 required transparency of scientific activities in this area. The BWC's efficacy rested on the notion of "intent," a so-called gentleman's agreement, thus requiring dual-use biological facilities, such as pharmaceutical plants, to remain accessible and transparent to international or country-specific investigators, but claims of proprietary secrecy trumped such visibility once these activities were transferred to the private sector. As will be discussed in more detail in Hurt's chapter, senior White House officials considered this move essential for safeguarding national security secrets as well as America's technological superiority.

Hence, Nixon administration officials were able to accomplish two formidable objectives in remedying the *legitimacy crisis* while simultaneously gaining credit for pursuing arms control agreements and reducing objectionable military research at the nation's universities. These efforts enabled the military to maintain its hand in biological research, at least for defensive purposes, while the federal government continued to be the majority supporter of basic biological research, over the past four decades providing far more funding than private capital to university and corporate labs. See Figure 1.1.

For the most part, the administration acted unilaterally, from Congress and capital, in the one arena in which it had considerable autonomy—military strategy and action—to foster a more general developmental strategy organized around an emerging *hybrid rule* strategy of classified research. The use of the private sector to reduce transparency and accountability has endured as an innovative state practice ever since. Indeed, these limited examples highlight the discrepancy between appearances and objectives as the Nixon administration promoted the ideas of deregulation, decentralization, and privatization, on the one hand, while simultaneously expanding and entrenching the executive branch and state power ever more, on the other.

Suffice it to say, this brief overview of the initial stage of the historical origins of privatization shows that a full-blown, multi-pronged *legitimacy crisis* confronted political elites of all partisan persuasions in the late 1960s as they negotiated a tumultuous and perilous landscape at home and abroad. This fraught societal landscape led many scholars and pundits to write extensively about the perils of the *legitimacy crisis*, speculating that the ripe political conditions would fundamentally remake American politics (Connolly 1984; Pye 1971; Lowenthal 1976).

Elite counterattack, 1970–1980

At the dawn of the new decade, political elites within and outside the government began developing strategies for a widespread and long-term "counterattack" (Dickson and Noble 1981) against the myriad forces that threatened the status quo. The Nixon administration's privatization policies were supplemented and bolstered by the growing rhetoric and influence of numerous elites, including but by no means confined to those who later became identified with the "neoconservative" movement (Mann 2004). Among the more prominent of these were Samuel Huntington at Harvard, Simon Ramo at TRW, and Lewis Powell, Jr., at the U.S. Chamber of Commerce. During the 1970s, their efforts were complemented by organizations such as the re-launched Committee on the Present Danger, media outlets such as *Commentary*, and think tanks such as the Heritage Foundation, to name just a few. Moreover, a number of prominent members of the Ronald Reagan, George H. W. Bush, and George W. Bush administrations cut their political-bureaucratic teeth in the Nixon White House – Donald Rumsfeld, Dick Cheney, Paul Wolfowitz, George Shultz, Casper Weinberger and Richard Perle, among others. These elites wanted to enhance the prerogatives of the national security state while protecting and restoring executive power, which had come under challenge by Congress and a restless public in the wake of Watergate. Foremost among their goals was the unwavering commitment to privilege national security considerations above all else by constraining democratic accountability. In so doing, the elite counterattack sought nothing less than the remaking of American democracy.

Already during the 1960s, in journal articles and in one of his best-known books, *Political Order in Changing Societies,* Samuel Huntington worried about the effects of too much democracy on the country's political stability.[15] However, not until publication of the famous Trilateral Commission Study of 1975, *The Crisis of Democracy*, did Huntington give full voice to these concerns. In his contribution to that volume, Huntington blamed the movements of the 1960s for an "excess of democracy," calling the results a "democratic distemper" (Crozier, Huntington and Watanuki 1973). He argued that the *"The vitality of democracy in the United States in the 1960s produced a substantial increase in governmental activity and a substantial decrease in governmental authority"* (ibid.: 68, original italics). Expanding further, Huntington wrote:

> The essence of the democratic surge of the 1960s was a general challenge to existing systems of authority, public and private. In one form or another, this challenge manifested itself in the family, the university, business, public and private associations, politics, the governmental bureaucracy, and the military services. People no longer felt the same compulsion to obey those whom they had previously considered superior to themselves in age, rank, status, expertise, character or talents.

He then asked, what was to be done? "Democracy is only one way of constituting authority, and it is not necessarily a universally applicable one," he argued. "In many situations the claims of expertise, seniority, experience, and special talents may override the claims of democracy as a way of constituting authority." In expressing a preference for a more technocratic form of rule, Huntington did not call explicitly for privatization. Nevertheless, he did favor restricting democratic access and transparency in order to remove some of the oxygen that had fuelled the fires of protest during the 1960s and threated the political order.

Many others besides Drucker shared Huntington's concerns. One of these concerns stands out: Lewis F. Powell, Jr.—later to become a Supreme Court Associate Justice—believed it necessary to counter an organized and dangerous threat to social and political order from "the left." In a now well-known memorandum written for the U.S. Chamber of Commerce in 1971, entitled "Attack on American Free Enterprise System," Powell warned:

> We are not dealing with sporadic or isolated attacks from a relatively few extremists or even from the minority socialist cadre. Rather, the assault on the enterprise system is broadly based and consistently pursued. The most disquieting voices joining the chorus of criticism come from perfectly respectable elements of society: from the college campus, the pulpit, the media, the intellectual and literary journals, the arts and sciences, and from politicians.[16]

As a remedy, Powell offered an extensive program, directed by "business," to respond to and, if possible, destroy this "tendency." What stands out in the memo is his following observation:

> One should not postpone more direct political action, while awaiting the gradual change in public opinion to be effected through education and information. Business must learn the lesson, long ago learned by labor and other self-interest groups. *This is the lesson that political power is necessary*; that such power must be assidously (sic) cultivated; and that when necessary, it must be used aggressively and with determination—without embarrassment and without the reluctance which has been so characteristic of American business.[17]

Furthermore, Powell argued:

> If our system is to survive, top management must be equally concerned with protecting and preserving the system itself ... . [I]ndependent and uncoordinated activity by individual corporations, as important as this is, will not be sufficient. Strength lies in organization, in careful long-range planning and implementation, in consistency of action over an indefinite period of years, in the scale of financing available only through joint effort, and in the political power available only through united action and national organizations.

These provocative statements prompt one to ask what might have been meant by "united action?" Here, Simon Ramo, founder and Chairman of TRW, Inc. and a senior advisor to presidents Nixon, Ford, and Reagan, suggested the creation of a "social-industrial complex" to replace the highly controversial "military-industrial complex" of the Cold War and to solve society's supposed problems by pacifying the American polity.[18] According to Ramo, pursuit of this new "complex" could restrict the sources of strife that had so divided the society while simultaneously expanding the capacity of the state to achieve national goals, particularly in the area of national security and defense. He predicted that policies put in place in the early 1970s would bear fruit in the 1990s once the social-industrial complex was fully developed.

Such problem solving would rely on trained teams of "poly-social-econopolitico-techno-managers," applying their expertise and skills in a "hybrid economy, part free enterprise and part governmentally controlled." Indeed, argued Ramo (1971a), the groundwork for transitioning to *hybrid rule* had already been laid:

> Almost everyone knows we are actually operating a hybrid society, part free enterprise and part government controlled ... . Consider that for most of the coming, large-scale advances involving resources and technology, effective use of private enterprise resources (even with

considerable government participation) will involve private corporations in cooperative efforts ... .

Moreover, the new social-industrial complex would encompass most of society, rather than being limited to the defense sector and its industrial contractors:

> The military-industrial complex, with its imperatives and yet its dangers, involved at most less than 10 percent of our gross national product. In contrast, half of our gross national product is tied in with the matters ... which the coming social-industrial complex will tackle ... . [M]ore of the nation's resources in general will be tied up in serving the social-industrial complex.

Ramo's invocation of government by expertise through institutional expansion did not represent a new idea (Burnham 1941; Galbraith 1967). During his tenure in the White House, Ramo supported a considerable infusion of federal funding for academic and industrial R&D, hoping it might defuse some of the opposition to various technological programs, such as ballistic missile defense and supersonic transport, among scientists, scholars, and students. Hence, he and other White House officials hoped that an increasing role for experts in management and oversight throughout the federal government would restore trust in and legitimacy to the existing political order.[19] Indeed, key policymakers, such as Ramo, made clear in their internal deliberations in the Nixon administration that their goal was nothing less than the "restructuring of traditional relationships [...] between business and government [in order to promote] reprivatization."[20] Ultimately, by the 1990s, the "social-industrial complex" hoped for and anticipated by Simon Ramo had come to fruition in myriad ways, fundamentally altering the institutional configuration of America's political economy while pacifying scientists, students, and the broader citizenry.

While privatization did not receive serious public attention in the United States until the 1980s, a broad "deregulation movement" was launched during the Ford and Carter administrations, with the Securities Acts Amendments of 1975, the Airline Deregulation Act of 1978, the Motor Carrier Act of 1980, and the Depository Institutions Deregulation and Monetary Control Act of 1980, among others. Deregulation complemented the movement toward privatization while obscuring the continuing growth of the federal government, and the power of the American state. In fact, not only did the state expand in size and scope, it also centralized political power in unexpected ways, with both serving the national security rationales of the day. Nevertheless, deregulation should not be viewed as only a shibboleth of Republicans; rather, it had widespread bipartisan support, including from progressive social movements, such as Ralph Nader's consumer safety initiatives. In a well-known law review article published in 1973, Mark Green and Ralph Nader accused

"Uncle Sam the Monopoly Man" of regulating in support of monopolies and oligopolies and against the interests of the consumer public (Green and Nader 1973: 871). Many of their arguments echoed those offered by conservatives, and inasmuch as the Democratic Party dominated Congress throughout the 1970s, the passage of the legislation listed above serves to illustrate the bipartisan breadth of support for privatization and deregulation. Although Green and Nader believed deregulation would reduce corporate power, it has since become evident that "deregulation" was replaced with re-regulation by other means (Vogel 1998).

These collective efforts sought to double-down on the rhetoric and policy of privatization reforms to persuade the American public that impersonal and unaccountable market forces served as a better guide for navigating a complex, modern society than did government management. What should not be lost amidst such claims is the success of the elite counterattack in transforming citizens into consumers and politics into economics, leading more and more toward the "managerial revolution" predicted so long ago. In a provocative reflection on the potential political consequences of the expanding privatization policies on American society and life, Kevin R. Kosar, author of a 2008 Congressional Research Service report entitled, "The Quasi Government: Hybrid Organizations with Both Government and Private Sector Legal Characteristics," noted:

> the emergence and growth of the quasi government can be viewed as either a symptom of a decline in our democratic system of governance or as a harbinger of a new, creative management era where the principles of market behavior are harnessed for the general well-being of the nation. One thing is for sure, however: debate between the competing management paradigms is over important issues, such as legitimacy and utility of the quasi government, and is likely to continue into the foreseeable future.
> (Kosar 2008: 32)

Needless to say, the potential consequences of hybrid rule not only increases state power but also renders representative institutions less important and the role of executive branch agencies more central. For the most part, however, scholars and pundits have treated privatization as a positive or politically neutral development. That privatization appeared to become global practice during this decade only served to illustrate the growing global hegemony of American principles and practices.

Our approach to the state debate: intellectual inspirations

Obviously we place the state, particularly the American state, at the center of our analysis; hence, we recognize the necessity of addressing the theoretical and conceptual approach to the state taken in this book. While debates about the state have raged within political science for decades, we refrain from becoming too mired in one perspective or another, given the depth of the debates as well as our commitment to the "analytical eclecticism" approach we promote in this book more generally (Rudra and Katzenstein 2010: 411–431). Our aspiration is to spark a new research agenda that brings together scholars from diverse theoretical viewpoints in order to generate fresh and innovative work on the impact of *hybrid rule* on domestic and world politics in the 21st century.

Meanwhile, we want to highlight briefly how our approach to the state moves beyond the stale ideas about flattening or gutting the state in an era of globalization and technological change (Friedman 2005; Evans 1997: 62–87). Indeed, we reject the zero-sum framing between state and society that persists in scholarship on the state today.[21] Rather, we seek to animate the state by engaging with its multifaceted capabilities to exert authority, influence, and power through innovative institutional and social relations. Part of our inspiration comes from Ira Katznelson's *American Political Science Association* presidential speech at the Annual Convention in September 2006 entitled, "At the Court of Chaos: Political Science in an Age of Perpetual Fear," wherein he lambasted scholars for their disciplinary failures of neglecting the state as a subject of analysis. Katznelson claimed that this disciplinary neglect left scholars unprepared to confront the myriad challenges facing the American polity in a post-9/11 world in which an atmosphere of perpetual fear, a burgeoning national security state, and a bevy of elites in the government, business, and military realms seemed increasingly unaccountable to the American public. While attributing the origins of the present crisis to the aftermath of WWII, Katznelson stressed that the persistent neglect of studying state power created an "unfortunate intellectual vacuum for political science at today's court of chaos, a void that would surprise the post-war students of power." The two students he had most in mind were C. Wright Mills and Harold Lasswell.

Katznelson argued that these two theorists of the state and power illuminated new developments that arose in the wake of the horrors of WWII with the onset of a permanent crisis based on the new realities of the nuclear age, genocide, and total war. According to Katznelson, Mills and Lasswell uniquely captured the institutional *zeitgeist* of an age that had broken from its past in forging an altered political configuration of frightening potential. In reviewing Mills' *The Power Elite*, Katznelson brushes aside the common methodological criticisms of the book while emphasizing how he "thought about power as a means to understand analytical problems and empirical puzzles distinctive to an age of perpetual fear, thus raising questions as vital now as they were then." More importantly, Katznelson stresses "analytically, Mills wished to better understand how constraint and agency intertwined in each of its aspects by treating power as a tiered variable, each level of which is defined by a field of tension established by poles of structure and action." Not surprisingly, Katznelson emphasized here the contribution of J. P. Nettl's famous formulation of the state as a "conceptual variable" by drawing out the state's multifaceted capabilities.

In stressing the substantive contributions Mills made in *The Power Elite* to understanding better the processes of varied decision makers on outcomes of American politics at the dawn of the Cold War, Katznelson also highlighted the enduring image Lasswell provided in his depiction of the "The Garrison State." According to Katznelson, Lasswell recognized the new "socialization of danger," wherein the centrality of military affairs merged "to unprecedented technological means and to a more unequal distribution of power." Lasswell's argument about the new normal captured the increasing dominance of "a world in which the specialists on violence are the most powerful group in society." By bringing together Mills and Lasswell's arguments on the elite, the state, and technology, Katznelson insists that industrialized societies, particularly the United States, had irrevocably crossed a Rubicon, so to speak, into a new era where the perception of risk and danger had become the organizing principles around which societies cohered. Katznelson's call to action among his fellow political scientists has not been taken up to the extent expected during these perilous and controversial times. This book represents a small gesture toward that end.

Our second intellectual inspiration comes from the work of Michael Mann on "infrastructural power" and Susan Strange's "structural power" approaches (Mann 1984: 185–213; Mann 2012; Strange 1998). These two theorists of state power provide a dynamic portrait of states that combine their capacities in security, economic, and information generation, moving away from traditional, static approaches of the state that rely on coercive power or zero-sum formulations. Mann's rejection of the "despotic power" approach and his embrace of "infrastructural power" enables him to dismiss the reductionist pull in much theorizing about the state by demonstrating the state's dynamic interaction with society rather than simply dominance over it. Mann's stress on the interaction between the state and civil society highlights how states penetrate society, remaking it in the process. This dialectical interplay, in other words, enables us to analyze more concretely the evolving relations between the public and private sectors in modern, industrialized societies. In particular, Mann's emphasis on the so-called military variable complements the security component of Strange's structural power theory, providing both with an opportunity to incorporate this critical dimension of the modern state into their analyses.[22] Due to our definition of *hybrid rule,* which positions the quest for security, broadly conceived, at its core, we benefit from these theorists acknowledgment that militarization and securitization are essential features of modern states, making them amenable to achieving that objective in anyway possible even if it means delegating some authority to the private sector in the process.[23]

Our third and final intellectual inspiration comes from the copious literature on state formation, particularly that of Perry Anderson, Hendrik Spruyt, James Scott, and Timothy Mitchell, among many others. We situate this project within these debates to highlight the institutional change that *hybrid rule* represents in world politics. Surprisingly, most of the state formation literature remains focused more on historical origins than contemporary change, yet, a recent revival of this line of research has emerged within political science to inquire about the changing logics and metrics of the state–society nexus in the 21st century. For instance, Spruyt has presciently remarked on how some scholarly debates have "confuse[d] changes in the autonomy of the state with changes in the institutional logic of territorial sovereignty" (Spruyt 2002: 142). While the former has witnessed some measurable changes, he notes, the latter "remains robust." Indeed, the surprising resilience of modern states has led to some notable recent advances in the literature on state formation.

According to Tuong Vu, these advances depart from those epitomized by the *Bringing the State Back In* "movement," as he calls it, which were too fixated on a static view of the public sphere (Vu 2010: 150). Accordingly, Vu argues that one of the most important advances in the current literature "define[s] states as institutional configurations in which political actors operate." Hence, the static nature of the autonomous state debates from an earlier era have been pleasantly eclipsed with a keener appreciation of the dynamic interplay between agency and structure, with greater attention being paid to political elites holding and manipulating the levers of power. Despite these scholarly advances, Vu notes that in too many of the earlier and contemporary iterations, scholars reduced or even eliminated the emphasis on legitimacy that Max Weber made so prominent in his analysis of modern state formation. Vu compellingly argues that this systemic removal of legitimacy from scholarly debates reduced Weber's analysis to an exclusively materialist one, thereby, eliminating the salient "ideas, beliefs, and rituals [which] do more than structure elite relations and produce physical coercion. They also serve to legitimize state power – a function that wars of conquest do not perform." Hence, Vu insists, "[t]he emphasis on culture and ideology [within the new literature] enriches our understanding of the modern state" (Vu 2010: 165). These two dimensions of state formation, the endurance of institutional logics coupled with the metrics of elites and ideas, represent a departure point for understanding our approach to *hybrid rule.*

These three important sources illustrate how political elites capitalize on ideas to shape, and thereby, legitimize state–society relations anew. They also help us to problematize the use of privatization as a new faith-based initiative that modern industrialized states deployed to reorient the citizenry's perceptions of the boundaries between the public and private spheres. The depoliticisation of the idea of privatization contributed mightily to nurturing passivity among the citizenry in the 1970s and beyond as complacency slowly set in after the ostensible democratic victories involving what was believed to be the reining in of government power excesses, best epitomized by the end of the Imperial Presidency in the wake of Watergate, the end of the military draft in the wake of defeat in Vietnam, and the end of the FBI's black bag

Bringing politics back in 37

jobs and the CIA's assassinations in the wake of the Church Committee revelations.[24] The American populace's belief that their hard-won efforts had resulted in a renewed balance between the elite and the governed in the public sphere, in state–society relations, meant that the valorization of the private sphere could move forward unhindered by the cultural baggage of an earlier historical moment. Only in retrospect, can we see more clearly now how *hybrid rule* re-legitimized public–private relations away from the body politic by draining it of democratic accountability and control.

Notes

1 Please see Beatrice Hibou's chapter in this volume where she discusses her use of the term "delegation" in this context.
2 Habermas' contributions drew directly from the first generation of Frankfurt School scholars of critical theory who studied assiduously the underbelly of Enlightenment thought. See, for instance, Horkheimer and Adorno 1991. For a relatively contemporary discussion, see Honneth 1991.
3 Memorandum: Patrick A. Moynihan, Assistant to Urban Affairs to The President, November 13, 1970, "CONFIDENTIAL" declassified 5/17/1982 E.O. 12065, Section 6–102. White House Special Files; Staff Member and Office Files; H.R. Haldeman; Folder: Misc Materials 1970, Box: 48, Richard Nixon Presidential Library, Yorba Linda, CA.
4 A photo of Johnson signing the bill at his ranch is available at the National Security Archive where they recount Bill Moyers recollection of the historical event: www.gwu.edu/~nsarchiv/news/20120704/.
5 Please see the National Security Archive's report at http://nsarchive.wordpress.com/ 2012/03/15/document-friday-kissinger-says-the-illegal-we-do-immediately-theuncon stitutional-takes-a-little-longer-but-since-the-foia-im-afraid-to-say-things-like-that/.
6 This list is certainly partial and does not even include the Chinese Cultural Revolution of 1967. Scholars, such as Jeremi Suri, have written extensively about the global cultural upheaval of this era and its indelible impact on political leaders within the U.S. and abroad. Please see Suri 2003, 2007.
7 We were reminded of Ralph Nader's involvement in the deregulation movement from Derthick and Quirk 1985.
8 Letter: Vincent Rock, Executive Secretary, National Research Council to Mr. H.R. Haldeman, The White House, January 31, 1969, White House Central Files, Subject Files, ND, folder, GEN ND National Security-Defense Beginning ... . 5/31/69, Box 1.
9 See Memorandum: Todd R. Hullin to Staff Secretary, RE: "P 1768, Wall Street Journal Article 5/27/71 Reprivatization," July 13, 1971, White House Central Files, Domestic Council FG 6–15, folder EX FG 6–15 Domestic Council [12 of 27, July 1971–September 1971] Tab C, Box 2, Nixon Materials.
10 For a cite to the above-mentioned quotes, see "Exhibit II, Report on National Growth Policy, Suggested Outline," in Memorandum: John R. Price to Committee on National Growth Policy, Subject: "Staff Recommendations for Future Tasks," July 27, 1971, White House Central Files, Domestic Council Files FG 6–15, folder EX FG 6–15 Domestic Council [12 of 27, July 1971–September 1971] Tab C, Box 2, Nixon Materials.
11 Memorandum: Alexander P. Butterfield to The President, Subject: Negatively Biased Productions by NET's "Public Broadcast Laboratory", July 12, 1969,

[marked "The President Has Seen"], White House Central Files, Subject Files, ND, folder, EX ND Beginning … 12/31/69, Box 1, Nixon Materials.
12 Memorandum: Henry A. Kissinger to The President, Subject: Daniel P. Moynihan's Recommendations Concerning the "Military-Industrial Complex", April 26, 1969, White House Central Files, Subject Files, ND, folder, EX ND Beginning … 12/31/69, Box 1, Nixon Materials.
13 Another element of the Doctrine was the arming of regional allies, such as Iran, to act as "policemen" in strategically important areas such as the Persian Gulf.
14 Memorandum: Douglas L. Hallett to Ray Price, Subject: "Possible Presidential Speech on Present Attack on Science & Technology," March 25, 1971, White House Central Files, Subject Files Science, folder […], Box 1, Nixon Materials.
15 At least until *The Clash of Civilization* in 1996.
16 The text of the memorandum can be found at ReclaimDemocracy.org. www.reclaimdemocracy.org/corporate_accountability/power_memo_lewis.html.
17 Emphasis added.
18 Simon Ramo received the Medal of Freedom from President Reagan in 1983. The "R" in TRW, Inc. stands for Ramo. TRW is one of the country's largest defense contractors. Ramo 1971b: 80–86; Ramo 1972: 313–318.
19 As Huntington points out, the Truman and Eisenhower administrations relied heavily on bankers, lawyers and corporate executives to staff Executive Agencies. Both Kennedy and Johnson began to include academics among their advisors, but still relied heavily on the private sector for advice. With the rise of technocratic agencies, such as the EPA, the role for science and social science grew even further.
20 See "Exhibit II, Report on National Growth Policy, Suggested Outline," in Memorandum: John R. Price to Committee on National Growth Policy, Subject: "Staff Recommendations for Future Tasks," July 27, 1971, White House Central Files, Domestic Council Files FG 6–15, folder FG 6–15 Domestic Council [12 of 27, July 1971–September 1971] Tab C, Box 2, Nixon Materials.
21 Within this zero-sum debate we also place the *Bringing the State Back In* perspective that too strictly separated the state and its institutional powers from society.
22 In particular, we draw upon Susan Strange's valuable insights about the U.S. emerging as a "non-territorial empire" in the wake of the Cold War. Her innovative analysis built upon her earlier insights about the myth of U.S. decline. Nevertheless, we think about the structural analysis of Strange in the international sphere as complementing Mann's structural analysis of the state in the domestic sphere. Please see Strange 1989: 161–176.
23 Interestingly and importantly, on a panel at the 2013 Annual International Studies Association Convention in San Francisco, California Stephen Krasner remarked that the two types of power that remain woefully understudied in political science are a) social relations and b) authority delegation. We concur with Krasner's analysis here. See the book based on Krasner's various power analyses by Finnemore and Goldstein (2013).
24 The historiography on all of these momentous events are vast but for a more recent discussion of the stakes involved in this re-legitimation campaign away from the public sector, see Rosenfelf 2012.

2 Roving elites and sedentary subjects
The hybridized origins of the state[1]

Iver B. Neumann and Ole Jacob Sending

> It must be possible to do the history of the state on the basis of men's actual practices.
>
> (Foucault 2007: 358)[2]

Introduction: the need for a historical and comparative approach

In the introduction to this volume, Hurt and Lipschutz ask about historical precedents for the present-day hybridization of state power and capitalist accumulation strategies and practices. As is well known, the emergence of capitalism was marked by a number of earlier and relevant shifts of governmental rationality, leading back to the break with mercantilism, which was decisive in singling out economics as a separate sphere in western societies. This process was a key drama in western state building during the mercantilist seventeenth and eighteenth centuries, and it was indigenous to those states. Similar processes emerged in other states only as a result of contact (trade, conquest, colonization etc.) with western states. Characteristically, at present non-western states have a less clear division of political and economic spheres than do western states, and in some states, it makes little sense to talk about separate spheres at all. One of the defining features of what are often called "fragile states" is precisely that the public and the private is not separate, thus contradicting the ideal-typical model of a Weberian state on which the category rests (Eriksen 2011).

The implication of this for hybridization should be clear. Hybridization is a process of imbrication between two spheres that are seen as previously existing and, ideally, self-contained. It follows that without the existence of separate spheres there cannot be hybridization. The corollary is that hybridization is a characteristically western phenomenon. In non-western states, politics and economics remain imbricated, whereas in western states the process is conceptualized as one where the two were once imbricated, then separated, and are now once again imbricated (hybridized). Western liberals tend to forget this difference in temporality, and so they naturalize a situation where spheres are separate, even though this is actually a historically specific phenomenon. As Hurt and Lipschutz also point out in their introductory chapter, conventional accounts of neoliberalism—whether on the right or the left—have no good account of how political power is transformed when the lines between the public and private are being redrawn. If we want to understand the evolution and effects of the relationship between the public and the private, however, we must not only historicize it. We must also seek to identify how the drawing and redrawing of the distinction the two spheres—hybridization—has a distinctive *productive* dimension. In this chapter, we will argue that the differentiation and singling out of spheres—state and society, public and private—is in fact a most central source of power. In so doing, we address head on what the editors single out as one of this book's main intended contributions, namely to account for the seeming paradox that neoliberal reforms have engendered the growth, not the reduction, of governmental intervention. We do so by treating public power as constituted in and through the drawing and redrawing of boundaries, of which hybridization is one key component.

A particularly apposite target for us is the Eurocentrism and, we would argue, weak knowledge of the western state's own history that permeate western discourse on the state. In western countries, the separation of the public and the private has become toxic. The classics on state formation and on the rise of capitalism—Hirschman's (1977) *The Passions and the Interests* and Tilly's (1992) *Coercion, Capital and European States* being cases in point—show us that the differentiation of state and society, public and private, was not an evolutionary process but the outcome of power struggles—politics—between (proto-) states and groups within them. The fact that patrimonial rule, which defies the separation between public and private, remains pervasive in present-day western states (Adams and Charrad 2011), is a reminder that any fixing or naturalization of the boundaries between the public and the private blinds us to the "metamorphosis of the state and the power it exercises" (Hurt and Lipschutz: Chapter 1, this volume).

We introduce a relational understanding of the social specified through a focus on the importance of boundary drawings. We argue that polities are constituted in and through boundary drawings—they are things of boundaries (Abbott 1995). We then discuss key theorists of state formation and situate our understanding in relation to theirs. Using one of the editors' principles for analyzing hybridization—periodization—we round off with an example how one particular state—what was to become Russia—emerged. This exercise yields three insights that are apposite to the volume's theme, which is present-day hybridization. First, politics: it is a constant of state building that the state attempts to arrogate to itself the right to draw the line between its own domain and the rest (what we now call society). Moreover, what we would now call private actors always challenged state authority, also when the state drew on its services. Second, causality: today's hybridization may be seen simply as the last phase of a long history whereby the western European state, once it had sufficiently firmed its hold some time in the late 1500s, tried to govern ever more by indirect means. And as we discuss briefly in the conclusion, our focus on boundary drawing has important implications for how to understand the causal mechanisms of how state governing practices change in an era of globalization: globalization generates small, often unintended, "sites of difference" which are the raw material for boundary (re-)drawings between state and society. What contemporary theorists refer to as "re-assemblage" of the state (Sassen 2008) is in our view a logic of boundary drawing organized around the state in a global age.

A relational approach: boundary drawing

As our stepping-stone, we choose perhaps the most satisfying account of state building on offer, namely Timothy Mitchell's (1991). Mitchell argues that the state is an *effect* of practices differentiating one sphere from another. As Mitchell puts it:

> The appearance that the state and society are separate things is part of the way a given financial and economic order is maintained. [...] The power to regulate and control is not simply a capacity stored within the state, from where it extends out into society. The apparent boundary of the state does not mark the limit of the process of regulation. It is itself a product of those processes.
>
> (Mitchell 1991: 90)

Mitchell does not offer an empirical analysis of these processes, though, save for some illustrative examples of how the architecture of public buildings and the uniforms and practices of the police and military is central to setting the state apart from society. Moreover, Mitchell does not specify the mechanisms through which the state emerges as an effect of delimiting one sphere from another. In drawing attention to boundary drawings, we take on the challenge of specifying theoretically what boundary drawing amounts to and how it can be traced empirically. In so doing, we hope not only to uncover the history of the "hybridization" of the public and private which this volume addresses, but also to highlight a more general social theoretical point about how boundaries constitutes entities and not vice versa.

If we ask what was to become the western state entails historically, the land was typically owned by "the crown", i.e. by the king. More specifically, throughout the Middle Ages, ownership of the land was the prize for which kinship-based groups with culturally specific and socially acknowledged claims on the crown fought. In what we may anachronistically refer to as Western Europe, such control took the form of feudalism, which meant, among other things, that this was not a straightforward winner-takes-all game. The entire point of feudalism was that the line between what was the crown's and what was the aristocracy's was the crown's to draw. So, when sovereignty emerged as a principle in the sixteenth and seventeenth centuries, one of the key practices constituting it was the right of the crown to draw the line between the domain of the crown and what lay outside it. The principle of sovereignty flowed from the principle of ownership of land, not vice versa.

Against this backdrop, we could very well have focused on the different changes in economic thinking from mercantilism onwards and the crystallization of a separate economic sphere. We could have discussed how the king's interests transformed into state interests, and also how fights between the aristocracy and the king resulted in the absolutist state (Anderson 1974). When we focus on the emergence of the state—public—in the first place, it is because we want to address a prior question that has bearings also beyond the issue of the distinction between the public and the private, namely how the state emerged in the first place, and what role boundary drawing played in that process. The main point will be that, from the humble beginnings of state formation to present day neoliberal reforms, states' "infrastructural power" (Mann 1984) stem from the drawing and redrawing of boundaries.

While it would be misleading to refer to early state builders simply as organized robbery, their goal was not only to take a cut of proceedings, but also to establish this state of affairs as their right. And to do so, boundary drawing was central. In short, we see the successful drawing of boundaries as constitutive not only of the emergence of separate public and private spheres, but also of the very authority of the state to decide where that boundary should run and how to adjust it over time. To do so, we focus on the issue of land ownership, since that was central to the gradual emergence of a separate economic sphere.

The question of the state's ability to decide where to draw the line between public and private nonetheless begs the more fundamental question of where the ability to draw the line comes from historically, and whether, in fact, the ability to first establish a boundary between spheres is constitutive of proto-states or polities in the first place. To answer this question, we need an analytical framework that does not take the public or the private as given entities or spheres. We thus foreground relations as that which constitute entities and analyze historically how the public and the private emerged as separate entities, using the example of early Russian state formation.

Our relationist argument, borrowed from Andrew Abbott (1995), is that we have to look at things of boundaries rather than the boundaries of things. We show that the role of proto-polities was central in constituting the private as separate from the public in terms of establishing practices of rule that could uphold an order where rulers' cut was secured and paying tribute was constitutive of the political order. The more general point is that early polities emerged *through* the ability to establish and draw up boundaries, thereby setting itself above and differentiating itself from its environment on which it feeds to fund its activities. The boundaries come first, then the entity (Tilly 2004: 226).

But asking about the emergence of boundaries, and the effects thereof in terms of establishing entities—here polities—with distinct identities and capacities, present us with a problem because the public and the private, the economic and the political were not established categories of the period we shall investigate—that of early Russian state formation. As we set out to explore a period around the turn of the first millennium, therefore, we must recognize that *our* analytical categories were not *their* categories of practice.[3]

Underwriting this challenge is another one, more fundamental: We ask about the emergence of private property and how its emergence was part of the rulers' attempt to single out a sphere, private property, the boundaries of which were for the ruler to determine and draw. But in employing such a narrative, we construct it from our perspective and reconstruct the story on the basis of what we now know. But social life is not lived backwards but forwards. The upshot of this is that in researching the differentiation of spheres and the drawing of boundaries—and thus the emergence of entities (here, polities)—we have to be attentive to small and seemingly unimportant differentiations. This is so because the drawing of boundaries is not made by some magic pencil. There must be some level of initial differentiation on which to build up or draw boundaries. Boundaries are drawn, and entities come into being, when a certain bundle of differences can be grouped together and make up a boundary. In Abbott's terms, the boundaries come first, then the entities.

By placing the accent on relations and on the practices that generate boundaries, we are in a position to account for changes between systems (feudal to state, say) and also changes within polities in a way that theories which take entities for granted cannot. As Jackson and Nexon (1999) have argued, explaining change in an entity when that entity is taken as the ontological point of departure for the analysis leads to unsatisfactory accounts. This is so because an entity has primary and secondary properties. A territory, for example, is a primary, defining feature of a state, whereas its form of rule (parliamentary, presidential) is secondary property, and variable. To account for the transformation from feudalism to statehood, then, substantialist accounts would have to vary primary features, but that undercuts the whole premise of taking entities for granted since primary features have to be invariant and constitutive. As a result, substantialist accounts of change typically rely on less satisfactory arguments about, say, exogenous shocks, as in punctuated equilibrium models (Krasner 1984)—these shocks functioning like a *deux ex machina* to account for changes in the entities (Jackson and Nexon 1999: 296–298).

In a relational perspective, what one gains in terms of analyzing the emergence and transformation of entities, one loses in specificity about which actors are involved in that boundary drawing. For the task at hand, however, the trade-off should be worth the candle, inasmuch as our primary objective is to identify the emergence of distinct entities or spheres, not to identify the behavior of or within pre-constituted ones. We shall highlight the importance of what Abbott (1995: 871) calls "yoking"—the connecting and formalization (or rationalization) of proto-boundaries or sites of difference. He gives as an example the creation of "social work", noting that this social space was "unstructured" and that in the late nineteenth century, a group of actors created the entity "social work" by hooking up:

> the female side of friendly visiting with the non church-affiliated side of the provision of social services with the non medical side of patient work in hospitals, and so on. The founding definitions of social work included one group from each of these disputes, placing that group "inside" the entity-to-be.
>
> (Abbott 1995: 872)

Abbott elaborates this point by noting that creating an entity involves rationalization, meaning that the connecting of differences to form a boundary (and inside and an outside that differentiates one entity from another) involves stabilizing and, in a sense, "black boxing" an entity through a variety of tools, both material and symbolic.

In their discussion of what they call "processual relationism", Jackson and Nexon (1999) note that the state can fruitfully be understood as an ongoing "project" that constantly draws and redraws boundaries which produces the state as a separate entity (cf. Mitchell 1991). While projects need not be conceived of as intentional, there may be a distinct intentionality at work: the state, as a project, is not the result of material factors alone, since boundary drawing and the efforts to rationalize them involves inter-subjective meaning. Thus, intentionality is to be understood not in psychological terms, but rather in narrative ones (Jackson and Nexon 1999: 308–309, 316).

We focus on land ownership, as that is a precondition for a separate economic sphere to emerge. Ownership is central here because it rests on an authoritative order with means of force to back it up and thus combines material with symbolic factors. Before ownership, therefore, there must be a socio-political order that places some actors in a position to draw up boundaries. But it is not the case that there was first an authoritative order and then land ownership. Rather, the two emerged simultaneously, with the capacity to demand tribute and secure surplus from activity on a certain piece of land being what made it possible to establish and institutionalize a certain order. And from the hierarchical position within that order emerged the capacity to later redraw and determine where the line was to be drawn: The central mechanism here was boundary drawing, which served to secure and institutionalize would-be-rulers' ability to receive tribute and thus the capacity to rule.

Historically, the precondition for establishing this right was to establish property rights. In the first section of the chapter, we review some classics on state formation with a view to highlighting the importance of property rights. In the second part, we demonstrate how this process played out in the case of Russia. State building in the areas that are now European Russia, Ukraine and Belarus has so far been neglected in IR, so the chapter may have some empirical value.[4] The point of the exercise is, however, first and foremost to demonstrate that the state comes first, and reactions from the ruled come second. Furthermore, we want to problematize the unspoken point of departure for much analysis of present-day state–society relations, namely that we are seeing a movement away from state control towards private control. The introduction to the volume highlights how this may be a Eurocentric summing up. We stress another aspect, which is that, historically, the state emerged as a way for what we would now (but not then) call a private group, namely a kinship-based polity, typically a nobleman and his entourage, to institutionalize its hold on a certain territory. It would not make sense to say that the state began as a private undertaking, for the idea of the private thus entailed belongs to a later age (cf. Gunn 1969). What we may say, however, is that the hybridization of the state was a goal of the early state builders, who concentrated on opening ever new (strictly hierarchical) interfaces between themselves and those from whom they took tribute, and from these interfaces, differences were yoked into proto-boundaries, later to be rationalized and black-boxed into boundaries. In doing so—and this is of the essence—an entity took shape which gave them a position from which a project of consolidating and institutionalizing a certain order around that entity could be launched. The right to draw the line between what was the affair of the king, and what was not, emerged out of a relational process of boundary drawing.

Three *Longue Durée* themes

Three *longue durée* themes emerge. First, it is a constant of state building that the state attempts to arrogate to itself the right to draw the line between its own domain and the rest (what we now call society or the public sphere). The state starts as a particularistic project, lodged in one kinship group. What we would now call private actors initiated it and what we would now call private actors were authorized by the king to be acting in its name. Actually, as stressed by Bourdieu (1999), the moment at which the king could add to the already existing nobility (*Uradel*) by appointing his own was a key moment in state formation. Second, today's hybridization may be seen simply as the last phase of a long history whereby the western European state, once it had sufficiently firmed its hold some time in the late 1500s, tried to govern ever more by indirect means. It did so by drawing and redrawing boundaries between itself and its environment as a means of governing in different ways (comp. Neumann and Sending 2010). Third, and this is a theme that comes out particularly strongly given that the case study here is Russia, what we would now call private actors always challenged state authority, also when the state drew on its services. The case in point in the following is how nomadic polities fell on sedentary Rus' polities from out of the eastern steppe, only to be roped in by the leaders of the latter (until, with the Mongols' arrival in 1238, a steppe empire established itself as suzerain and remained so for the next 250 years or so). In reviewing works on early state formation below, the key point is that, although the question of ownership stretches back to time immemorial, it takes on a rather different hue once societies change from being nomadic to being sedentary.

A note on method seems appropriate. The material is by necessity circumstantial, since the period in question is the period at the turn of the first millennium AD. Some of the well-established facts from this period are the pervasiveness of nomads and the gradual emergence of sedentary polities. We thus reread central sources on the period and highlight mechanisms that in our analytical framework constitute boundary-drawing strategies. We stress that the transition from nomad to sedentary polities were essentially one of redrawing boundaries for what constituted a polity. Here, a key practice mediating between the nomadic and sedentary, and helping secure resources for the institutionalization of a new boundary, was the royal tour where the head of a polity fed off his subjects. By polities we mean a group of humans that has a self-reflected identity or "we-ness", a capacity to mobilize resources and a degree of institutionalization and hierarchy (Ferguson & Mansbach 1996: 34).

Nomadic to sedentary polities: extant accounts

Nineteenth-century theorizing about social evolution came to a head when, in 1877, Morgan published his *Ancient Law*. Morgan here hypothesized that what we may call polities change from a nomadic to a sedentary form. Morgan writes in what we take to be a processual perspective when he argues that:

> all forms of government are reducible to two general plans [...] . The first, in the order of time, is founded upon persons, and upon relations purely personal, and may be distinguished as a society (*societas*). The *gens is the unit* of this organization; giving as the successive stages of integration, in the archaic period, the gens, the phratry, the tribe, and the confederacy of tribes, which constituted a people or nation (*populus*).[5] At a later period a coalescence of tribes in the same area into a nation took the place of a confederacy of tribes occupying independent areas. Such, through prolonged ages, after the gens appeared, was the substantially universal organization of ancient society; and it remained among the Greeks and Romans after civilization supervened. The second is founded upon territory and upon property, and may be distinguished as a state (*civitas*). The township or ward, circumscribed by metes and bounds, with the property it contains, is the basis of unit of the latter, and political society is the result.
>
> (Morgan 1963: 6; see also 61, 66)

The key point here, as we see it, is that Morgan's reflections capture how different entities emerges in and through how boundaries are drawn to form units, with polities being distinct based on whether the boundaries are drawn territorially (property) or between groups or people (gens, tribe, etc). In *The Origin of the Family, Private Property and the State* ([1884]1985), Engels latched onto Morgan's reflections on property and synthesized them with Marx's analyses of capital accumulation.[6]

Following the way Morgan analyzed the shift from nomadic to sedentary, or, more exact, territoriality's synthesis between the old principle of genealogy and the old principle of property, Engels laid out how:

> In his new constitution, Cleisthenes ignored the four old tribes founded on gentes and phratries. In their place appeared a completely new organization on the basis of division of the citizens merely according to their place of residence, such as had already been attempted in the *naukratiriai*. Only domicile was now decisive, not membership of a kinship group. Not the people, but the territory was now divided; the inhabitants became a mer political appendage of the territory. The whole of Attica was divided into 100 communal districts, called *"demes"*, each of which was self-governing.
>
> (Engels 1985: 151)

Note how Engels stresses that "a completely new organization" emerged *because* of a new division, or boundary, was established on the basis of territory rather than people. As the territorial principle, with its property element, became, so to speak, the new bases for the formation of an entity, the identify of the political institution also changed.[7] This institution is the state, and note here how Engels hones in on cleaves and divisions as constitutive of the state:

> At a definite stage of economic development, which necessarily involved the cleavage of society into classes, the state became a necessity because of this cleavage. [...] The central link in civilized society is the state. Which in all typical periods is without exception the state of the ruling class and in all cases continues to be essentially a machine for holding down the oppressed, exploited class.
>
> (Engels 1985: 212, 215)[8]

We need not subscribe to the ideas of historical irreversibility, progress, etc. in order to appreciate these insights. Barry Hindess is amongst the many who have recently reminded us that the assumption that, to-ing and fro-ing aside, people will normally be settled in the society to which they belong, is not historical. On the contrary, periods like the present one, which are marked by extensive migration, have alternated with periods where sedentariness was the rule. In fact, Hindess points out that:

> large-scale population movement is as normal a feature of the human condition as is long-term territorial settlement. [...] Nevertheless, the

system of territorial states and the techniques of population management developed within it have turned the movement of people around the world into an exceptional activity, something that can and should be regulated by the states whose borders they threaten to cross.

(Hindess 2000: 1494)

True, but where Hindess draws attention to this in order to live down the idea that migration is exceptional, our point here is a different one, namely that the state formation that follows sedentariness is part of a wider institutionalizing thrust that changes the meaning of nomadism irrevocably by changing the political terrain on which it happens. In terms of polities, territorial units are probably not the end of the story, but what will come after it will certainly not be what went before it. Note that Weber's definition of the state as that unit which claims to hold a monopoly on the use of legitimate force, as well as Schumpeter's definition, which turns on the state's claimed monopoly on taxation, are compatible with Morgan's (and, classes aside, also with Engels's) account, inasmuch as they highlight the importance of subduing competing polities and of uniquely collecting tribute, respectively.

Neither Morgan and Engels nor Weber and Schumpeter have much to say about the relationship between rulers and ruled, beyond characterizing it as extractive. An insight from another founder of sociology, Emile Durkheim, may complement them on this point. Durkheim's point of departure is how the rulers extract from and lay down the law for the ruled, but contrary particularly to Engels, he sees this as inevitable and obvious. As he puts it:

> Every society is despotic, at least if nothing from without supervenes to restrain its despotism. Still, I would not say that there is anything artificial in this despotism; it is natural because it is necessary, and also because, in certain conditions, societies cannot endure without it. [...] From the moment the individual has been raised in this way by the collectivity, he will naturally desire what it desires and accept without difficulty the state of subjection to which he finds himself reduced.
>
> (Durkheim 1992: 61)

To Durkheim as to Spinoza, human autonomy consists in insight into the incontrovertible character of this process (Durkheim 1992: 91). And to Durkheim, it is exactly the state which plays the key role of inculcating the subject (Durkheim would probably say the citizens) with this insight. In order to do so, the state must incorporate itself as a small cadre, organized independently of society: "... the State is nothing if it is not an organ distinct from the rest of society. If the State is everywhere, it is nowhere." Moreover, and very much in line with our stress here on boundary drawing, Durkheim notes that "The *State comes into existence by a process of concentration that detaches a certain group of individuals from the collective mass*" (1992: 82; emphasis added). In present-day IR literature, the Durkheimian Alexander Wendt (1999: 209) makes the same point: "State actors are differentiated from their societies, but internally related to them: no society, no state."[9]

When the state is young, it has few ties to society, "it is above all the agent of external relations, the agent for the acquisition of territory and the organ of diplomacy" (Durkheim 1992: 85). The state becomes more and more conscious of itself, establishing narratives latched onto material factors deployed in the project of drawing and redrawing boundaries as a tool of institutionalizing order and of governing. Durkheim's work on the state has been curiously overlooked by subsequent generations. Just like the reception of Morgan and Engels has been so marked by controversy over their teleological view of history that their insights have often disappeared from view, so the reception of Durkheim has tended to be so hung up on his unfortunate organicism that his insights into the formation of the state have been largely lost.[10] This is our loss.

Durkheim is on the money when it comes to specifying how state formation begins as a business undertaking by some clan or lineage (in this sense, it is "private"), only to transmute into something more "public" through a process of rationalizing proto-boundaries to establish a distinct entity (whatever that may mean in each specific case). Although Morgan and his popularizer have been influential in drawing attention to the key role of property rights to state building, it is nonetheless Weber's work that has been at the core of theorizing about early state formation. The benefits of drawing on Weber are obvious, but that reception has also come at a certain cost. One is the occlusion of the importance of property rights, taxation and tribute collection that may be a corollary of a focus on the use and function of the use of force violence. Another is the ontologizing of territorially bounded units (Walker 1992, Appadurai 1996, Barkawi, forthcoming). Neo-Weberians like Charles Tilly have explored how a Weberian approach may be combined with an approach whose genealogy stretches back at least to Hintze (1975), where the focus is on how different possible collectors of tribute vie for control of the same areas and the same populations. In so doing, one must part with the idea of given units that are "doers" of something and rather focus on how entities take shape through processes where proto-entities are unfolding from within, stressing that that within is what is being created, not something that is actually there from the outset.

It is instructive to revisit the reception of Morgan in discipline of anthropology here. As is well known, evolutionism and diffusionism fell into disrepute in the first half of the twentieth century, but returned with a vengeance with Leslie White's (1949) *The Science of Culture* and Julian Steward's (1955) *Theory of Culture Change*. They focused on bands, but their neo-evolutionary approach soon spawned works that focused on states. Morton Fried (1967) came close to the Darwinian idea of mutation as the motor of evolution when he talks about the "leap" of chiefdoms to archaic states. This leap is often brought about by population pressure—a possible side effect of sedentary organization—which serves as a key precondition for hierarchisation. Earle

(1997) notes how intensification of agricultural techniques may link the two; another possible link is warfare. For our purposes, it is of particular interest that Fried (1967: 232) refers to states which emerge in settings where there is not such thing before as pristine states. This is important because—as noted above—no boundary can be drawn from thin air, and the raw material out of which it emerges is often local, unintended and haphazard "sites of difference" that can be brought or yoked together to draw a boundary.

Elman Service (1975) worked out a typology of evolutionary stages—bands, tribes, chiefdoms, states—that is still the coinage in evolutionary circles and beyond.[11] Service's debt to Morgan is obvious, and he demonstrates his debt to Durkheim when he underlines how the origins of the state may be traced to how a small band of warriors take tribute from a larger population which thereby enter into a subaltern position, but which at least in principle gains military protection from other marauders (Service 1975: 300). Here Service is aligned with historical sociologists like Tilly, who quips that war makes states, and states make war.[12] Marshall Sahlins, who started his career as Service's collaborator, went on to do groundbreaking historical work on chiefdoms in the Pacific. Sahlins also inspired a key work on the transition from chiefdom to state (Earle 1997). On the basis of wide-ranging comparative work, Claessen and Skálnik (1978: 640) defined the early state as:

> a centralized sociopolitical organization for the regulation of social relations in a complex, stratified society divided into at least two basic strata, or emergent social classes—namely, the rulers and the ruled—whose relations are characterized by political dominance of the former and tributary obligations of the latter, legitimized by a common ideology.

It is no coincidence that the state, in this conception, rests on a stratified society and a particular set of relations between the ruler and the ruled. In our view, this suggests that statehood fundamentally rests on establishing and institutionalizing boundaries, either between "social strata" or between "ruler and the ruled".

In 1977, there emerged an important alternative way of framing studies of the early complex state, when Jane Schneider (1977) brought Immanuel Wallerstein's world-systems model of a core, semi-peripheries and peripheries into the field (Peregrine 2007). A rich literature has since ensued, the key positive factor of which is to highlight the importance of *relations between* polities as a key factor for their development (previously, relations were first and foremost brought into play as a precondition between some unspecified and generalized "model" state on which secondary states formed), i.e. an idealized relation, not one dependent on specific, constitutive practices that should be at the centre of study. However, in a highly effective critique Gil Stein (1999) points out that world-systems theory can be faulted for its logical fallacies. The three preconditions of world-systems theory—that the system has a core that dominates the peripheries, that exchange is asymmetrical (and, it may be added, zero-sum) and that exchange of goods is the key factor of social change—are all demonstrated to be theoretically and empirically highly questionable (Stein 1999: 10–26 *et passim*). Most of the time, in most places, distance and technology have simply not allowed for the kind of projection of military power needed to dominate peripheries directly. Exchange has taken various economic and political forms which may not be directly linked to trade and which may not translate into dominance.[13] As Stein (1999: 37) puts it, "The power of core areas is often overestimated because researchers tend to conflate ideology, politics, and economics, so that if evidence for one form of influence is found in the periphery, by metonymic extension, the other forms are presumed to be present as well." To take but one example, the Byzantine domination of its geographical peripheries, such as it was, depended on the spread of religious and legal practices more than on trade and military conquest (the Byzantines always tried to leave the use of force to allies from the steppe).

The alternative presented by Stein himself is to analyze early states by means of relational approaches other than world-systems theory such as the peer polity interaction model of Renfrew and colleagues (Renfrew and Cherry 1986) where the point is to study the emergence of, say, Sumer and Greece as a case of *emergent clusters or systems of polities*, rather than on an individual basis. This mode of analysis is, we think, consistent with the one we employ here. Our focus on boundary drawing as constitutive of entities seeks nonetheless to specify the process through which changes in entities occurs without resorting to ad-hoc theorizing. Stein draws on Abner Cohen's (1969) work on trade diasporas to draw up his model, a "parity-distance model" which zooms in on the relative military and economic power of the parties as well as the distance between them in order to study trade relations. Reading these anthropological theories, it is of particular interest to IR theory to see how it seems to be in the middle of a relational turn, where the importance of the relations between and boundaries of entities take precedence over substantialist accounts of polity formation.

Armed with these insights, let us now take a look at how early state formation looked in one of the cases that are crucial to an understanding of property rights, namely those that are to do with a change from nomadic to sedentary social organization. Welcome to the area where the westernmost reaches of the Eurasian steppes ran up against forest. Welcome to the area around the rivers that we now call the Dniepr and the Volga. Welcome to the happy hunting grounds of Persian, Jewish and Viking slave traders. Welcome to what is now the territories of Ukraine and European Russia, in the eighth and ninth centuries.

The case of Russia

The area where Rus' early state formation takes place is the forested zone on either side of the great rivers Dnepr and Volga, from the Baltic Sea in the north to the Black and Caspian Seas in the south. The forest density was such that the rivers were crucial for communication. Finno-Ugric peoples were indigenous to the area. Other peoples started to trickle in as the huge glacier left by the last ice age started to recede from the Pontic steppe to the east of the forest zone around 4000 BC (Vernadsky 1943: 15).[14] The Pontic steppe is but the westernmost part of a contiguous steppe land stretching all the way to Altai and the Pacific. Vernadsky (1943: 27) speculates that empires may have been formed here already in the Neolithic age, and that the Hittites passed through the area some 2000 BC. The first peoples we have certain information about are Kelts and Cimmerians (who were probably also an Indo-European people), and the first confirmed steppe empire in this area dates back to around 700 BC and belong to the Scythians, who were followed around 200 BC by another Iranian people, the Sarmatians. Around 200 AD, the Sarmatians were followed by the Goths, who were replaced in 370 by the Huns, who lasted to 454 (Vernadsky 1943: 49).

Making an argument from silence, we may assume that the Khazars were the first permanent tribute-taking polity in the area. They came looking for tribute during the eighth century. Kiev, which two centuries later was to become the key centre of the state formation, was founded by the Khazars as an outpost under the name of Sambat. When Slav-speaking tribes like the Polyane migrated to the forest zone from the steppe, the Khazars were there to exact tribute. Thus, being sedentary, the Khazars could control movement of peoples and goods to a much larger degree than could nomads travelling through, one effect being the ability to take tribute of those passing through. The practices of tribute-taking constitutes in our interpretation an instantiation of boundary drawing where material and symbolic forces are brought to bear to construct a boundary out of an initial "site of difference", and here, the key point to emphasize is the fact that there was intense competition between different sets of actors to establish itself as the actor with a right to differentiate itself from others through tribute taking.

Ethnically, the Khazars seem to have been predominantly Turkic, with Hunnic elements and elements authochthonous to the Caucasus thrown in. We know that the Scandinavians (also known as the Norsemen, the Varangians, the Vikings or the Rus') and the Khazars were competitors for tribute and trading partners. We also know that the Rus' borrowed practices from the Khazars. What we do not know is the exact relationship between the two polities and the degree in which the Rus' borrowed from the Khazars. Since we need to know what kind of practices the early state building in the area consisted of, this matters. The Vikings were not only in direct competition with the Khazars over exacting tribute, but also over trade, the other key economic activity in the area. The Khazar empire, like all the steppe empires, sustained itself on tribute and trade. As pointed out by Kaplan:

> These peoples [the severally religiously and linguistically oriented tribes] were *held together largely by the advantages of Khazar trade and the*

society built upon it. Once that trade began to decline and the prosperity of the kingdom to wane, the heterogeneity of its peoples would have led to the dissolution of the existing organization. When the Varangians, therefore, carried on their process of attrition against Khazar commerce, *they loosened the bonds that held together the tribal unions* of the Khazars. The *political unit which they had formed began to disintegrate*, the various tribes probably broke away from one another, regrouped, reformed, and sought a new identity [or rather, form of political organization].
(Kaplan 1954: 9. Emphasis added. Cf. Barfield 1989)

We take this to indicate that when the material basis for the continual production of a boundary holding these entities together began to fade, the boundary became less strict and thus up for grabs: the loosening of the bonds that held together the tribal unions led to the disintegration of the polity. The Vikings had some military advantages, such as superior weapons and, above all, their command of the waters. Once the Viking began to appear in mass on the riverways, the Khazars had no way of combating them as long as they stuck to their ships. The Rus' challenge to the Khazars was also waged by means of practices they had taken over from the Khazars themselves. Brutzkus (1944: 124) goes as far as seeing the Kievan administration, army and laws as being generally founded on Khazar tradition.

Given all the other possibilities, this seems exaggerated. There are, however, a number of specific cultural and symbolic loans to consider. The trident, which was the common heraldic emblem of all Kievan princes except the princes of Suzdalia (who used a lion), may be traced back to the Khazar kagans (Vernadsky 1959: 181). More substantially, the polity of the Rus', the first political entity larger than the tribe to appear in this area, was the Rus' khaganate.[15]

By assuming this title, Vernadsky (1943: 282) speculates, "the ruler of the Rus' most likely wanted to emphasize his independence from the Khazars".[16] It is difficult to interpret the move towards signalling independence as one not aimed at redrawing the boundaries, thus forming a new polity. Novoseltsev (1982) and Noonan (2001) make the case that the title of khagan was not only taken over from the Khazars (of which there is little doubt), but that it was specifically intended to ease the transfer of tribute-paying from one (Khazar) khagan to another (Rus') and generally to stake a claim first to equality and then to succession. We need not postulate a full-fledged *translatio imperii*, as does Noonan, in order to make the point that the Rus', upon their arrival, confronted the major power and insisted on their own equality with that power.

The crucial period in centralising tribute collection by driving out the Khazars, taking over their role as tribute taker and their base in Kiev as well as increasing the regularity of their payment was the tenth century. The Ryurikid prince Igor and his widow Olga, their son Sviatoslav, and his sons Iaropolk, Oleg and Vladimir presided over the Kaganate in this period.[17] The

Byzantine emperor reported that the Russian prince made the rounds to collect tribute (*polyudie*) (Porphyrogenitus [*c*.950] 1967: 63). It has been suggested that what we have here is an example of a practice that is "one of the focal points of the embryonic state", namely the royal tour:

> This phenomenon, named *gafol* or *feorm* in Anglo-Saxon, *veizla* in Ancient Scandinavian, *poludie, poludavanie,* or *goszczenie* in the Ancient Slav dialects, *makahiki* in Hawaiian, etc., was spread almost universally. [... It] is an institution whereby the ruler—the political or ritual head of the Early State (chief priest, sacred king)—or some other person acting in his place (his heir, vice-roy, vice-regent, envoy, etc.) makes his rounds of his dominion (the subject communities) following a prescribed traditional route to perform his duties and enjoy his privileges.
> (Kobishchanow 1987: 108)

Money was gathered from locals and then redistributed to the king's entourage. In effect, the king and his people peripatetically dined off their subjects. In our perspective, this seems to be of central importance: the royal tour represents, we think, an intermediate practice following the key nomadic practice of the (often seasonal) raid. But it was transformed into tribute, which later paved the way for the more differentiated practice of taxation on the other. These successive changes in practice through which resources were extracted entailed that the polity in question changed in identity, from being nomadic through and through (raids), to the semi-sedentary one of the royal tour of demanding tribute, to the sedentary of taxation.

Note that in Old English, *gafol*, or *gafol-geld*, came to mean tax (Ward 1954: 308). Sure enough, the first money payments seem to have complemented payment in kind. The first general tax we know from European history is, according to the general view, that of Danegeld, which fastened sometime in the early eleventh century. Ward (1954: 301) speculates that the ushering in of a universal tax in both England and Rus', though undoubtedly unpopular, contrasted favourably with the previous system (of which *gafol* was a key ingredient) in that it made for more predictability: It "paid for a well-organized government, administered by a body of officials, who received regular pay for their services, the proceeds of that tax". Less speculatively, she establishes that "in Russia *dan'* [tribute] was paid annually in the late tenth century just when it was being organized in England" (Ward 1954: 302). At this early point in time, there was little or no difference between the early formations of polities.

At the end of the ninth century, the Bulgars and the Pechenegi succeeded in pressing the Magyars westwards, and the waterways from Kiev to the Black Sea opened up for more intense trade and tribute-taking. Oleg (or someone we know by that name) conquered the Slavic-speaking tribe of the Severyans ('Northerners') and forbade their further payment of tribute to the Khazars'. The years after, upon learning that another tribe, the Radimichians, paid tribute to the Khazars, Oleg simply transferred that tribute to himself. Oleg also collected tribute from a Finno-Ugrian tribe that is consistently mentioned on a par with the others (regardless of the fact that they obviously spoke a non-Slav language), the Meria.

Given the formative and centuries-long Rus' experience with trying to form and maintain a polity at the very edge of the Khazarian empire, Prince Sviatoslav's victory over the Khazars at their own fortress of Sarkel on the Don River in 965 must have been a major Rus' breakthrough. When it subsequently proved instrumental in bringing down the entire Khazarian empire, one major hindrance to Rus' tribute collection and hence political consolidation was gone.

If Prince Sviatoslav's victory is a testament to the centrality of warfare and coercive capacity for boundary drawings, this should not detract attention form the importance of the symbolic or social sources either: While there is no direct textual evidence to the effect that Rus' saw itself as a successor state to Khazaria it seems a fairly safe bet that there was some sense amongst the Rus' of some kind of succession from Khazarian to Rus' political control in the forest zone bordering the steppe. Such a supposition is strengthened by the fact that, when Prince Vladimir followed Sviatoslav's successor Iaropolk as prince of Kiev in 980, the Khazarian empire's demise seems to have been one of the factors instilling in him a newfound interest in religion. As Martin (2007: 6) points out with reference to the invocation of symbolic resources in an effort to form and institutionalize a distinct entity:

> Having witnessed the recent collapse of Khazaria, which had lacked religious unity, and evidently appreciating the advantages of identifying himself with the broad spectrum of gods worshiped by his diverse subjects, Vladimir sponsored the erection of a pagan temple on a hill at the very heights of the city.

Vladimir subsequently found Christianity to be a better social glue. In 988, he forced baptism of all the subjects in Kiev. By instituting a singular religion—thus redrawing a new boundary on the basis of manifestation of religious beliefs, the polity took yet another form. It also further institutionalized and secured the strength of the polity inasmuch as the right to determine the character of the boundary was here strengthen, witness Vladimir's shift from paganism to Christianity as demarcation of the polity.

Conclusion

Ownership of land makes possible a separate economic sphere. Early state building turns on the state's attempts to arrogate to itself the right to decide where the line between state and society—be that between the state and the economic sphere or the state, the state and the religious sphere or any other sphere for that matter—should be drawn. Once the state has arrogated this right to itself, state building may no longer be referred to as "early", for the state is then in a position to control the further emergence of spheres, and we have plenty of examples in later periods of state formation about how that position of strength was used to erect new and redraw old boundaries of states.

Note, however, that from the very beginning, this process is not cordoned off from the surroundings. It makes little sense to discuss the earliest Rus' state building without reference to Khazaria—a point that we should like to stress given the importance of identifying the initial "sites of difference" of which Abbott speaks as raw material from which to draw boundaries. The existence and importance of (historically varying) external forces to Russian state building—Byzantine, Mongol, Polish, Swedish, French, British and American—continue unabated until this day. These two points may be generalized. The state, and this includes today's hybridized state, arrogates to itself to draw the line between itself and society, and it has to relate to external models and experiments for what the state should entail and do. Today's discussions of state building sometimes veer off course by discussing these factors as exceptional. This is not so. In the degree that there are historical constants to state building, this is it.

In this light, our effort here should be read as an attempt to capture the mechanisms through which the state emerges as distinct from the society over which it rules. Leaning on Mitchell and Abbott, we have those mechanisms in the continual production, reproduction and changes in the boundary between state and society. A key implication of this, and this is a point argued convincingly by Saskia Sassen (2008), is that in an age of globalization it is inadequate to treat the state as a given entity whose influence is either on the increase or decrease. Rather, globalization offers new raw material out of which boundaries may be redrawn or new ones established. In so doing, a re-assembling of governing practices (for Sassen, a re-assembling of the relationship and role of territory, authority and rights) takes place. Such re-assemblage of governing practices, we hypothesize, result from new boundaries being drawn in and through the competition and negotiation between different actors, national and foreign, public and private.

Boundary drawing, then, was not only central for past state formation processes, it is also central to the hybridization of the state in a global age. Indeed, what sets neoliberalism apart from liberalism as a strategy of rule is that the former does not see the market as a naturally evolving, autonomous sphere. Rather, it sees the market as a strategy of rule that requires active intervention and regulation (by the state) (Hurt, this volume). So-called New Public Management is precisely about such redrawing of boundaries, where market principles are made inserted into and made integral to the work of public institutions—"results-based management" being a case in point. As such, neoliberalism hinges on the ability to carve out and redraw boundaries between what constitutes the private and the public also inside the state itself.

Roving elites and sedentary subjects 57

In their introduction, the editors stress periodization, causality and convergence as three key analytical principles to unpack the nature and effects of hybridization. We have stretched the periodization to early state formation, thereby seeking to uncover a general mechanism of how entities and spheres spring into being and become institutionalized, thus re-ordering the positions and power of different types of actors: if markets become the litmus test for effective security management (Leander, this volume), then some actors win and others lose in terms of shaping public policy. Thus, we have tried to specify the causal mechanisms, and politics, involved in boundary drawings historically but also in the contemporary era.

Notes

1 We should like to thank the other contributors to the book, as well as Stein Sudstoel Erkisen for comments. Thanks to Ingvild Johnsen for research assistance.
2 See Foucault 2007.
3 We recognize, of course, that proximity between the two (practice and analysis) is no guarantee for the validity of the analytical tools. Often, the reverse is the case. Here, however, there is a distinct danger of reading historical developments into categories of analysis whose assumptions about the social and its organization simply don't hold.
4 Rosenberg's (2006, comp. Hobson 2011) plea for changing IR to a Trotskyite historical sociology does, however, draw on general works on the issue to illustrate where Trotsky found the inspiration for his idea of combined and uneven development.
5 "Throughout the latter part of the period of savagery, and the entire period of barbarism, mankind in general was organized in gentes, phratries and tribes. These organizations prevailed throughout the entire ancient world upon all the continents, and were the instrumentalities by means of which ancient society was organized and held together. Their structure, and relations as members of an organic series, and the rights, privileges and obligations of the members of the gens, and of the members of the phratry and tribe, illustrate the growth of the idea of government in the human mind" (Morgan 1963: ii).
6 "... Engels's text *The Origin of the Family: Private Property and the State* began as the very modest project of making available to a wider readership the research—thought by Engels to be important and controversial in its implications—of a neglected anthropologist" (Barrett 1985: 12).
7 In light of the Hintzean and Tilleyean reflections which will follow shortly, note that Engels (1985: 195) saw the birth of the state as changing the character and function of war. Whereas for nomads, "War settles external conflicts; it may end with the annihilation of the tribe but never with its subjugation", for sedentary polities with states, subjugation is the entire point, because it is a precondition for collecting tribute.
8 "Exceptional periods, however, occur when the warring classes are so nearly equal in forces that the state power, as apparent mediator, acquires for the moment a certain independence in relation to both" (Engels 1985: 210).
9 For an exchange about this, see Neumann 2004 and Wendt 2004.
10 Note how social anthropologists working on these themes often want to keep the concept of evolution but shear it of its teleology; Claessen and van de Velde (1987: 1), for example, define it as "the process by which a structural reorganization is effectuated through time, eventually producing a form or structure which is

quantitatively different from the ancestral form". That's what the rest of us call structural change. Comp. Service 1975.

11 For example, in his primer on political anthropology, Lewellen (1992) defines "bands" as undifferentiated groups of about 25–150 individuals and "tribes" as "uncentralized systems in which authority is distributed among a number of small groups; unity of the larger society is established from a web of individual and group relations", different from bands by dint of "the existence of pan-tribal sodalities uniting the various self-sufficient communities into wider social groups" (Lewellen 1992: 31). "[U]nlike *band, chiefdom,* and *state*, the concept of *tribe* really does not—and cannot—refer to a particular type of political organization' (Lewellen 1992: 32); '... the chiefdom level transcends the tribal level in two major ways: (1) it has a higher population density made possible by more efficient productivity, and (2) it is more complex, with some form of centralized authority' (Lewellen 1992: 37).

12 Service (1975: 297) even tips his hat in the direction of diplomacy when he writes that "political evolution can be thought to consist, in important part, of 'waging peace' in ever wider contexts".

13 Wallerstein's definition of culture is "the ways in which people clothe their politico-economic interests and drives in order to express them, hide them. Extend them in space and time, and preserve their memory" (quoted in Stein 1999: 19). It is hard to imagine a more vulgar Marxist way of making the superstructure point.

14 The Pontic steppe is roughly the area between the forested areas at the Dniepr in the west, the Black Sea and the Caucasus in the south to, the Urals in the east and the taiga in the north.

15 The best introduction to the Rus' Khaganate and its historiography is actually http://en.wikipedia.org/wiki/Rus_Khaganate.

16 The quote continues as follows: "... in contrast to the submission to the Khazar kagan of the Azov As and Rus prior to the coming of the Norsemen". Vernadsky holds that there were two groups of Slavic tribes who together made up what was to become the Rus', and that the Rus' khaganate as well as a polity forming at Tmutorokan on the Crimea should therefore both be given their due heed as precursors of the Rus' state. This view has received little scholarly backing.

17 As to the exact timing and names of the political leaders between Ryurik and Igor, there is confusion. Igor is said to be Ryurik's son, and Oleg is supposed to have ruled in the interim, but however way you look at it, the time stretch between the alleged times of Ryurik's arrival and Igor's appearance on the stage is too long (Franklin and Shepherd 1996: 57).

3 Neoliberal bureaucracy as an expression of hybrid rule

Béatrice Hibou

The title of this chapter may appear paradoxical or even oxymoronic: a whole swathe of neoliberal rhetoric is based on the critique of state bureaucracy and of direct administrative intervention in the economy: 'cut the red tape' is undoubtedly its most important slogan; indeed, one of the key arguments of neoliberalism hangs on the necessity of transforming state interventions. But 'state administration' must not be confused with 'bureaucracy': this latter term also characterises enterprise, the private sector, the market economy, and the organisations of so-called civil society... . In fact, to anyone who lives, produces or consumes, anyone who seeks relaxation, education, or health care these days, one thing is clear: bureaucratic practices, structures and procedures are becoming ever more ubiquitous. How else, after all, are we to describe the ever-increasing demand for paperwork (ever more omnipresent as it becomes immaterial), whether one is travelling, signing up to some institution, or benefiting from insurance (including private insurance)? Or the incessant confrontation with formal procedures, whether one needs to access credit, electricity, or a computer network, to rent a flat, to grade banks or businesses, or to go to law? Or the need to respect norms and rules, so that the accounts of a particular business can be certified, a vegetable classified as 'organic', or an article accepted for publication? The examples are numberless.

In the following pages, I show how this specific form of bureaucracy is one important aspect of the hybrid rule this book studies. It may prove useful to return to Weber, and to combine his analysis of the relation between bureaucracy and capitalism with Michel Foucault's investigations into the arts of governing, and Claude Lefort's discussion of bureaucracy as a concrete milieu, a social formation, and a system of behaviours: contemporary bureaucratisation should not be understood as an institution or administration—in other words, as a hierarchised apparatus proper to the state—but as a set of norms, rules, procedures and formalities that includes not just the state administration but the whole of society; seen as such, bureaucratisation constitutes one of the main facets of neoliberalism and the public–private hybridisation that characterises it. In this chapter I want to discuss the main argument of Shelley Hurt and Ronnie Lipschutz's introduction, that public private hybridisation is a political project whose goal is to restore or enhance state authority and sovereignty. The entrance through bureaucracy undeniably shows a public private convergence and a transformation of the exercise of state power. But it also suggests that the process of hybridisation is much more complex, that it's not only, even not so often, a political project that is explicitly stated and carried on. It is not mainly operating through colonisation of the private sector. Beside the production of unintended effects, neoliberal bureaucratisation proceeds also from autonomous dynamics from other actors such as computer or security companies, enterprises and banks, NGOs and associations, consumers, academics or citizens, and so forth, as I will show throughout this chapter. Bureaucracy does not occur outside society, bureaucratisation is not imposed from above; it takes effect through the very actors who are its target and who, consciously or not, are accomplices of this process. I will try to show that the term 'project' carries too much intentionality. Of course, political projects and even state projects exist: they often are projects of control, rationalisation, normalisation through the development of hybrid rule. But I want to show that this process of neoliberal bureaucratisation also results from non-political behaviour or logic of action, from non-state actors; for instance it can be the fruit of economic and financial dynamics, profit seeking and logic of market share, professional interest, or citizens' demand for transparency.

The bureaucracy of the market and enterprise: a central mode of the neoliberal art of governing

It is well known that neoliberalism is not the same as *laissez-faire*. In the line of interpretation of neoliberalism as 'intervening liberalism' (Foucault 2008), much research has since underlined this dimension by talking of 'government at a distance' (Barry, Osborne and Rose 1996; Rose 1999), of 'the privatisation of the state' as the redeployment of the latter and a 'new interventionism' (Hibou 2004), of 'entrepreneurial government' as a 'new rationality' (Dardot and Laval 2014). As Hurt and Lipschutz underline, this mode of government finds expression in a sort of hybridisation between public and private. Through an analysis of the bureaucracy, I want to show that this process assumes a particular form: the spread of the norms of the 'private' sector, the market, enterprise and competition. Neoliberalism is an art of governing that aims at restricting and shaping any interventions in accordance with these norms that are those of the private sector. A whole series of measures is thus promoted, from the privatisation of enterprises and public services on the one hand to 'new public management' on the other, via the development of various public–private partnerships, the drawing up of rules favourable to enterprise and to the mechanisms of the market, and the establishment of rules of the game that correspond to the demands of the private sector. According to the co-editors of this book, I can say that one is, here, witnessing a political project, which aims to metamorphose the state, not by colonising the private sector but by adopting its rules and its logics of action. I show how the two inseparable sides of the neoliberal art of governing—namely the critique of state administration and government practices on the one hand and, on the other hand, the development of practices aimed at an interventionism that pays proper respect to the environment of economic activities, and conformity to market needs and to enterprise—produce this specific form of bureaucracy, a private bureaucracy understood as the expression of order within the market and enterprise.

The bureaucracy of a 'frugal' government

The first side, directly linked to the permanent critique of government action, flourishes in the practice of the permanent reform of the state and the quest for a 'frugal' government (Foucault 2008). Concretely, these permanent reforms follow two complementary directions when traditional state bureaucracies are critiqued: 'discharge',[1] aiming at a smaller level of direct intervention in the economy with programmes of privatisation, concessions and public–private partnerships; and the homothetic transformation between public and private designed to ensure that the market economy will be the principle of internal regulation of the state (Foucault 2008) with what now tends to be called 'new public management'. But these two modes of state reform are exceptionally bureaucratic. As far as concessions and other forms of delegation and public–private partnership are concerned, bureaucratisation is manifest throughout the life of these contracts.[2] It is embodied firstly in the management of invitations to tender and the minutely detailed verification of the respect for competition, transparency, and good governance. It is then realised in the definition of terms and conditions, and in their regular assessment, in the management of amendments to the contract and other forms of negotiation that punctuate the life of a partnership resulting from the difficulties raised by the asymmetries of information, the differences in approach and the logic of action shown by the parties, the different interpretations and understandings of the nature of the partnership, and the tariff formulae or formulae of regulation. It also takes the form of procedures of certification and normalisation as well as of their follow-up. It is, finally, sustained by the production of data, reports, counter-reports, the use of experts and consultants by different actors should any conflict arise … . Bureaucratisation, thus, is simultaneously sustained by at least three dynamics: by the very formula of delegation, since the latter rests on a contractual logic; by the several uncertainties and recurrent revisions of the contract in the course of its life, the investments realised, the risks incurred that necessitate not merely assessment and production of data, reports and documents of every kind, but also the establishment of agencies of supervision and regulation; and by the rules of private management. 'New public management' (NPM) is the clearest expression of the quest for rationalisation by calculability and foreseeability, and in so doing, the clearest expression of hybrid rule. Behind the critique and dismantling of the rules of public administration, it develops a whole set of procedures, norms, rules and principles, disparate in kind but mainly emerging from practices (self-proclaimed 'scientific knowledge') in the form of 'management' and new modes of rationalisation obeying an entrepreneurial logic.[3] As a result, it is translated into yet more bureaucracy (Hood 1994; Hood, James, Peters and Scott 2004; Bruno 2008; Bezes 2009; Eyraud 2013; Pierru 2007; Belorgey 2010). The NPM expanded in Western countries in the 1980s, but is not new; in fact, it's an exacerbated form of a process of modernisation that started in the 1960s and mainly in the 1970s. For example in France, the RCB ('la rationalisation des choix budgétaires', i.e. the rationalisation of budgetary choice) or in the United States the PPBS ('planning, programming budgeting system') drew their inspiration from the world of enterprises: the state decided to import management methods for public services and administration (Ogien and Laugier 2010; Fourquet 1980). The idea was (and still is) to make the objectives of the administration more explicit by calculating and planning the cost of operating.

Bureaucratisation is first spread by organisations involved in reforms: cabinets, services of general management, services of the finance ministry, teams of experts, ad hoc commissions, co-ordinations with round-table discussions, representatives from so-called civil society, and so on. It is then sustained by the instruments set up to guide reform, in particular increasingly precise, norm-governed and automatic structures of evaluation, tabulation and graphic representation, in lists of histograms and comparisons between public policies. It is also sustained by the techniques of quantification and benchmarking that necessitate the collection of data, the composition of manuals of procedure, the signature of conventions, the coordination of numerical data, negotiations on the creation of norms, indicators, and methods for evaluation. It is, finally, maintained by the spread of techniques of assessment and control: there is a boom in the number of audits, questionnaires, inspections, demand for reporting from central administrations, the creation of performance indicators, the setting up of procedures of equivalence, the request for reports, for documents needing to be continually updated ... in other words, as in the world of enterprise management, government by numbers. The NPM and state reforms are sometimes called 'postbureaucratic' administration' (Bezes 2007: 477) sometimes 'new technical bureaucracy' and 'bureaucratisation by the margins' (Benamouzig and Besancon 2005: 301 and 308), sometimes 'postbureaucratic public management' (Trosa 2006: 15), sometimes 'reweberianisation' or 'weberianism in a new habitat' (Hood 1994: 125–41). Over and above the differences in the way 'bureaucracy' is defined, these critical analyses show the predominance of the following: norms of management, rules produced by the many different public–private partnerships, and disparate measures taken in the name of pragmatism in the process of rationalisation, efficiency and professionalism aimed at showing that the public sector can and must behave like the private sector, that they are both to be governed by the same norms and the same principles. And this is what I call neoliberal bureaucratisation.

The management process of state reforms expresses a political project and is a perfect illustration of the idea, proposed by Hurt and Lipschutz, that hybrid rule translate a form of state colonisation of the private sector. This project seeks to destroy an old form of ascendancy over the society, a form that existed since the end of the Second World War and rested on the supremacy of ministries and central administration and on the hypothesis that public sector and public interventions were specific and needed specific modes of operating. It pretends to establish a new political order based on the principle of efficiency, of lower cost, of results, and so doing to transform politics and the relations between state and society (Ogien 1995). It is based on a process of detailed quantification of state actions and strong power devolved to managers. New Public Management imposes an expert definition of the general interest that is reduced to their financial dimension.

The bureaucracy of de/re-regulation

The second side of the neoliberal art of governing is the development of practices aimed at an interventionism meant to bring the environment of economic actors into line with the rules of the market and make it propitious to enterprise. It is the inflation in the number of norms and regulations concomitant with the development of capitalism. This process embodies one of the main forms of neoliberal bureaucratisation precisely because it assumes the form of a definition of the rules of the game and an institutional and normative framework produced by this public-private hybridisation. An examination of the practices of regulation of the private sector shows that things happen less and less in the domain of laws, public structures and rules defined by national or international laws, and more and more in the domain of norms and rules established by agencies (of regulation, of certification, of notification), commissions, associations and other 'hybrid organisations'. Here also, following Hurt and Lipschutz, one can admit that a political project exists; yet this political project finds itself an expression not in the colonisation of the private sector by the state but in the adoption and ownership of practices and logics of actions directly stemming from the complex world of enterprise by state actors. Moreover, there is a strong cooperation between these two worlds, so much so that it's difficult, even impossible, to distinguish between their mode of actions and behaviour. These modes of intervention are highly specific: on the one hand they operate less on the economy than on its environment; on the other, they contribute to a major blurring of the distinction between public and private, not only at the boundary between those supposedly separate spheres but also, and perhaps especially, in the very way they are defined. The process of bureaucratisation that accompanies them is less marked by direct interventions on the part of public administrations than by the imposition of norms, criteria and rules simultaneously defined and implemented by public and private actors. It is not possible here to provide an exhaustive analysis,[4] but insofar as the world of agencies and 'hybrid organisations' has been studied more and is better known (Thatcher and Stone Sweet 2003; Koppell 2003; Christensen and Laegreid 2006; Graz 2008: 230–45; Gilardi 2008), I chose quite a different example, the case of ISO norms.[5] Created in 1947, the ISO (International Organization for Standardization) is a public establishment, including an increasing number of countries whose activity has been galvanised by neoliberal globalisation, in particular with the intensification of the WTO negotiations. A first important point for our discussion of hybrid rule as a new form of the political is the periodisation one. As for NPM, government by standards and norms extended from the 1970s. The deepening of globalisation, mostly in services and transportation, the growing use of subcontracts, delocalisation and decomposition (and internationalisation) of production processes, the development of both management rules and information and communication technologies, all these evolutions run in favour of standards and gave stronger authority and autonomy to the ISO: the institution started producing not 'ISO recommendations' but 'international standards' (Murphy and Yates 2009; Ruwet 2011).

A second point concerns the nature of hybrid rule. The ISO standards are, however, not defined either by public technicians or by private ones but by the 'consensus' of an extremely complex and plural professional world (manufacturers in every sector of industry, commercial companies, distributors, importers and exporters, the associations that represent the latter as well as the industrial associations that represent SMEs); university researchers and other types of research institutes or laboratories; consumer associations at the national, regional or international level; governments and regulatory bodies at the national or regional level; interests that deal with societal, environmental or other issues represented by NGOs. States are not represented as such but by their agencies of standardisation, which, depending on the country, may be public, private or mixed. Furthermore, the experts—precisely because the area of competence is very narrowly defined—often pass from one 'sphere' or from one institution to another: they may be in a business for a while, then spend time in an administration or an agency, etc. Finally, the process of standardisation set in motion by agencies, generally at the request of private actors, may see itself being imposed on the set of actors at the request of the public authorities.

Standardisation rests on the principle of paradigmatic traceability: it means the power to recognise and go back to the procedures that permit the production of a product or a service; so it is a mechanism of control that requires ways of doing things to be carefully noted, and compared with the rules that are known and accepted in the profession.[6] Of course, a certain form of traceability has always existed; there was always a desire to control, supervise and keep watch on. But the way this traceability is done has changed radically; before, it was done by institutional organisations governing areas such as customs, internal revenue, the suppression of fraud and the protection of the environment. Since the 1970s—and every day more—it's been done by a set of bureaucratic and legal rules. Thus, quality is not the recognition of a result; it is merely the presence of procedures (that must be, and are often not, used) and the granting, by a higher category of experts, of a certificate to the firm's employee or 'apprentice' who keeps the procedural rule book. This process of traceability concerns businesses, but other private actors (consumers) as much as public actors (i.e. States, in the name of consumer protection) extend its use. Clearly, at every link in the chain there is an interweaving of interests and a blurring of the lines between public and private. Generally, the need for a standard is expressed by the private sector, which transmits its request to the specialised (often public) entity in its country, which in turn passes on the request to the ISO. The construction of the standard occurs by consensus. The organisation publishes documents, organises regular revisions and just as regularly updates its catalogue of all standards. 'Up to now, 16,000 standards, comprising over 620,000 pages in French and English' says the ISO website (www.iso.org). This presentation and its formulation immediately suggest the fundamental bureaucratic dimension of this process of standardisation. Internally, the production of ISO standards is the result of perfectly clearly demarcated procedures: a committee entrusted with the 'preparatory project' meets; then successive 'committee projects' that have to reach a consensus and open up the possibility of creating a 'projected standard'; then come the negotiations, the vote, and approval, in accordance with defined criteria; finally, the publication of the standard and its revision three years later, then every five years. A committee to regulate the indications of conformity to the standard—whose aim is to provide consumers with information—establishes general principles and standards, principles of labelling that themselves follow strict standards, etc. This whole bureaucratic process is brought together in a guide for the preparation of Standard Methods for Measuring Performances.

But the bureaucratic dimension is to be found of course—and above all—within the enterprises that adopt ISO norms. The bureaucrats involved need first to embark on a planning process, fix aims and objectives, intermediary targets, and construct plans to attain them. These then need to be implemented, and what is done must be verified as in conformity with the planned objectives, via various indicators. And inevitably, the objectives, criteria and measures need to be adapted in accordance with the results of verification. The bureaucratic process is pursued with the quest for certification, i.e. the acknowledgment, on the part of an independent national organisation, that the enterprise is applying the norm properly. This certification requires an audit of the management system and verifies that it conforms to the demands specified in the norm. Only at the end of this audit can the agency deliver a written assurance that the norm is being respected, and register the certification in its register of clients. The audit is, in reality, a self-validation of a frame of reference produced by an organisation that is itself certified.

The ISO case exemplifies an apparent paradox: through the choice of norms coming from the private sector and more or less standardised, public intervention intends to deregulate and diminish the presence and interference of public administration but it becomes a bureaucratic machine. This process is not direct since it's not imposed from the state or from the private sector. It's a process of normalisation coming from both parts. On one side, the economic world (or more exactly the most powerful actors of a globalised economic world) tends to impose theses standards because they are tools of economic domination. On the other side, these standards impose themselves and they become essential because state entities give them authority and use them more and more frequently (for example in tenders and public markets) (Weiss 2003; Ruwet 2011). The nature of the process is different from the NPM's one; it's more subtle and difficult to qualify. It's an illustration of the privatisation of the state I analysed some years ago: the use of standards can be analysed as a new mode of government, a form of redeployment of state intervention, but unlike NPM, this process of privatisation is not the result of a precise decision; it results from the necessary adaptation to constraints and from projects of various non-state actors. This is an important point. What makes the difference between Hurt and Lipschutz conceptualisation (project of colonisation) and my conceptualisation (privatisation of the state/neoliberal bureaucratisation) is the question of intentionality.

For the former, a project, a decision, a more or less explicit rationale and thought exists; for the latter, there was not, at the beginning, a project of substituting direct intervention from administration by indirect intervention through norms and standards. The use of norms and standards is neither decided, nor programmed, nor forecast, nor considered; it's the result of relations of power between different actors, economic conditions and wheel-work of behaviour, negotiations, compromises and previous decisions. In the case of standards, there is no project, no decision coming from the government to use standards from the private sector. But these standards became gradually unavoidable as a result of three processes: 1) political delegitimation of direct intervention by public entities, 2) ideological hegemony of the idea that market rule and enterprise standards are the best principles to follow for good government, and 3) economic practices and rationalisation processes that increasingly use standards as a way to control and supervise productivity, efficiency and profit. These three processes legitimate the 'government by norms'.[7] It's not an explicit will from state institutions and actors to use standards as public action, it's an expression of a much more diffuse *imaginaire* in the society for which 'the private' is the absolute reference. It's a true co-production in which it's difficult to assign responsibility to public or private actors. Instead, the interweaving of public and private actors in this bureaucratic process sustains itself through the complexity of its procedures. There is an effect of reinforcement and 'irreversibility' (Callon 1998).

At present, the market operates according to norms that not only comprise the capitalist system, but are also proof of rationalisation, modernisation and technical domination. In these conditions, to impose itself in the economic domain the market needs to go through the production of new norms. And for a new norm to gain acceptance, it needs to be compatible with existing norms, including the management norms that structure capitalist economic life.[8] The growth in norms is also fuelled by the essentially unfinished nature of standardisation. This is always in progress, since improvements can always be envisaged and new norms regularly make an appearance. The growth in the number of procedures, rules and norms is the result of a complex process that combines technical improvements, the 'market' effect, and the effect of competition through innovation, by the protection of innovation and the attempt to create 'niches', and by the effect of distinction and marketing, and so on. Finally, the growth of norms is fed by the way the process of standardisation fits into another characteristic of contemporary capitalism: externalisation, outsourcing, and the internationalisation of these processes. In a configuration that always comes with government at a distance, the increased resort to contractual relations, a product of this new organisation of production, requires the development of norms that will make it possible for people to get things done and to have control. Those who give orders must be able to give orders unambiguously, to follow, monitor, 'trace' and be sure of their subcontractors. And these norms themselves must be harmonised so that the doubling up of evaluation and control does not lead to contradictory injunctions, and also so that the evaluation and control of these norms can themselves be outsourced. Within this context, it is necessary to have ever more detailed and shared norms, and ever more sophisticated procedures of traceability, auditing arrangements and certifying techniques. In this movement, 'bureaucracy creates its order. The more fragmented activities become, the more diverse, specialised and compartmentalised the departments, the more numerous the storeys of the building and the delegations of authority on every storey, the more we find—by reason of this very same dispersal—that bodies for coordination and control multiply, and the more bureaucracy prospers' (Lefort 1960).

What is neoliberal bureaucracy?[9]

This bureaucratic dimension of neoliberalism, which may appear paradoxical or even shocking with regard to current ideology, is nonetheless familiar to specialists of the historical sociology of state formation and to readers of the great classics. Thus, the analysis of the snowballing effect of rules and norms mentioned earlier is now more than a century old, dating back to when Max Weber showed that, historically speaking, liberalism had created inflation in the number of economic institutions. Karl Polanyi drew on this tradition when he brought out how liberalism stimulated an unprecedented increase in the number of legislative and administrative measures, with the particular aim of allowing obstacles to the commodification of land, money and work to be dismantled.[10] Following the same line of argument, Michel Foucault points out that the market 'was [...] invested with extremely prolific and strict regulations':[11] an art of governing based on the market cannot be embodied in any form of *laissez-faire* but rather in a 'framework policy' (Foucault 2008: 140) opening the way to an 'active governmentality' necessary to making the whole of society conform with the principles of enterprise, competition, and the market.

Return to Max Weber

I feel it is worth returning to Max Weber, so as to put paid once and for all to a widespread idea: contrary to the common view, his critique of bureaucracy does not concern merely the administrative apparatus of the state. Far from it: Weber adopts an extremely broad and complex view of bureaucracy, and considers it to be a multi-dimensional and general phenomenon: admittedly, his most frequently quoted works—especially the works that set out to interpret Weber's thinking—do concern state apparatuses alone;[12] but his political writings (Weber 1994) and other entire passages from *Economy and Society* (Weber 1994: second part of text) show that bureaucratisation does not pertain to state administration alone, and that judicial and administrative constraints (another way of characterising bureaucracy) also characterise big businesses and capitalism. Weber notes that capitalist enterprise presents bureaucracy with a privileged framework for development insofar as 'the demand for as rigorous a calculability and foreseeability as possible favours the rise of a special layer of administrators and imposes on the latter a certain type of structuring' (Lefort 1960: 292). He goes so far as to speak of bureaucratisation 'in *all* fields', and mentions political parties, clubs, lobbies and interest groups, churches ... (Weber 1978: 223). He underlines the way that, vis-à-vis its older forms, modern bureaucracy is distinguished inter alia by the emphasis placed on the division of labour, specialisation and rational technical training, and assessment through impartial procedures.[13] For Weber—who on this point disagrees with Marx—bureaucracy is not a parasitical organisation; it is a necessary and fundamental element of capitalism (Lefort 1960). It is characteristic of the process of rationalisation, of the rise of calculation, of writing and of assessment in modern societies;[14] and it is, moreover, properly established only when capitalism dominates society. In Weber's work, there is an identity between the bureaucratic movement and the capitalist process of rationalisation. 'The future belongs to bureaucracy,' he concludes (Weber 1994), if we accept that 'bureaucracy is *the* means of transforming social action into rationally organised action' (Weber 1978: 987, Weber's emphasis).

Upon rereading these fundamental texts, how can anyone fail to think of the norms of what is called 'new public management', of the procedures of normalisation and certification that are, these days, required in businesses as well as banks, of the procedures active in universities and research, and of the structures of participation in development or good governance? How can we fail to remember the rules that each and every one of us must respect in order to be considered as a citizen, as a legal immigrant or as a refugee eligible for the right to asylum? In Weber's words, we really are in the presence of a process of 'universal bureaucratisation' (Weber 1978), or in the words of Bruno Rizzi, in the Marxist tradition, of a 'bureaucratisation of the world',[15] or, if we follow Cornelius Castoriadis and the work produced by *Socialisme ou barbarie* (Castoriadis 1990), a 'bureaucratic society'. It is in this sense, and with these theoretical reference points in mind, that I speak of a 'new' form of bureaucracy, a bureaucracy by norms, by rules, by a whole set of structures of control that do not pass mainly through state administrations but more through the normative and organising structures of society themselves. What gives them the stamp of neoliberalism and enables me to speak of 'neoliberal bureaucracy' is the fact that these norms and these rules to a large extent arose from the 'private' sector or, more precisely, that they are as often as not co-produced by what people continue to call the 'public' and the 'private' sectors, but which can be defined and identified only with difficulty, so intense are the processes of hybridisation, or more precisely of the overlapping and transformation of the meanings of both of these notions. In other words, neoliberal bureaucracy is one of the strongest expressions of hybrid rule that characterises the current political situation.

The neoliberal bureaucratisation of society

The order of the market and of enterprise, in particular management, extends to the world of the state with 'new public management', as we have seen—but it also invests the whole of 'society as such, in its fabric and depth' (Foucault 2008: 145). It constitutes the 'new spirit' of neoliberalism (Boltanski and Chiapello 2012). Justice and security on the one side, participation and voluntary work on the other, and, finally, knowledge both theoretical and practical constitute interesting illustrations of the neoliberal bureaucracy: they suggest the diversity of dynamics that produce the process of hybridisation, the diversity of logics that underpin hybrid rule. These dynamics don't go altogether in the same way, and above all are not necessarily carried on by the same actors.

The example of justice and security illustrate perfectly the thesis that Hurt and Lipschutz have propounded in their introduction. The 'zero tolerance' policy is a political project that replaces the welfare state in the hope of restoring and enhancing state authority and sovereignty. This project is not conducted by a will to colonise the private sector, but is the result of the diffusion of private manners of thinking to state actors: it is the result of an analysis that draws an analogy with the 'zero default' policy of the chains of production, and an analysis of behaviour that denies the freedom of the subject in the name of security. Hybridisation means, here, a process of de-differentiation, a loss of specificity of the public good, and the public interest. This policy of social intolerance thus transforms justice (especially penal justice) 'into a total bureaucratic system', notably by the mechanisation of punishment (Sainati and Schalchi 2007: 11; Garapon 2010): the decision is no longer delivered on the basis of the facts but following the principles of the 'treatment' of delinquency, of the last-minute 'management', of the 'execution' of punishments in real time without any regard for their social usefulness; appeal court judges have to write reports on the management of the court, with indicators of performance and the splitting of magistrates and civil servants into 'full-time equivalents' (Marshall 2008: 25–35). This policy turns the magistrate into a manager whose job it is to increase his 'portfolio of proceedings'. It also creates bureaucratisation, since justice sees itself being subjected to all the processes of bureaucratic rationalisation and systematic assessment characteristic of NPM, in particular with a demand for information to be put into figures and statistics (figures for questioning, for elucidation …), the assessment of judges, the production of information on the number of verdicts reached, on the ratio between people sentenced and judges, and on the costs of prosecutions. Justice even experiences an application of the quality drive in the private sector, with the application of the system of official norms: sentences are certified ISO 9001.

The blurring of the boundaries between public and private, the practices of overlapping, and the way in which conflicts of interest are becoming commonplace (and even legal) increase this bureaucratisation by norms. In France, for example, the promoters of 'zero tolerance' are the CEOs of private companies giving security advice.[16] But this is found in Latin America as in Africa, with the development of private companies which guarantee the exploitation of natural resources, protect certain districts and certain citizens, enable the pursuit of economic activities in an environment of extreme violence … and, of course, in the United States, with the delegation of the pursuit of war, intelligence and even torture to private enterprises.[17] Given the general political disaffection noted in European countries, for example, new structures of participation are being set up, and formal procedures are meant to improve the operation of democracy: the codification of the place of citizens, of the relation between the citizen and the administration by technical procedures (local elections, referendums, citizens' charters, etc.), the definition of the rights of citizens or of the responsibilities of civil servants. When an investment has been decided on, one with effects on the environment, highly specific procedures are set up, formalised and standardised, described in detail in the laws on the assessment of impact on the environment (Callon, Lascoumes and Barthes 2009): consultations have to be organised, the direct and indirect effects of the investment evaluated, and procedures of compensation defined. Whereupon, a standardising and formal bureaucratisation of participatory procedures is set up, in other words, a 'bureaucratisation of participation' (de Vries 2000: 325–42) by the imposition of rigid deadlines (consultation must intervene at a very precise moment), the precise formulation of what the populace is supposed to be expressing its feelings about, the definition of the criteria and norms on the basis of which people can make their voices heard.

This bureaucratisation also concerns participation in development. In the name of 'appropriation' and 'ownership', projects, programmes or policies financed by donors increasingly have to go through a sort of 'discharge' on NGOs and by the demand for the formal and obligatory establishment of mechanisms of participation.[18] This process takes various forms, such as the setting up of local NGOs,[19] the reactivation of village councils, and the organisation of participatory meetings or public consultations. NGOs are now integrated into what Jayasuriya calls neoliberal 'economic constitutionalism', in other words into the hegemonic logic of commodification (Jayasuriya 2005). Even if this participation takes place unbeknownst to the people involved in non-government activities, they do not represent an alternative, a counter-hegemonic project, but are part and parcel of the neoliberal order, increasingly involved in workfare around micro-credit activities and the logic of micro-entrepreneurship (Elyachar 2005; Servet 2006; Bugra 2007: 33–52; Bono 2010a; Berkovitch and Kemp 2012) and demanding a professionalisation of their personnel, rendered necessary by the quest for finance and by constraints linked to the support of donors who, in increasing numbers, delegate their social policies to these representatives of civil society (Bondi and Laurie 2005; Hély 2009). The operational modes of the donors and enterprises that support these organisations are transferred to NGOs in return for the respect of procedures able to facilitate control of their activities (Riles 2000). As a result, the boundaries between the world of NGOs, the world of enterprises, and the world of the state blurred, and there is a process of 'bureaucratisation of NGOs'. By becoming ever more integrated into the market, by participating in this logic of increasing commodification, NGOs also become integrated into this world of norms, rules and bureaucratic structures inspired by private management. This is especially clearly brought out by the increasing role of normed procedures that are summarised in these manuals, précis or guides which NGOs have to follow scrupulously if they are not to lose out on additional funding; by the generalisation of norms of management and even prudential norms (notably in the case of micro-credit); by the development of the culture of invitations to tender that require extremely strict replies, in accordance with definite procedures that are framed by rules of management, financial rules, but also a well-defined mode of thinking (Bono 2010b). And this bureaucracy, of course, extends to the brokers, experts and 'beneficiaries' in villages and town districts, who need to be able to fill in the forms, find out information, draw up documents, master the procedures for invitations, and so on (Jacob and Lavigne-Delville 1994: 169–81).

The neoliberal bureaucratisation of society suggests a complex dynamic. Privatisation of the state, transformation of the exercise of power and redefinition of the political through hybrid rule are fuelled by processes that don't come from the state and are not entirely control by it. Thus, this 'participation' of the society to new forms of government open the field of the possible: sometimes, it can shift the emphasis or a form of the political project, sometimes it can reorient it or even subvert it, but it can also—and it's most often the case—consolidate it.

The bureaucratic production of indifference

I would now like to try and understand the various types of political momentum that underlie this process. The disciplinary dimension and the functions of control and surveillance traditionally associated with the analysis of state administration also concern the neoliberal bureaucracy analysed here. Michel Foucault's emphasis on the 'conjunction between the disciplines and liberalism' (Foucault 2008) is yet again an echo of Max Weber's analysis: for the latter, in a modern society, 'complete dominance' is achieved in everyday administration, and 'is distinguished from other historical bearers of the modern, rational way of ordering life by the fact of its far greater *inescapability*' (Weber 1994: 156). Every bureaucracy creates a milieu of power by virtue of a specific mode of behaviour, based on the respect for rules, a hierarchy and a system of command. In other words, it is an institution, an ethos, and a set of practices in the service of the dominant (Weber 1978). There are many examples of this, and they are often foregrounded by work that is critical of neoliberalism. So I will not dwell on them; this attention to the disciplinary mechanisms of neoliberal bureaucracy is now perfectly real.

What I feel is more important to analyse at present, because it is subtler and often imperceptible, is definitely the contribution of neoliberal bureaucracy to the production of social, political and moral indifference. This indifference is created by the combination of the quest for efficiency, for technological sophistication, for distancing, for the primacy of instrumental rationality and the normality of everyday work. Historians in connection with Nazism and the genocide of the Jews have pointed out this process. But it is much more diffuse than that is believed, it's not circumscribed to exceptional situations precisely because it emerges from an extremely commonplace configuration characteristic of all modern societies: the coupling of the 'functional division of labour', of the 'substitution of technical for moral responsibility', and the 'good performance of the job in hand' (Bauman 1991). It obviously concerns situations of conflict, for example today in Afghanistan with the use of drones, those unmanned planes that are guided from American offices, which leads to the very notion of war and human losses itself being lost. But it also concerns the daily aspect of our lives, especially at a time when technical norms and procedures are becoming ever more dominant with neoliberal bureaucratisation. Less visible, its effects are, in this sense, more insidious and laden with consequences.

Thus, the moral and political sense of the social question or of inequality eventually disappears into the complexity and technical aspect of bureaucratic practices. Without going into a detailed analysis, I emphasise here how commonplace it is, based on the way poverty is turned into a technical and numerical problem—and I thus hope to suggest how much these technical and expert arrangements, combined with a desire for modernisation and rationalisation, can easily legitimise bureaucratic actions (on the side of public actors such as NGOs, experts and other specialists) who also transmit an authoritarian exercise of power. This production of indifference results simultaneously from the absence of relation between the purpose of the action and technical and bureaucratic engineering, from the dissociation between the efficaciousness of the action and the moral and political assessment of the latter's objectives, of the distancing of the objects of action vis-à-vis technical procedures and arrangements.[20] The depoliticisation of the (highly sensitive) question of poverty now involves its quantification (Ferguson 1994): poverty must be measured in order to assess its development and the impact of the actions set in motion to reduce it, and to target the beneficiaries of measures and establish comparisons. Lines and thresholds of poverty are defined, separating the poor from the non-poor in terms of income, health, education and access to goods, in a denial of society and social categories. Social safety nets are set up, targeted at a population that has been identified on the basis of quantified criteria. Indifference also stems from a vision that considers poverty as a residual phenomenon arising from the individual responsibility of the poor themselves. This is why the poor are encouraged to get a grip on themselves, and in particular to become autonomous entrepreneurs through a whole arsenal of norms, rules and measures aimed at leading the 'beneficiaries' to improve their 'capabilities' for management and to become 'responsible' in a logic of 'empowerment' and 'ownership' spread through training programmes and various documents.[21] These bureaucratic techniques and practices constitute a machinery for producing moral, political and social indifference, one that makes decent, presentable and acceptable a phenomenon that is not. It is not a matter of highlighting and studying wretchedness, poverty and marginalisation and understanding their social and political dimensions. Instead, through a managerial and economistic analysis, through quantified instruments, kits explained in manuals, tools of development, through the establishment of reproducible models, 'programmes' need to be set up, and 'lessons' drawn from comparable experiences; people are encouraged to apply 'recipes', to pursue 'good' economic policies and find the formulae of 'good' governance. The violence of social relations, political conflicts, the many different vectors of inequality are all concealed by distancing and the chain of acts, decisions, men and measures that end up obscuring the purpose and the outcome of the actions of development undertaken. All that is left are neutral techniques that euphemise the political and social complexity of poverty and perpetuate the relations of domination that lie at the basis of its acceptance. The case of the fight against poverty shows the political nature of this bureaucratic production of indifference. It's a kind of process of depolitisation understood not as a denial of the political, but as a very political process which redefine what can be considered as political and what cannot be considered as political, what can be discussed and what is too objective, neutral, technical or marginal to be qualified for political debate. In other words, it's a process of 'pacification of the political' as analysed by Hurt and Lipschutz. The obsession of control, the over-valorisation of rationalisation and quantification, a technical and narrow conception of social dynamics, an apolitical vision of the economic life, all this ends up in a shrinking of the places, the subjects and the actors of public debates and political participation.

Looking to neoliberal bureaucratisation thus is also a way to explore the depoliticising dimension of hybrid rule. For in all these cases, indifference ensues from the depoliticisation concomitant with bureaucratisation of police, humanitarian, judicial and legal organisations, but also of medicine and psychology. This depoliticisation is very ambiguous and deceptive since it is, in reality, the expression of a particularly normalising exercise of power, of a (re)definition of the political marked by exclusion. Current movements of civil disobedience, for example in France vis-à-vis the law against foreigners (but also against managerialism) are very interesting for our analysis (Ogien and Laugier 2010). They suggest the extent of the depolitisation process since all classical channels for discontent seems to be neutralised, unable to give voice to protesters; but simultaneously they suggest that the production of moral indifference can end in such a feeling of dispossession that it can feed new dynamics of political participation.

The bureaucrat as neoliberal subject, bureaucracy as the moving locus of power

So doing, hybrid rule appears more and more ambivalent. The fact is that the process of bureaucratisation is also fuelled by requirements of autonomy and accountability, by the belief in the benefits of procedural rationality, and by the responses; however, these may be clumsy in relation to demands of emancipation and liberty. This explains why an increasing number of people from the society participate in this process of bureaucratisation and in the definition of hybrid rule. The examples of asylum seekers and of research have suggested that bureaucratisation does not occur outside society but takes effect through the very actors who are its target and who, consciously or not, are accomplices of this process. The neoliberal art of governing proceeds through the intermediary of individuals and it is in this sense that we can say that we are not witnessing a bureaucratisation 'from above', but a much broader and more complex process of 'bureaucratic participation' (Riles 2000: 17). This participation springs from different dynamics, but these later converge to shape bureaucratisation.

Bureaucratisation cannot be reduced to a process of the pure and simple acceptance of norms, procedures, rules and formalisms that can be clearly identified, that have their own power and operate as an exterior constraint. In fact, the norms are often vague, the rules fluctuating and random, and a pick-and-mix approach to techniques, 'good practices' and ad hoc arrangements inevitable. And this leaves room for much more latitude than would at first sight appear to be the case—and many more possibilities for interpretation and improvisation too, as is suggested by the sociological analyses of new public management. Furthermore, bureaucratic normalisation needs to be understood within its own dynamic, as a complex process on the more or less mastered set of rules based on norms that are indefinite in the sense that they 'are not pre-established or preconstituted', but 'produce themselves and define their way of proceeding as they act closely, *in situ*, on the contents they aim to regulate', developing 'by means of the same antagonistic process that makes and unmakes the forms of this human life' (Macherey 2009: 131). This dynamic understanding of norms undermines any static, passive vision of the latter. Norms are not fixed in advance, they do not prescribe normal life in society; they assume meaning only in their concrete exercise, in individual experience. Only in this way do they affirm their normative value. And this is another way of emphasising that we are not just in the presence of retroactive actions, of circumventions, of homemade fixes, of interpretations and adaptations, but that actors also have a degree of autonomy, a capacity for fabrication in the true sense of the word—a fabrication which, while integrating and drawing on the constraints imposed upon them, permit the expression of something singular following independent logics.[22] This is the case with documents, symbols of bureaucracy for procedures, which can open up, in both the metaphorical and literal senses of the term (Bagioli in Riles 2000: 127–57); they have a life, are produced but also read, and by different persons with different interests, preoccupations and visions; they can also be interpreted in many different ways. In other words, as Robert Harper would put it, these documents have a 'career': their material and social forms are transformed, as are the meanings attributed to them, the ways they are read, the uses that are expected of them in function of different places (from one department to another of an institution, from one institution to another) and of different times (Harper 1998). Finally and above all, perhaps, these neoliberal bureaucratic procedures are not implemented in a normative and regulative no man's land; they are part and parcel of a set of practices produced by a specific historical trajectory, so that the proliferation of rules, laws and practices makes it possible for choices to be made, accommodations reached, and the interplay between contradictory norms and procedures realised.

Conclusion

All these dynamics explain how a bureaucratic inflation is eventually produced—an inflation in the number of regulations, of norms, of procedures. The situation is one of a simultaneous process of bureaucratic 'anarchy' (Blum and Mespoulet 2003) and bureaucratic 'outbidding' (Samuel 2009), which creates a process of perpetual reform with ever more details, ever more measures, new indicators, new mechanisms of control … . In these conditions, the political horizon of neoliberalism could be considered to be completely dark, with an increasing number of mechanisms of control, surveillance, discipline and normalisation. But the neoliberal art of governing, as has been said, is also a permanent critique of government action, in particular a critique of disciplines, of the procedures of control and coercion, a fundamental scepticism vis-à-vis the capacities and concrete possibilities of being perfectly well-acquainted with what needs to be governed and vis-à-vis the modes of intervention. This explains how, simultaneously, we are also witnessing 'the appearance in this new art of government of mechanisms with the function of producing, breathing life into, and increasing freedom, of introducing additional freedom through additional control and intervention' (Foucault 2008: 67).

This does not prevent neoliberal bureaucratisation from creating new internal splits between actors: it redefines the tensions, the conflicts, the internal places of opposition. By authorising the expression of divergences and even confrontations, they make it possible for proper logics to be deployed. And because these logics do not question the political and moral economy of norms and procedures, they legitimate their normative power by broadening the possible modes of power relations.

The example of neoliberal bureaucratisation complicates the analysis of hybrid rule. It confirms that the historical process of convergence between private and public spheres doesn't lead to the retreat of the state but to the redeployment of state power, and often to an increase of disciplinary and normative ambitions. But it shows also the ambivalence of bureaucratic practices and the diversity of bureaucratic actors; so doing, it suggests also that hybrid rule is an indeterminate process which gives place to relations of force.

Notes

1 I have taken the concept of 'discharge' from Max Weber's historical works (my French term 'décharge' translates the German terms *Verpachtung* and *Überweisung*): Weber (2003/1923). For my reinterpretation of this term, see 'Preface to the English edition' in Hibou (2004/1999: vii–xvi).
2 Hart (1995); Hodge and Greve (2005). For a concrete analysis based on a particular case of the delegation of public service, see Hibou and Vallée (Dec. 2006).
3 On the way the NPM promotes 'home-made', improvised solutions, see Hood (Spring 1991: 3–19); Merrien (Spring 1999: 95–103); Bezes (Feb. 2007: 9–29).
4 For more examples, see Hibou (Feb. 2009: at second European congress of FASOPO) as well as the other presentations given that day and Hibou (2014).
5 On ISO norms, see Brunsson and Jacobsson et al. (2002); Hallstrom (2004: 233–60); Dudouet, Mercier and Vion (June 2006: 367–92); Murphy and Yates (2009); and personal research.
6 On traceability, see Cochoy (2007: 91–101); Bartley (May 2010).
7 Thévenot (1997: 204–42). See also, following on from Thevenot: Dunn (2005: 173–93); Dunn refers to a 'normative governmentality'. Murphy and Yates (2009) and Brunsson and Jacobsson et al. (2000); these writers emphasise how the realm

of norms has spread beyond the industrial and more broadly technical sphere to management, the environment, and social questions. Brütsch and Lehmkulh (2007: 9–32); the authors here use the term 'norm-based momentum' and point out that the number of legal norms is increasing at the international level—as do Schemeil and Eberwein (2009).

8 Hence the particular importance of the norms ISO 9000: Demortain in Schemeil and Eberwein (2009: 131–51; Murphy and Yates (2009).
9 I am clearly alluding here to the title of Lefort's article, 'What is bureaucracy?' (1960).
10 See Polanyi (1944), which says (p. 145) that there was nothing natural about 'laisser-faire', and Bugra, 'Polanyi's concept of double movement and politics in the contemporary market society' in Bugra and Agartan (dir.) (2007: 173–89). See also Braudel (1974) and Rosanvallon (1999).
11 M. Foucault, *The Birth of Biopolitics* (2008), lecture of 17 January 1979: 30. On another occasion he indicates in particular that this production and this management of freedom constitute 'the conditions for the creation of a formidable body of legislation and an incredible range of governmental interventions to guarantee production of the freedom needed in order to govern' (lecture of 24 January 1979: 63–5).
12 Weber (1978). There are problems with both French and English translations of Weber's work. For an exception that proves the rule, see Kalberg, 'Max Weber's type of rationality: Cornerstones for the analysis of rationalisation processes in history', *American Journal of Sociology*, 85/5, pp. 1145–79 and *Max Weber's Comparative-Historical Sociology* (Chicago, IL: Chicago University Press, 1994).
13 'Historically, too, 'progress' towards the bureaucratic state [...] stands in the closest relation to the development of modern capitalism. The main inner foundation of the modern capitalist business is *calculation*. In order to exist, it requires a system of justice and administration which, in principle at any rate, functions in a *rationally calculable* manner according to stable, general norms, just as one calculates the predictable performance of a *machine*.' In short, progress towards bureaucracy exists in a capitalist economy as much as in state administration, according to Weber, underlining the way that 'modern high capitalism' arose 'in places where the judges began as advocates. Nowadays, however, bureaucracy and capitalism have met and belong together intimately' (Weber 1994: 148–9) 'Parliament and Government'.
14 This is clearly brought out in two recent books: Riles (2006); Gardey (2008).
15 Rizzi (1985/1939). His analysis underlies that of Burnham in the same period— Burnham (1941)—and was taken up later by Jacoby (1973/1969).
16 The cases of Claude-Jean Calvet, CEO of Espace-Risk Management, and especially of Alain Bauer, the head of AB Associates, are good examples. Their careers are studied in Mucchielli (2002); Rimbert (2004: 235–76); Bonelli (2010).
17 The bibliography on this topic is vast. For example: Krahmann (2010); Valcarce Lorenc (2011); R. Banégas (1998: 179–94).
18 The process of NGO-isation is described in, for example, Berkovitch and Kemp (2012).
19 Destremeau studies the case of a female consultant who had six months to set up 600 NGOs in Mauretania, at the demand of donors: B. Destremau (2009). See also J.P. Olivier de Sardan, 'La gestion communautaire sert-elle l'intérêt public?', *Politique africaine*, 80, December 2000, pp. 153–68; Jacob and Lavigne-Delville (1994).
20 These elements are highlighted by Bauman, ibid.; Ginzburg (2002: 157–72), (the expression 'series of relations in which we are all caught up' is taken from this work: 166) and Traverso (2009).

21 On the analysis of the conceptualisation of poverty in the neoliberal order, see Hibou (1998); Procacci (1996: 405–16); Peñafiel (2008). For a critical analysis of the structures of the fight against poverty, see Samuel, (2009); Egil (2005: 97–115); Giovalucchi and Olivier de Sardan (2009: 383–406); Bono (2010b).
22 This is clearly also the lesson of *The Practice of Everyday Life* and the other works by Michel de Certeau.

4 Post-Fordist hybridization
A historical-materialist approach to two modes of state transformation

Ulrich Brand

Introduction

The concepts of hybridization of the state and hybrid rule seek to explain recent state transformations, focusing on features beyond the "privatization of public authority" and the overly abstract question of whether the state loses or gains power as a result. The convincing starting point is to the argument that a *"hybrid rule strategy* seeks to safeguard the state's legitimacy through valorization of the market as a primary mechanism in pursuit of myriad political objectives."[1] How we understand such transformational processes as well as the relationship between the public and the private depends strongly on the theoretical approach we take toward the state and its role and functions in society *and* our understanding of state power. From an historical-materialist perspective, the modern capitalist state is *always* a hybrid, but the concrete character of "really existing" and its social functions are contextual and contingent and it changes over time. At a middle-range level of abstraction,[2] the post-Fordist, internationalized competition state must be regarded as both a contested product and an integral part of domination-shaped social restructuring and *re*-hybridization. This means that the transformation of diverse social relations, such as those between capital and labor, the international division of labor, gender relations and related forms of societal reproduction, ethnic relations and migration policies and social forms of the appropriation of nature and dealing with the ecological crisis are all affected by hybridization and hybrid rule.

As a starting point for this chapter, I argue that historically concrete forms of hybridity and state intervention depend largely on historical developments, relationships of forces and the reproductive conditions of those forces, for example, the reproduction of industrial capital during Fordism or recent financialized and globalized capitalism and the integration of local or national economies into the world market. In the second section I outline a theoretical understanding of state and hegemony and, against this background, briefly discuss my understanding of hybridization. After this I offer a sketch of recent state transformation, that is, the internal restructuring and internationalization of the state—or better said, its internal structuring through the inter- and transnationalization of societal relations—as well as its changing practices. Note that hybridization becomes a means through which the "state" becomes internationalized and something more than merely an aggregation or interplay of particular and notionally independent national states.

In this chapter, and somewhat in contrast to the other formulations in this volume, I focus on two dimensions of hybridization that I consider crucial (but not exclusively so): the *public–private* and the *national–international*. Fordism was the hegemonic mode of development in the West and East during much of the 20th century, beginning in the 1920s. It was not, however, institutionalized internationally until the 1950s and 1960s. During the latter period, often regarded as the "Bretton Woods" phase, hybrid rule and relations were stabilized primarily at the national level, but these also came to be embedded in the international political and economic relations of both *Pax Americana* and *Pax Sovietica* (Cox 1986). As noted elsewhere in this volume, during the 1970s this national–international Fordist system came into crisis. In the 1980s, the power-shaped restructuring of both dimensions of hybridity strongly reshaped societal relations, a process that accelerated after 1989. Subsequently, neoliberal or "post-Fordist" hybridization along "public–private" and "national–international" lines became more or less globally hegemonic, a structuring moment for many social relations. In the wake of the Great Recession, more recent post-Fordist efforts to stabilize societal relations of domination through certain modes of development have come into crisis, as well. It is too soon to determine, however, whether "post-neoliberal" forms can effectively address what appears to be a chronic global crisis of underconsumption and over-accumulation (Brand and Sekler 2009). This most recent (and continuing) of post-Fordist capitalism is again both shaping and destabilizing manifold social relations, without any obvious outcome in evidence (Demirović et al. 2011; Brand and Wissen 2012: 327–345).

Against this background, (the shaping of) hybridization and hybrid rule should be understood as elements of both politics and policies that motivate and follow changing conditions of societal reproduction and power relations (hegemony) as well as related discourses and governmentalities. In particular, the enhancement and reconfiguration of private property rights is a key dimension in the hybridization of the internationalized competition state, evident in ongoing enclosure of "knowledge commons" and the high visibility of intellectual property rights claims. These changes, diffused from the U.S. national context into the international realm, must be understood against the background of both changing relationships of social forces and relations and changing patterns and practices of accumulation and regulation reproduction. The latter, especially, goes beyond a narrow understanding of political economy as concerning merely trade and markets; instead, political economy embraces many other social spheres that are generally not located at the center of the accumulation process (Brand, Görg, Hirsch and Wissen 2008; Sum and Jessop 2014).

The strategic-relational approach developed by Bob Jessop (2007) makes clear that one crucial mode of historically concrete and contingent hybridization can be seen in the actual practices taking place in strategically selective forms and forums (Jessop 2007). These practices prioritize specific interests, values and identities and therefore shape and reflect the contents and forms of politics. In this sense, hybridization and hybrid rule also reflect shifts in power techniques and technologies, a point often ignored in governance debates but of particular importance here (see the Lipschutz chapter in this volume). Shifts toward the market and related forces as well as the internationalization of societal relations can be understood against this background.

The state as a contested social relation

In most of the scholarly literature, the state is a settled given. Amongst such scholars, we find debates and struggles over the organization of the state and its characteristics, the meanings and significance of state "sovereignty" and arguments that the state form is "in decline." Few bother to interrogate "the state" at any more fundamental level. By contrast, an historical-materialist conceptualization of the state is linked to consideration of the manifold and dominant forms in which people live together and organize social life, visible in forms of production and consumption: the social division of labor: dominant and marginal orientations, values and identities: the capacity of various actors to act, which depends on social power relations and access to specific means to pursue goals and create normalities; and the forms for dealing with those problems and crises related to the manifold social relations (Marx 2004/1848).

Social life under capitalist conditions or, more precisely, under the dominance of the capitalist mode of production is—according to tendencies that are more or less contested—structured by particular capitalist social forms: wage labor, commodities, capital, money, a capitalist state and the specific subjectivities that arise as a result.[3] Over some period of time, these forms can stabilize contradictory and crisis-driven societal relations and processes. Societal and political dynamics and conflicts are the result of the many forms in the societal division of labour, which, in turn, constitute societal dynamics, social domination and latent or manifest conflicts. This does not mean, however, that the entire social process and its relative durability are purely capitalist or that other modes of production do not persist but, rather, that these capitalist forms have the tendency to dominate those of a non-capitalist nature.

In that sense, among gendered, ethnically and nationally structured social classes, "vertical" conflicts arise over the appropriation of socially produced wealth, wage rates, dominant forms of non-wage labor and, consequently, over labor and living conditions, taxes, welfare, redistribution, etc. But "horizontal" relations and potential conflicts also need to be stabilized, for example, among the owners of capital or among segments of the public through cooperation, competition and conflict. An essential moment of societal dynamics consists of the constraints imposed on private firms: under threat of going bankrupt, each must compete successfully with other private firms. Consequently, as Marx and Engels pointed out, societal conditions are permanently revolutionized in the endless search for increased productivity and profit. Furthermore, horizontally organized forms of the division of labour and competition among territorial spaces (countries and regions) may also lead to conflict and struggle. Tensions and conflicts are also a result of capitalism's tendency to turn all aspects of life, including non-human nature, into commodities, permitting them to be valorised.

In order to understand more clearly dominant structures and processes, the concept of hegemony is helpful, especially as developed by Antonio Gramsci (1991). In this instance, "hegemony" means a "modern" form of bourgeois domination, in which elements of physical force and coercion step back behind forms of consent (Thomas 2009) and power becomes, according to tendency, less apparent or even invisible (see Leander in this volume). Under bourgeois-capitalist conditions, hegemony is an important condition for a dynamic growth model, relying on broad acceptance of hierarchies, from without and within the ruling forces, as well as the capacity of and the willingness of various groups and classes to compromise as foundational to domination. In addition, the concept of hegemony means that social order and dynamics can be stabilized only over a limited period of time, and only so long as the interests, values, and identities of the ruling forces can be pursued generally without interference from others. During periods of rapid technological and social change both hegemony and stability may come under challenge, leading to various forms of intrasocietal struggle.

One question about hegemony asks how and why subaltern groups and social forces become inscribed into diverse social structures. The answer is neither economistic nor a matter of "false consciousness" but, rather, points in the direction of material social practices and everyday consciousness, both of which are organized and stabilized through explicit or implicit moral, ethical, economic and political consensus as well as compromise and the shaping of subjectivities and political will.

To better understand the hybridization of the state along the private–public and national–international axes, it is useful to differentiate between *conflicts over hegemony* and *conflicts under conditions of a hegemonic constellation*. The former involves widely accepted forms or rules of social interaction and development that assure societal domination and socio-economic dynamics, including forms of institutional politics. The latter involves established forms of societal reproduction and conflict resolution that relevant social forces are unwilling or unable to modify. Hegemony emerges through the "hegemonic projects" of ruling classes and forces, though complex strategies, compromises and alliances which, when successful, are consensually accepted by relevant dominated actors.[4] The relations of forces themselves, as constitutive and a hallmark of a hegemonic constellation, are based on consent, as such. If these hegemonic projects can be established in most sectors of society and ensure a dynamic constellation of economic growth, we can speak of a "mode of development" or, in Gramsci's terms, an "historic bloc" (Gramsci 1991: 1045). Although highly uneven in time and space, the neoliberalization of societal relations in many societies since the 1970s and 1980s represents such a successful project.[5] An established hegemony also implies that relevant societal conflicts *are dealt with in a rule-guided way* and that parties in conflict adhere to those rules. This also means that forms of marginalization and the use of physical violence are socially less visible or receive passive consent. Whether or not conditions of hegemony exist in a given society is highly relevant for the forms and contents of social and political developments. In addition to these means of addressing conflicts, another element vital for consensus in capitalist societies is economic growth, which mitigates many potential and primarily distributional conflicts. Related to this, the valorization of nature is another deeply embedded element of consensus, inasmuch as it is a condition of a dynamic growth model.

In exploring hybridization of the state, I focus on conflicts *over* hegemony, the first form enumerated above. The primary argument here is that, since the 1980s, the hybridization of the state along the lines private–public and national–international has been fundamental feature of societal transformations and the effort to restore a particular form of hegemony. But such hybridization also produces the instabilities and risks responsible for today's multiple crises. During a crisis of a hegemonic mode of development, such as post-Fordism, the dominant forces in society begin to recognize that they may have to reformulate their interest, values and identities. It is over these matters that conflicts over hegemony are fought. In historical-materialist theory, this point has been emphasized, in particular, by regulation and Gramscian theories.[6] Latent conflicts, more or less suppressed or dealt with successfully under conditions of a hegemonic growth model, now become manifest, and offer (collective) actors the chance to articulate themselves against existing conditions. These forces try to transform those conditions even as others defend or to modify them in ways that will sustain their hegemony. At this point, I come to my primary object of interest in this chapter (and this volume). From an historical-materialist perspective, the state must be regarded as an unstable institutional, discursive and subjectivizing structure and practice.[7] The state is understood as one crucial social form in and through which people and collectives articulate and fight over conflicts of interests, values and identities. In that sense, the state is a perpetual terrain of struggles, contestation and asymmetric compromises as well as a process of privileging, co-optation and marginalization. There are, of course, many other terrains of contestation in social life, such as the work place, the public sphere, religion, forms of social self-organization and, not least, the subjectivization process itself. However— and this is a critical point—the state does not stand apart from other societal relations—e.g. the economic is co-constituted by state practices through laws, regulations and other means. Rather, as a specific social form and institutionalized social relation, the state plays an important role in regulating the manifold societal tensions and conflicts that permeate society and gives a certain durability to dominant or even hegemonic societal orientations and relationships of forces. But this does not mean that the state stands somehow apart from these orientations and relations.

In modern societies, the state and its myriad dimensions appear as a heterogeneous apparatus or institutional ensemble. As a complex practice, the state is itself a *specific social form*. It constitutes an institutional ensemble which—through law, material, administrative and knowledge resources, as well by the fact of being acknowledged as such—disposes of specific means so as to function as a terrain for dealing with and giving a specific form to the manifold social conflicts. The state provides a specific framework through which conflicts can be fought out without threatening the overall social order. On this terrain, the state's (political) decisions are claimed to be generally binding, and its units dispose over the legitimate (and, if necessary, violent) means to enforce those decisions. Such a relational understanding of the state highlights the point that it is part and parcel of the manifold social conflicts and not external to them.

With respect to its class dimension, the capitalist state is an institutional ensemble through which the bourgeoisie, as the dominant class, is politically organized as an entity through which it performs its political domination. But given its members' relationship of competition with each other, the bourgeoisie cannot organize itself autonomously and, as a rule, does not exercise its power by coercive means alone but rather, through law. The state is thus the form through which the bourgeoisie organizes as a power bloc, and where conflicts are fought out and projects and compromises are formulated between the different ruling fractions as well as with the ruled (for a feminist historical-materialist understanding of the state, (Ludwig, Sauer and Wohl 1985; Sauer and Wöhl 2011) with respect to societal relationships with nature) (Brand and Görg 2008). As Poulantzas put it, the state can be understood as "a relationship of forces, or more precisely the material condensation of such a relationship among classes and class factions, such as this is expressed in the state in a necessarily specific form" (Poulantzas [1978] 2002: 159).

When the modern capitalist state is not the instrument of particular forces or the site through which social wealth is appropriated—as in many countries with a "state class" and a state-led, rentier economy—this relative autonomy gives the state the appearance of standing "beside" or "above" society, appearing to be a specific social relation and practice in the name of a general will and a societal common good. This general will—the general interest in and of a society to maintain and enhance economic competitiveness in the world market—somehow appears to exist autonomously from society. In fact, the state consists mainly of the generalised interests of ruling forces.

This appearance of autonomy also means that the state and its officials seem to be the initiators and driving forces in political life, but this overlooks the fact that political initiatives often arise from societal actors and that hegemonic social relations constitute a kind of a corridor to legitimate and viable state action (Demirović 2011). As said above, then, from a historical-materialist perspective the state is not a neutral entity that stands above society but, rather, is a crystallization point of social disputes and relations of forces. In this way, the state becomes a material condensation of societal power relations (Poulantzas [1978] 2002; Gallas et al. 2012). As Demirović puts it:

> The state is the specific form in which the bourgeois class is organized as a class and its social power is given the form of a collectively binding will. In this respect the state is in itself a specific and autonomous social relation. The boundary between this relation and other forms of social relations is always contingent and drawn by social struggles between movements of the subalterns and the dominant classes. The autonomy of this particular social relation 'state' and its distance from other social relations—those of production, those between the sexes or generations, or between "white" and "black" people (so-called race relations)—is not fixed but always shifting.
> (Demirović 2011: 44)

Again, echoing Poulantzas, the state can be understood as a material condensation of relationships of social forces, their interests and strategies, and of generalised and accepted discourses. The materiality of the state consists of trained officials and bureaucrats, enduring institutions, the tax basis and financial capacities, and the legal and coercive means of knowledge and discourses.

"Condensation" is a concept that remains rather opaque in Poulantzas' work (Demirović 2007); it means that particular state apparatuses deal with specific asymmetric social power relations and their attendant contradictions, which in turn transforms them into more or less coherent policies—and that the idealized, clear lines of authority and policymaking are largely illusory. Sometimes the same apparatus pursues contradictory policies as a result of the complex condensation of societal interests and power relations, often with contradictory results. But this does not mean that the state as such is a coherent entity. It consists, instead, of many such apparatuses that may be in relationships of tension with each other, of state officials and networks with opposing interests, of mechanisms by which non-decision decisions are made, of symbolic policies that contradict actual ones, and so on. These are a consequence of the internally incoherent structure of the state and its highly complex and contradictory social relations. The "unity" of the state is never final and needs to be constantly (re)produced.[8] It is not a given, however, that the state is the central strategic terrain on which social forces deal with their conflicts, formulate compromises (so that dominant forces don't completely marginalize others) and/or sustain a certain continuity in specific societal power relations and discourses. To be sure, the state is the strategic terrain of dominant forces—those that control the means of production and wealth—but this arrangement can fail. Compromises among fractions of the ruling classes in a particular power bloc cannot be established when they lack a common interest in reproducing their domination (Demirović 2011). Moreover, the state's institutional and discursive apparatus offers specific opportunities and constraints and particular selection biases, which make it more visible and receptive to certain interests and values as opposed to others. This is linked to the contexts and conjunctures of strategic action, the relationships of forces and the related strategizing of different actors as well as restrictions on particular actors given that context and conjuncture (Jessop 2007). Hybridization in the form of "pure" public or private-public action and its reach is then manifest through changing selectivities of the state via its changing materiality as reflected in the orientation of state officials, laws and procedures, both institutionalized and informal access to state apparatuses by particular actors, and the effects of the latter within the former.

Consequently, the state *always* consists of many public–private forms. Crucial to this is Gramsci's account of the state as both "political society"—the state in its narrow sense—and "integral state"—the broader sets of structures and practices that are not part of the state in the narrow sense and comprise "civil society." From the Gramscian-Poulantzian perspective presented here, hegemony and the state are connected, with state structures and processes forming elements of hegemonic conditions. In particular, the consensual elements of these arrangements are created in civil society, in the highly politically and economically organized, but also highly sectoralized, everyday life structures and practices (Demirović 1997). In spite of the particular dynamics of state policies, which often take place via party competition and internal power struggles, the concept of hegemony hints at state-institutional "channels" created by society through struggles and conflicts—which is what concrete private–public hybridization is about. When we understand the state as a social relation, we must pay closer attention to modes of societal reproduction (capitalist, patriarchal, racist, society and nature, etc.), the existence of more or less constituted social forces, and dominant or even hegemonic discourses and orientations as well as governmentalities.

If we are to detect and identify the various forms in which public–private and national–international hybridization appear, we need to remember that the societal projects of dominant actors, such as strengthening of privately organized activities or creation and enhancement of strong international economic mechanisms, must be transformed into state action and/or a state project through, for example, the successful instanciation of new forms of property (which only a state can authorize). If such efforts are successful, the state, with its manifold practices, comes to supports processes and practices that, formally speaking, exist outside of the state apparatus. In other words, the concrete functioning of the state, as practices, is not merely the consequence of societal relations but is also a result of contestation within the state administration among individuals, groups, networks and political parties (Poulantzas [1978] 2002: 167; Demirović 2011: 43–47; Offe 2006).

During such struggles, some state apparatuses and the groups dominant within them may try to become more dominant and powerful (e.g. military, finance technocrats) and with the support of societal groups may succeed (e.g. Chile in 1973 and after). The activities involved can include: manipulation through regularized, bureaucratic processes; rapid or drawn-out decision-making and non-decisions; (non-)creation of knowledge; and control of information flows or their suppression. State officials are recruited to act within specific institutional fields and according to more or less strict rules and habits. During the era of neoliberalization and internationalization of the state, particular orientations and strategic actions became dominant within the state, and among different state apparatuses standing in an asymmetric relationship to each other, a phenomenon that can be called "governmentalization" (Foucault 1977–78; Mitchell 2010).

How can these theoretical considerations on hegemony and the state be related to international politics and the internationalized state, and contribute to our understanding of hybridization and hybrid rule? According to Robert W. Cox, we can speak of "international hegemony" when there exists a dynamic correlation among relations of production, states and political world order, that is, a hegemony that is, to some extent, conditioned by coherent ideas, social power relations and institutional configurations (Cox 1986: 204–254). A corresponding "international historic bloc" emerges when the manifold strategies of a large variety of actors and societal institutions form into a more or less, dynamic whole, by contrast, sees a more integrated form and places more emphasis on the transnational character of dominant classes and the power bloc.[9]

From an historical-materialist perspective, the accumulation and attraction of capital as well as the creation of competitiveness of particular societies are structural features of global capitalism. Class alliances and a certain social coherence at the national level become possible only as a result of more or less successful integration into the world market. Specific national societies compete and cooperate with each other, while their various actors are integrated differently into the world market and the international division of labor, which shapes orientation of their politics. Consequently, international policies can be simultaneously both cooperative and competitive.

For our understanding of hybrid rule, one point is crucial: the "international state" of which we speak here cannot be equated to our understanding of the "national" state. The different scales of the state are not predetermined; rather, their constitution and significance are themselves parts of power strategies.[10] Even though the national state came to be predominant during in the 20th century, following the fall of empires and state creation via decolonization, the national principle is not necessarily the state's only possible scale. In this sense, hybridization must be understood as one element in a struggle to restructure relationships between the national and the international. This is due primarily to the internationalization of capital but it is also a result of the recognized international character of problems such as the ecological crisis and migration.[11]

The two dimensions of hybridization: public–private, national–international

The term "hybridization" runs the risk of suggesting that the state once was an homogeneous entity at the national scale. As argued above, the state has never been a coherent or singular entity; rather it is a fluid, more or less stable set of social relation that is part of and participates in the contested structuring of other social relations, such as class and capital, gender, ethnicity, citizenship, and the household. From this theoretical perspective, therefore, hybridization is *always* taking place, albeit in specific concrete forms that must be identified and named. What becomes important are both the manifold and power-shaped forms of the social division of labor and dominant orientations and values, such as hetero-normative gender relations or understandings of progress through economic growth.

I propose, therefore, that we understand the state and recent state transformation through two processes of hybridization, the first along the public–private divide and the second along national and international scales. This division is not comprehensive because the "local" state remains important and is being transformed, but this distinction sheds light on two crucial dynamics. Historically concrete processes of hybridization can be interpreted as specific forms of the condensation of asymmetric societal relationships of forces, which result in specific, time-limited constellations and orientations. But hybridization can also be treated as the means through which hegemony deals with and institutionalizes, in particular societal contradictions, the creation of an historic bloc that assures a certain stability and dynamic in modern societies.

Public–private hybridization: the neoliberalising of society and the state

We should not regard hybridization as the coming together of public and private, of two distinct, pre-existing things or spheres. Each is co-constitutive of the other, and each is a specific form of societal organization and domination as well as state intervention. Hybridization is both subject and consequence of social conflict over where, precisely, the line between the private and the public should be drawn, whether this involves industrial sectors in which the state should be active, developing distributional mechanisms that determine which part of the wage relation are part of primary incomes and which are secondary and provided through state agencies or the household as a site of unwaged labor, or if specific forms of knowledge are to be created through state apparatuses or private entities. We also need to consider under which circumstances particular social relations are organized by and around the state in specific public–private forms. Some are to be avoided because, for example, if competition is too severe and destructive, capital might ruin itself, or if social crises, struggles and dysfunctions threaten the survival of society itself. These are not abstract matters but must be dealt with and understood in specific historical conjunctures: which social strategies and struggles by specific forces and which resistances and compromises lead to a historically concrete state as part of the organization of the power bloc.

The question of the societal relationships among forces and their conditions of reproduction—as elements of state, economic and ideological structures— is crucial for understanding hybridization, because concrete forms of state apparatus and specific public–private relations are shaped by social relationships of forces and related social orientations and discourses. From both the Gramscian and Poulantzian perspectives, the critical question is not so much if and how specific goods are delivered in private or public forms but, rather, what are the specific social functions of such private and/or public processes and deliveries, and which interests stand behind them. Gramsci argued that hegemony must first be organized at the "private" level, in the sense that dominant actors have to overcome their different economic-corporatist interests and must be able to formulate strategies and compromises and organize a power bloc. This "ethical-political phase" (Gramsci 1991: 1567) might lead to the "hegemonic or state" phase in which this power bloc formulates a political programme and reorganizes the state as the center of the bourgeois political.[12]

We see this process in the post-World War II state—often called "Fordist"— based primarily on a specific form of class compromise in the countries of the Global North, through enormous intensification of the production and work process ("Taylorism"), dominance of industrial over financial capital, and unprecedented exploitation of natural resources, especially petroleum.[13] The resulting intensive accumulation made dynamic economic growth possible and made Fordism hegemonic (Aglietta 1979, 2000). In gender relations, Fordism relied on a nuclear family with a male "breadwinner" and subsidies to capital through the unpaid work of women in the home (Chorus 2012; Sauer 2012). Notwithstanding specific differences among Northern societies, the dominant form of state was both interventionist and welfare-providing, leading to a considerably expanded public sphere. This form was functional for relevant societal actors, made socio-economic dynamics possible and created a strong consensus. But this constellation came into crisis during the 1970s, with first responses in many countries consisting of greater and stronger state intervention, primarily via Keynesianism but also through greater commitment to industrial policy. During the 1980s, scholars like Claus Offe proposed that the modern state, especially in its Fordist form, had gone through "paradoxical proliferation" because it was precisely the growing size and scope of that state that undermined its rationality and sovereignty, for two reasons (Offe 1987: 309–320). First, the state was forced to deal with societal actors and, second, the project and image of an authoritative and unitary state, oriented toward the general well-being, failed. After a century-long process of centralization and near-successful assertion of the legitimate monopoly of violence, centrifugal processes began to break the state apart, leading to a tendency that, today, is often called "governance" but which we understand as hybridization (Offe 1987: 309–320). From an historical-materialist perspective, we need to remember that hybridization is not merely a consequence of the over-stretch of the welfare state but also and primarily a power-shaped and interest-driven change in the mode of societal reproduction.

In this sense, practices such as privatization and outsourcing are responses to the accumulation crisis of the economy as well the legitimation crisis of the state, linked to the crisis of Fordism and the (re)shaping of power relations within the state and society (Atzmuller et al. 2013; McNally 2009; Jessop 2007; Hirsch 2005; Dorre and Röttger 2003). Neoliberalism consequently was adopted as the new strategy of political elites, with a contested neoliberalization of manifold societal relations shaping and redrawing the public–private divide. This process developed unevenly in different fields and societies, according to existing structures and power relations. Within the public realm, new steering mechanisms were deployed, for example the new public management while, in the private realm, the political economy of neoliberalism privileged finance-led forms of investment and accumulation (Aglietta 2000; Boyer 2000; Sablowski 2009). At the same time, a certain stabilization of public–private hybridization during Fordism came under pressure. Privatisation of formerly state or public enterprises and the strengthening of the private in general became a major strategy to overcome the crisis, i.e. to restore capital profitability and to shape societal power relations. However, this did not lead to a new form of stabilization of the public–private hybridization but caused many smaller crises and then the major crisis from 2008 onwards.

Of course, the post-Fordist, hybridized state is no more an homogenous entity than was the Fordist one; rather, by necessity it is heterogeneous because very different societal interests have been condensed within the state apparatus and its discourses—some pro-privatization, others pro-state—with resulting social contradictions being addressed by various state apparatuses. Policies might (continue to) contradict each other; as Jessop highlights in his work, the articulation of eventual hegemonic projects with "state projects" is a political process, and not one that happens automatically or spontaneously (1990: 315ff). We can even regard the hybridized state itself as part of such a state project, one that bundles different strategies and deals with contradictions. It is for these reasons that, between 1970 and the present, the state has "sought to strengthen capital and foster marketization" (Hurt/Lipschutz, this volume), as specific social forces (economic, political and intellectual ones) were able to make this a hegemonic and state project. This does not mean that the state has been "retreating," as often suggested, inasmuch as in some policy areas, such as security, surveillance and migration, the state role continues to expand. Indeed, Poulantzas's diagnosis, in the 1970s, that an "authoritarian statism" was emerging and undermining liberal-democratic processes, remains as valid today as then, as seen, for example, in the growing economic-security surveillance activities of the American government (Poulantzas [1978] 2002: Ch. 4; Hurt/Lipschutz in this volume; Lipschutz in this volume; Lipschutz 2009).

There remains, however, one crucial difference between public and private fulfilment of specific tasks: the former is usually connected with broader accountability and legitimacy, with reference to comprehensive societal interests, whereas the latter forms are legitimately bound to particular interests and accumulation and are often proprietary and secret. In this sense, at the core of the neoliberalization of society and state we find not only enhancement of private property rights and related interests and forces but also a strengthening of dominant social forces through a decrease in public accountability (Hurt in this volume) and a transformation of non-democratic processes in the name of competitiveness. Thus, what is often described affirmatively as "governance," in the sense of greater participation, inclusiveness and problem-oriented forms of politics, as through "global civil society" is, in fact, a new formation of political will and decision-making. This is seen in the sense that non-transparent networks of experts and elites can pursue their interests more easily and rapidly (the bank rescue packages and state "haircuts" of the past few years indicate how "governance" often operates). The relative informality, unaccountability and fragmentation of governance structures and processes thus become a mode of domination by powerful societal groups that, in comparison to formal-democratic and public politics, is less subject to compromise (Demirović 2011).

Recent state transformation through its internationalization

As argued above, the state is not just an institutionalized entity but also a materially condensed relationship of societal forces; in this sense, it is not external to class, gender or other societal relations but, rather, integral to them. In addition, different scales of the state are not predetermined but contextual and contingent as a result of their constitution and significance, both of which are also part of power strategies. This is why the institutionalized forms of international politics are termed the "material condensation of societal power relations of second order" (Brand et al. 2014; Brand, Gorg and Wissen 2011: 149–175). During much of the 20th century, under Fordism and based on a particular class compromise, the national scale became especially dominant in the countries of the Global North (Aglietta 1979/2000). Nationally organized societies and states relied heavily on the distinction between the national (internal) and the international (external) to secure dominant and even hegemonic societal relations.

From roughly 1945 to about 1975, international political and economic relations took the form that John Ruggie has called "embedded liberalism," through which coordinated and Fordist social relations supported specific material condensations (Ruggie 1982: 379–415). The Western growth model was based on a particular class compromise and the hegemony of industrial capital, buttressed by strong regulation of financial markets, the stabilizing mechanisms of IMF, the predominance of the U.S. dollar, trade liberalization through GATT and specific development strategies pursued by the World Bank. The more-recent "post-Fordist" transformation of capitalism implies a reshaping of societal power relations, especially those between capital and labor, which were deemed necessary to overcome the crisis of Fordism. Here, the growing internationalization of socio-economic relations, especially the restructuring of the global division of labor, has been key to overcoming accumulation problems and strengthening the geopolitical power of the Global North (Hirsch 2005).

As a result, today's Gramscian power blocs have become less organized at the national scale than in the post-World War II decades. If we consider the state as crucial to organizing the power bloc and social domination, and disorganizing weaker actors, the internationalization of the state is no surprise. In contrast to the implicit functionalism of many historical-materialist analyses, which assume the internationalization of politics due to the transnationalization of capitalist relations, it seems more promising to consider the contested character of inter- and trans-nationalization (Cox 1981). Nowadays, "inner" (national) and "outer" (international) relations remain an important mode of development and domination in capitalist societies—class compromises are organized primarily within national societies but the compromising forces themselves are unevenly internationalized. The shaping and reproduction of socio-economic as well as political domination both take place, however, in more hybridized forms, and national and transnational power blocs are increasingly organized through multi-scalar structures and processes. One crucial dimension of the internationalization of the state is, therefore, the emergence of international state apparatuses.[14] With respect to the spatial scale, that is, national–international hybridization, in the post-war era the national scale was of great importance because it was in line with the power bloc and with large fractions of wage earners (Shaw 2000). More recently, the internationalization of production and consumption and, related to that, of class relations, has been a key element in the reconfiguration of social power relations. Parallel to and in support of this, international state apparatuses have emerged or been strengthened in order to stabilize those changing patterns. A "relativization of scale" has developed. This does not mean that the international scale was of no political importance in earlier times; merely that it was less important for the organization of national ruling forces. Against this background, we should imagine a "multiscalar" state and conceptualize contemporary state modes of existence as acting and functioning on multiple levels. To this extent, we can speak of an *internationalized state* (Hirsch 2005), one that reflects the fact that international political institutions and, accordingly, the state apparatus, are growing in importance.[15] This is accompanied by a process through which, due to the changing power constellations, nation-states are also transformed, leading to a form of *internationalized competition state* (Hirsch 2005: 145–151).

At the institutional level of state apparatuses, we can identify changing strategic selectivities of the state toward specific forces and interests, toward "market-oriented" solutions and toward international scales (especially in the EU). Stephen Gill has called this tendency "global constitutionalism," an international politico-juridical structure that universalises a liberal constitutional order, through which property rights are increasingly secured by international institutions and cooperation is pursued in order to regulate capitalist competition in a specific way (Gill 1995; Hurt, Lipschutz in this volume). As part of this process, national states as well as societal power and production relations are becoming both more internationalized and more "interiorized," as external constraints and shifting internal power relations feed into domestic politics. The constant creation of competitiveness is a structural feature of the modern state but it has become ever more important, serving specific social actors and alliances.

New international state apparatuses (INTSA) are being created and existing INTSAs are being transformed, as their creation and functioning are part of the contested politics of rescaling. The dominant or hegemonic actors try, in particular, to fortify their interests and to impose their strategies not only through changed relations of forces on the existing levels but also through the shifts of spatial scaling. Consequently, hegemonic and state projects such as global constitutionalism emerge increasingly in a multi-scaled form and manner, as they are formulated and secured by negotiated compromises in different places and at different levels (think here of the multi-scalar authority of the WTO). In this respect, the dominant national states are of fundamental importance. At the same time, the international projects that they and other powerful actors support and push forward become progressively more significant in guaranteeing the coherence of national projects, for both the international political system and the specific functioning of the world market. That is why the neoliberal-imperial state project must also be established *within* the INTSAs, or what we conceptualize as a "material condensation(s) of societal power relations of second order" influenced by national constellations, even as the former is also shaping the latter (Brand et al. 2014). The INTSAs do not constitute a centralised world state but function, instead, as organised, specialised agencies acting with means (recognition, money, law, force, knowledge) and a Western-bureaucratic mode of existence and action, to instantiate the "internationalized" state.

Even so, neither hegemonic nor state projects are rigidly imposed prearrangements. They are constantly under (re)negotiation and adapted to changing circumstances, crisis and critique. In this way, the capacity and willingness of the leadership of the ruling states and social forces are quite important at the international level. At the same time, as a result of the strong spatial and social-structural fragmentation of the actors at an international level, the terrains on which compromises are elaborated have an even larger significance. Among these are the World Economic Forum, which began to meet annually in Davos, Switzerland during the 1970s, the Trilateral Commission, which was also established during the 1970s as well as countless conferences, publications and network meetings that take place on a daily basis (Gill 1990). These have all contributed to establishing consensuses among the elites that are, more or less effectively, based in every single society as well as internationally (van der Pijl 1984).

The actual crisis

As sketched out here, the hybridization of the state along the lines of private–public and national–international beginning in the 1970s were crucial elements of post-Fordist transformations. Neoliberal strategies became central in overcoming accumulation problems, restructuring societal power relations—especially through weakening of organized labor—and re-hybridizing the state. At the same time, these strategies not only reshaped the then-existing social compromise, they also produced new instabilities and risks responsible for the actual multiple crises that have followed. In a serious crisis, both the role of the state becomes contested again even as economic forms of state intervention increase dramatically. This is not, however, necessarily in the form of "state-managed capitalism" (Hurt/Lipschutz in this volume). We can see this if we analyze the actual state interventions that have taken place from the perspective of the still deeply embedded neoliberal orientations (competitiveness, world-market, flexibility, etc.) as well as the still favourable relationships among those that have benefited from the developments of the last 30 years. Subaltern actors, especially trade unions, remain subaltern and bound by the dogma of competitiveness. The same is true for what can be called the imperial mode of production and living (Brand and Wissen 2013: 687–711) and gender relations (Wichterich 2013). The socio-economic power relations that have been the basis for historically specific forms of state intervention do not change (Brie 2009; Demirović and Sablowski 2013; Candeias 2011). Therefore, and not by chance, the state is a last-resort crisis manager in support of dominant societal interests and forces.

In sum, in the continuing financial upheavals, we see that the dominant actors in financial capitalism continue to frame the crisis in particular ways and to push for concrete forms of intervention in support of their interests and not of the system as a whole. During the sub-prime crisis, financialized capitalism explicitly reproduced itself in everyday life, while other actors were too distant from financialized relations (e.g. industrial capital) or too weak (e.g. trade unions) to do the same. A similar situation can be seen in the "Euro crisis." The specific, more or less hybrid state policies that emerged after 2008 offered the imaginary and illusion of a "neo-Keynesian state," both of which were incorrect, because what has been underestimated and misperceived is the transformation of both state and society themselves over the last 35 years.

Outlook: governance, hybridization and counter-hegemony

Governance and multi-scalar governance are concepts used to analyze the transformation of policies through recognition of the internationalization and re-scaling of politics, the emergence of new actors like NGOs, new problems like the ecological crisis, and claims for more participation, democratization and accountability. Some fraction of the governance literature focuses not only on processes and policies but also on the reshaping of political structures, claiming that changing modes of governance are, at least in part, the expression and lock-in of shifting social power and domination. Nonetheless, the majority of the research and literature on governance and multi-level-governance is limited to a focus on various modes of institutionalized cooperation and problem-solving. In this respect, such work cannot tell us very much about either power or change. The concept of hybridization offered in this book could, consequently, enhance our knowledge of governance in several ways:

- Examining not only established modes of governance but also the domination-shaped making of changes in those modes, with a focus on state power and its extension through fusion with private entities, and the role of governmentality and biopolitical management in all of this (Kutting and Lipschutz 2009).
- Using hybridization to understand the policies, institutional structures and other, non-political structures and processes in governance, rather than focusing only on the "steering side" of policies as promoted by institutionalism, discourse theory and regime theory (Brand 2013; Jessop 2014).
- Focusing on a specific, albeit crucial, aspect of the governance debate in which hybridization is central, such as the relationship between the private and the public and its scale.
- Showing that, by contrast with the governance debate, which is oriented normatively towards accountability and transparency, contributions in the field of hybridization that focus on "new forms of public–private fusion" indicate that non-transparency and authoritarian rule represent not governance failure but highly functional methods of rule by the internationalized competition state and its societal foundation (Buckel 2011: 154–169).

The perspective I have outlined in this chapter, of (re)hybridization of the state through internationalization and the shaping of private–public relations, helps us to understand better the interest- and power-driven transformations that have emerged out of the crisis of Fordism. As I have argued, moreover, these have been important dimensions of post-Fordist hybridization but they are not the only ones that have been critical to that process. My arguments could, as well, frame future lines of research, especially into the concrete selectivities of the two modes of state transformation and, even to a partial shaping of the post-Fordist hybridization of the state.

Notes

1 Please see "Introduction" to this volume for the complete definition of "hybrid rule."
2 At a "middle-range level of abstraction" we try to detect common elements of social relations in a particular historical phase (e.g. Fordism) without denying differences among concrete societies, acknowledging that, in different historical phases, those social relations change (as the state is assumed to have changed in the Western capitalist countries from a national welfare state to an internationalized competition state). At a more abstract level, concepts like the "capitalist mode of production" are deployed in order to provide analytical categories for the continuities of societal reproduction over time, and not to claim that all states or modes reflect the same particular forms. "In order to achieve a precise analysis of the forms of regulation under capitalism, it is necessary first to define an intermediate concept, less abstract than the principle of accumulation … ." Please see Aglietta (2000: 68).
3 The concept of social form enables us to understand capitalist societies not as outcome of the actions of the ruling classes and forces but as a result of interdependent and asymmetric social relations. The value form makes opaque the social character of the production process, i.e. as part of a domination-shaped division of labor. Commodities seem to be things and contain their value as such things. The political form reproduces according to the tendencies of specific forms of politics—those via the state and the bourgeois public influenced by societal actors with asymmetric power resources—allowing some to dominate and others to be marginalized.
4 The notion of "consensus" to hegemony is a complicated one, involving both a degree of consciousness of domination and a "common sense" that it is to the benefit of society and the dominated.
5 For a discussion of the concept of neoliberalization, please see Castree (2008: 131–152); Brenner, Peck, Theodore (2010: 327–345).
6 See for example Lipietz (1985: 109–137) This aspect has also been underlined by the theory of reflexive modernization, which focuses on the non-intended consequences, as well as on the possibly crisis-producing, self-perpetuating dynamics in singular areas of society. Please see Beck, Giddens and Lash (1994).
7 In fact, there is a broad debate within historical-materialist state theory on the state: Gallas et al. (2012); and Bratsis (2002); Brand, Görg and Wissen, (2011): 149–175; Demirović (2011: 38–59); Sauer and Wöhl (2011: 108–128; Jessop (2007); Hirsch (2005). I outline here a specific understanding.
8 Although this description might sound very similar to the "bureaucratic politics" models of Allison (1971) and Halperin (1974), those presume that coherent policies emerge from the end of the bureaucratic pipeline and reflect some sort of organized process, whereas the condensation model includes structural incoherence and contradictions, as well.
9 Cox in Gill (1993: 49–66). By contrast, Gill sees a more integrated form and places more emphasis on the transnational character of dominant classes and the power bloc; please see Gill (1995: 399–424).
10 Here lies the decisive difference between, on the one hand, the so-called multi-level approach or multi-level governanc and, on the other, scale as a concept in critical geography. In the first case, the geographical levels of scale are supposed as given,

whereas, in the second case, their domination-shaped constitution is taken into account.
11 Up to now, a relevant difference exists between the nation-state and the international level of politics, which is to say, the missing monopoly of legitimate use of violence by the latter. What continues to dominate here is the principle of national sovereignty, because violence and open coercion continue to be interpreted as violations of that sovereignty. We also see here the source of the strong orientation toward "inter-governmental cooperation" in social science theories addressing international relations and policies. There are two important exceptions: on one hand, the capacity of intervention maintained, in certain cases, by international political organizations, and, on the other hand, the U.S. government's efforts to develop the U.S. state, together with the NATO, into the centre of an international legitimate monopoly of violence.
12 Of course, from the perspective offered here, the "private" level is not free from the state, especially inasmuch as dominant forces are organized politically by the state. More than Poulantzas, however, Gramsci emphasized the relative autonomy of organization within civil society, especially of dominant economic forces.
13 Indeed, from the late 1940s through the 1970s and beyond, control of oil was a primary means of creating and supporting hegemony.
14 Or in more conventional terms, "regimes," please see Krasner (1984).
15 For the concept, see Brand in Kütting and Lipschutz (2009: 100–123).

Part II
Empirics

5 What's at stake in the privatization debate?

Enclosing the public domain through hybrid rule

Shelley L. Hurt[1]

> Most panelists agreed that the US life sciences research community was more or less "over its Vietnam-era distrust" of the national security establishment and would be open to more collaboration.
>
> U.S. Central Intelligence Agency 2003[2]

> The market has been the outcome of a conscious and often violent intervention on the part of government which imposed the market organization on society for noneconomic ends.
>
> Karl Polanyi[3]

On November 1, 2012, President Obama issued a notice, for the fourth time since entering the White House, which continued a "declared national emergency with respect to the unusual and extraordinary threat to the national security, foreign policy and economy of the United States posed by the proliferation of nuclear, biological, and chemical weapons (weapons of mass destruction) and the means for delivering them" (Obama 2009). This notice built upon Executive Order 12938 that President Bill Clinton first issued in 1994 and then amended in 1998, followed by an additional amendment by President George W. Bush in 2005 (Clinton 1994; G. W. Bush 2004). This nearly twenty-year national emergency, with no discernable end in sight, is interesting and important for two reasons. First, it harkens back to a 29-year national emergency that President Harry Truman launched in 1950.[4] That heady and enduring national emergency cast a long shadow over the pivotal years of the Cold War, impacting civilian, commercial, and military life. Second, both national emergencies placed science and technology, particularly "weapons of mass destruction," at the center of their claims (Drew 1994). In keeping with the dire warnings laid out in NSC-68 as well as NSC-20/4, President Truman called for a full-scale mobilization of the country to confront the challenges posed by an expanding communist menace, including the partnering of private industry toward this end. Even though it is well known that the private sector played a major role in the Cold War and post-9/11 military buildups, Americans tend to consider the state's involvement with the private sector in terms of telecommunications surveillance and eavesdropping rather than having to do with those aspects of science and technology identified as "WMDs."[5]

This chapter seeks to remedy this oversight in the scholarly literature. In particular, the chapter hones in on the biological sciences as a representative area of WMDs, considering its overlooked importance during the Cold War era up to the present day. The chapter shows how the private sector came to serve as a shield for the national security state for domestic and international audiences as the U.S. government pursued technological superiority in biodefense capabilities at all costs. Indeed, the seeming paradox of the private sector serving to enhance rather than diminish state power in American life appears at first glance to be a blatant contradiction. Yet, the partnering of business and government that began during WWII for national security purposes accelerated dramatically in the 1970s and beyond, despite the rise of neoliberal ideology and policies.

The chapter examines two pivotal moments in American political history to illustrate how this partnering unfolded in relation to federal science policy in the biological sciences. The two events emerge in the wake of President Richard M. Nixon's decision to convert the nation's Biological Warfare Program into the Biological Research Program on November 25, 1969.[6] Nixon's conversion decision altered U.S.–Soviet relations as the U.S. pursued intelligence information on its rival's science and technology pursuits, especially in the biological sciences. Hence, the first of the two pivotal moments entails the Nixon administration's deftly using the private sector during détente and arms control negotiations to outwit Soviet scientists and spies from gathering crucial information on the status of U.S. biodefense activities. The second pivotal moment involves the establishment of two seemingly contradictory events, with deregulation and privatization of molecular biology experiments on the one hand and centralization of federal science policy oversight on the other hand. Both of these policy changes facilitated the private sector's ability to begin conducting a wide range of molecular biology experiments without public accountability or access. This section also shows how the move toward centralization of federal science policy enabled national security agencies to capitalize on these new regulatory changes, since Nixon's decision and the Biological Weapons Convention of 1972 prohibited the military from directly participating in molecular biology experiments. The chapter concludes by reflecting on the post-9/11 era when Project Bioshield arose in the wake of the October 2001 anthrax attacks. Through an analysis of this new federal science policy we can see how Cold War-era patterns of industry–government relations fostered the emergence of hybrid rule to enhance state power. Therefore, these two historical moments in the 1970s highlight an enduring dimension of the national security state's deployment of the private sector for achieving its political aims. Before examining these moments, the chapter reflects briefly upon three lessons from WWII when the national security–private sector nexus first formed.

The National security–private sector nexus: dynamics of continuity and change

Scholarship on American politics is witnessing a "growth industry" of studies that probe the 1970s in an effort to redefine the decade as a watershed period for the country (Schulman and Zelizer 2008; Stein 2011; Cowie 2012; Borstelmann 2013; Schulman 2001; Perlstein 2008). These new analyses suggest that researchers have concentrated too heavily on the historical ruptures of the 1960s and the ideological shifts of the 1980s, neglecting the fertility of the 1970s in U.S. political history. One of the greatest consequences of this neglect, in my view, has been reflected in a misunderstanding of the national security policies that supposedly altered the landscape throughout the decade toward greater democratic oversight. For instance, scholarship on this period frequently stresses how Congress and the judiciary heroically placed brakes on the "Imperial Presidency" after Watergate and how the Church Committee hearings reined in the CIA and NSA, effectively providing a definitive correction to an abuse of state power. Despite these popular portrayals, far too little attention has been paid to the policy changes that accelerated and expanded national security prerogatives, altering the political economy landscape irrevocably while upholding President Truman's declared national emergency from 1950. Not surprisingly, yet somewhat counter-intuitively given the prevalent views that democratic accountability and government worked, these policy changes led to a dramatic expansion of state power.

Nowhere is this expansion clearer than in federal science policy. During the 1960s, Americans became increasingly skeptical about science and technology due to its persistent relationship to war (Mendelsohn 1993: 151–173; Moore 2008). By the late 1960s, policymakers confronted an increasingly hostile public that questioned the presumption that science produced more benefits than harm. Throughout the 1970s, policymakers, scientists, and business elites joined forces to counterattack these negative views through a systematic public relations campaign to accompany the broad-based federal science policy reforms. In 1981, David Dickson and David Noble argued that this 1970s campaign went far beyond just persuading Americans about the public benefits of science; rather, these forces sought to reform the very basis of American democracy:

What is at stake in the current struggle over science and technology policy is not merely the technocratic redefinition of reason but the redefinition of democracy itself. What has been altered by elite counterattack is not merely the pattern of choice within a limited area of government policy but the entire shape of American politics (Dickson and Noble 1981: 267).

Indeed, federal science policy reforms in the 1970s helped to lay the groundwork for the accelerated ideological shifts the country witnessed in the 1980s.

What does a refocus on the 1970s tell us about the national security–industry nexus in federal science policy? How can a reperiodization of policy change contribute to a fuller understanding of hybrid rule and state formation in the American context? This chapter attempts to answer these questions by revisiting the period when public–private relations acquired a distinct life of their own. Drawing upon archival evidence, oral histories, a FOIA request, secondary literature, and material widely available from the public record, I argue that the geopolitical and domestic political stakes of the biological revolution, which began in the 1960s, changed the strategic calculations policymakers made about federal science policy. In challenging the conventional wisdom about the American state's national security prerogatives being curtailed by democratic processes, the chapter tries to provide a fuller understanding of the state-driven policies that fostered a newfound alliance between the public and private sectors that fueled the growth of American state power. This fuller understanding leads us toward a critical dimension of hybrid rule and state formation, namely the state's attempt to valorize the market for political, particularly national security, ends. Hence, by linking biotechnology to its military past, the chapter throws into relief many of the scholarly and popular assumptions about the 1980s being the decade when biotechnology suddenly became the new high-technology frontier, once the neoliberal era unleashed the private sector's entrepreneurial spirit. Hence, the following brief section on the three national security lessons of WWII (secrecy, privatization, centralization) serve to highlight the institutional antecedents that inspired fundamental change in public–private power during the 1970s.

National security lessons of WWII

While scholars have written extensively on a variety of the national security lessons springing from WWII,[7] this chapter frames the following historical narrative in terms of just three: secrecy, privatization, and centralization. These three lessons represent the backbone of the federal science policy reforms that were enacted during and after WWII to position the country on a permanent wartime footing even when formal hostilities ceased to exist. These three lessons also represent our point of departure for understanding the cultural and institutional changes in federal science policy that emerged in the wake of Nixon's conversion decision. While the literature on secrecy during this formative period is well established, less is known about the roles of privatization and centralization as it pertained to the institutionalization of policies and practices established during the mobilization of WWII. Significantly, these three lessons are not mutually exclusive domains of federal science policy; rather, they represent interrelated policy tools that senior decision-makers deployed for sustaining the mobilization of the country's national resources throughout the Cold War. This brief discussion provides me with an opportunity to highlight the organizing features of the chapter and its relationship to hybrid rule.

Secrecy

The controversial legacy of secrecy became one of the most enduring features of federal science policy during and after World War II. In its wake, a vast and "largely invisible military framework" was erected in the midst of our democratic society (Dennis 1994, as cited in Krige 2006: 11–12). Historian Michael Dennis notes, "Looking at the civilian in postwar America is much like looking at a map of an archipelago composed of discrete islands of civilian life connected by a larger, largely invisible military framework" (as cited in Krige 2006: 11–12). The real-world implications of this postwar regime of secrecy provide substantial autonomy for state actors when they deliberate over federal science policy decisions. While the Nixon administration is infamous for its secrecy, far too little is known about the high stakes of converting the Biological Warfare Program into the Biological Research Program, which contributed significantly to this outcome. For instance, in a recent oral history confirming this view, Morton H. Halperin, staff member of the National Security Council (NSC) in 1969, mentions that the "impetus for the formal system" of the NSC, which National Security Advisor Henry A. Kissinger created, "came out of many [issues], including biological weapons" (Daalder and Destler 2000: 9). Lee A. DuBridge, Nixon's science advisor, also reflected upon the prevalence of policy secrecy during his time in the White House: "The public at large and even most of the scientific community remain unaware of the nature and extent of the activities of the White House Science Office" (DuBridge 1980: 70). While senior policymakers are oftentimes shrouded in a veil of secrecy, affording them high levels of autonomy, they still remain beholden to the pressures of American electoral politics. As a result, state actors sometimes engage in public relations campaigns to legitimize their actions to the American public in the hope of winning elections, extracting resources, and sustaining their chosen policies.

The public relations campaigns of WWII are well documented; however, they have not received the scholarly attention they deserve.[8] The success of these campaigns, and the lessons learned from them, provided senior policymakers with a blueprint for promoting and legitimizing federal science policy decisions throughout the course of the Cold War. Prominent examples, such as the Manhattan Project, the Apollo Program, and Atoms for Peace, demonstrate that policymakers were keenly aware of the power of these campaigns to achieve national goals. Historian Kenneth Osgood recently published a path-breaking study of President Eisenhower's enthusiasm for deploying a far-reaching psychological warfare campaign at home and abroad (Osgood 2006). Osgood remarked upon his "surprise" when discovering copious declassified material, demonstrating that these campaigns showed "domestic audiences were as important as international ones."[9] Indeed, Osgood persuasively documents Eisenhower's involvement in every aspect of the psychological warfare campaigns in "shaping, influencing, and manipulating public opinion" to ensure widespread political support for his national security strategy. Not surprisingly, Osgood mentions Vice President Nixon's support of these campaigns.

As will be discussed in the two case studies below, secrecy came to represent a constitutive feature of numerous public relations campaigns surrounding the biological sciences while federal science policy continued to change during the emergence of hybrid rule.

Privatization

The second national security lesson of WWII focuses on privatization or rather delegation to the private sector. In some respects this lesson seems counterintuitive because of the central role played by the public sector in wartime. However, this wartime mobilization taught policymakers and military leaders the value of partnering with the commercial and civilian sectors. In 1946, General Dwight D. Eisenhower points out in a memo entitled "Scientific and Technological Resources as Military Assets":

> The armed forces could not have won the war alone. Scientists and businessmen contributed techniques and weapons, which enabled us to outwit and overwhelm the enemy. Their understanding of the Army's needs made possible the highest degree of cooperation. This pattern of integration must be translated into a peacetime counterpart, which will not merely familiarize the Army with the progress made in science and industry, but draw into our planning for national security all the civilian resources, which can contribute to the defense of the country.[10]

The American state drove this integration process, acknowledging that it would maximize the country's military capabilities and readiness. As the country embarked on a thorough reform of the nation's R&D enterprise for wartime purposes, "the laissez-faire relation between science and government [...] vanished" (Bell 1976: 385). The institutionalization of this partnering has been referred to as the military-industrial complex, the defense-industrial base, and public-private partnerships, but all three of these terms connote the permanency of this integration since WWII. Aaron L. Friedberg argues that during the Cold War, the "arrangement" set up by the government to pay "private individuals and entities to design and build new weapons might not exactly be 'free enterprise' but (especially when compared to the alternative of complete state ownership of the means of military development and production) it was the next best thing" (Friedberg 1996: 112). This chapter focuses on how the ideas and practices of privatization ushered in a major institutional shift in the U.S. R&D enterprise wherein the post-WWII military—university partnership that had prevailed for nearly three decades was replaced by an industry—university partnership in the wake of Nixon's conversion decision. This institutional transformation accompanied a greater reliance on the private sector to act as a shield for the national security state.

The Nixon administration referred to both of these related changes as "reprivatization" ostensibly referring to the *laissez-faire* capitalism economy of the pre-WWII era.

Centralization

The final national security lesson addresses centralization of the nation's R&D enterprise. This lesson complements the other two by showing that policymakers sought a stronger hand at the helm for guiding federal science policy toward particular outcomes. In Eisenhower's 1946 memo, he asserts:

> Success in this enterprise depends to a large degree on the cooperation which the nation as a whole is willing to contribute. However, the Army as one of the main agencies responsible for the defense of the nation has the duty to take the initiative in promoting closer relation between civilian and military interests. It must establish definite policies and administrative leadership which will make possible even greater contributions from science, technology, and management than during the last war.

Eisenhower clearly meant to emphasize that the leadership he envisioned would concentrate decision-making and authority in the public sector as these new relationships between the public and private sectors were worked out. Gregory Hook and Merritt Roe Smith reinforce Eisenhower's perspectives in identifying the state and the military as agents of industrial change. Hook suggests that in the postwar period, the state became a "player" rather than just an "umpire" in directing the R&D enterprise toward the pursuit of "its own agenda" (Hook 1990: 359). Roe Smith takes an even longer view, suggesting that dominant explanations of science and technology that center on "industrial capitalism" in producing change "tends to deflect attention from the important nexus that exists between government institutions and industrialization. Particularly slighted in this respect is the role of the military as an agent of technological innovation and industrial consolidation" (Smith 1985: 1–37). The view adopted in this chapter borrows from Sanford Lakoff and W. Erik Bruvold with their emphasis on the "primacy of politics" wherein civilian policymakers and military leaders come together to forge new public–private partnerships while centralizing power and authority in the state (Lakoff and Bruvold 1990: 382–411).

Evolution of hybrid rule through federal science policy in the biological sciences

Private sector as foil for national security secrecy

This first section focuses on the Nixon administration's efforts to utilize and partner with the private sector to enhance national security secrecy surrounding the conversion decision. It examines the intricate, sophisticated, and duplicitous tactics used by the administration in negotiating with the Soviet Union when it established several science and technology agreements under the auspices of the newly established Biological Weapons Convention as well as under détente. This section emphasizes the emerging rationale for delegating public authority and responsibilities to the private sector in an attempt to protect the prerogatives of the military as well as the civilian policymakers who were intent on ensuring the country not be caught by technological surprise. These strategic initiatives were undertaken with the challenges of public perception foremost in senior policymakers' minds.

Secrecy aids public relations campaigns around conversion process

After unilaterally renouncing an entire category of weapons, Nixon yearned to persuade a war-weary nation that he stood for peace and cooperation with the Soviet Union. In seeking to capitalize on his disarmament efforts with biological weapons, Nixon hoped a modicum of legitimacy would be restored to national institutions, particularly those of the presidency. Hence, Nixon straddled a fine line between protecting the country's technological superiority in the biological sciences while appearing to adopt a dovish posture in associating molecular biology advances exclusively with civilian concerns, such as disease eradication. After all, it was President Nixon who launched the War on Cancer in 1971 and turned part of the former biological weapons lab in Fort Detrick, Maryland, into the National Cancer Institute (Semple 1971: 28). These efforts resembled those made during the Eisenhower administration when he launched an aggressive campaign to promote "Atoms for Peace" (Osgood 2006: 153–180; Osgood 2000: 405–433).

Accordingly, several policy decisions emerged soon after Nixon's announcement, which signaled his administration's plans for developing the Biological Research Program despite the new disarmament policy. For instance, Melvin R. Laird, Secretary of Defense, endorsed a revision to the controversial Mansfield Amendment, telling the Senate, "this revised amendment will allow us to maintain our chemical warfare deterrent and our biological research program, both of which are essential to the national security" (Weaver 1969: A1). Laird's comments echoed the calculations made in NSDM 35: "In any event, we would need some research on offensive agents as [the] basis for study of defensive measures and to protect against technological surprise" (ibid.). Kissinger also reiterated these porous, definitional boundaries as the basis for the new policy:

> The United States bacteriological/biological programs will be confined to research and development for defensive purposes (immunization, safety measures, et cetera). This does not preclude research into those offensive

aspects of bacteriological/biological agents necessary to determine what defensive measures are required.

(Wampler 2001: #26-a, henceforth cited as Wampler only)

To negotiate this tenuous balance, Nixon decided, "The term Chemical and Biological Warfare (CBW) will no longer be used. The reference henceforth should be to the two categories separately—The Chemical Warfare Program and The Biological Research Program" (ibid.).

To ensure agencies complied with these new definitional boundaries, Laird sent out a memo in December, insisting the terminology be implemented immediately: "I notice that current documents of various U.S. Government Agencies continue to refer to CBW, i.e. chemical and biological warfare. Such terminology, I believe, is seriously misleading and should be stricken from our lexicon" (Wampler—a). He went on to stress:

> While terminology may seem to be a minor point in some cases, this is one instance in which precise terminology is important. I would hope that in referring to the United States program the term chemical warfare and biological research would be used. I would also hope that in referring to other nations' programs, or to the general field of activity, chemical warfare and biological activities of whatever nature would be differentiated and treated separately. To do otherwise will continue to confuse the American public, our allies, our potential adversaries, and even those in our own government responsible for defense programs.

While this qualification made crystal clear the intent of the administration in separating biological research activities from any connotation with warfare, the U.S. government proceeded aggressively with research and development to ensure the country did not fall behind the Soviet Union in this burgeoning area of science.

Henceforth, during the many months between Nixon's disarmament decision in 1969 and the launch of détente along with the Biological Weapons Convention in 1972, senior government officials remained acutely aware of U.S. vulnerability in the face of rapid advances in molecular biology. For instance, in November 1970, the Interdepartmental Political-Military Group provided the president with the "Annual Review of United States Chemical Warfare and Biological Research Programs" (Wampler—b). Therein, the Joint Chiefs of Staff (JCS) "proposed a program [...] aimed at remedying CBW defensive deficiencies with respect to our military forces." The military was particularly concerned in the wake of Nixon's decision that it might be vulnerable to technological surprise, considering the rapid pace of developments in the biological sciences, particularly molecular biology at the time. For instance, the November 1970 Review analyzed several components of the newly established "Biological and Toxin Research Program" alongside "Foreign Capabilities and Threat[s]." It added, "The Director of Central

Intelligence shall continue to maintain surveillance of the biological and toxin warfare capabilities of other states." In terms of foreign country capabilities in this area, the review highlighted the Soviet Union's growing interest in this area:

> Soviet interest in various potential biological warfare agents has been documented and the intelligence community agrees that the Soviets have all the necessary means for developing an offensive capability in this field. Useful intelligence on actual production, weaponization, and stockpiling remains nonexistent, and information on the Soviet biological warfare program remains incomplete in almost all important details. In view of the US renunciation of biological and toxin warfare, the need for greater attention and priority to collection of intelligence in this area is particularly important.

This assessment of Soviet interests and capabilities in molecular biology had become an increasing concern of U.S. policymakers since the mid-1960s once the Soviet Union officially declared the end of the notorious Lysenko Period.

While the Nixon administration pressed ahead with sweeping conversion plans, the White House also confronted a growing anti-science and anti-technology sentiment gripping the American public. Senior government officials' concerns about this issue coupled with the sensitivity of the conversion process during international arms control negotiations led John N. Irwin II, chairman of the National Security Council's Under Secretaries Committee, to inform the president about the Department of Defense plan to conduct a study "to develop appropriate guidelines for the public information program on US chemical warfare, and biological and toxin research" (Wampler—c). At the same time, White House officials were responsible for overseeing the conversion process of the nation's largest biological weapons facilities, such as Fort Detrick and Pine Bluff Arsenal, toward defense-related purposes. Peter Flanigan, assistant to the president, described Fort Detrick as "ideally suited, [with] a large segment of the personnel […] well suited, for carrying on work in communicable diseases and other biomedical problems."[11] DuBridge highlighted the political benefits of converting Fort Detrick: "There will be an important public relations advantage in converting a war-time biological laboratory into a peace-time laboratory devoted to agriculture and health problems." While senior policymakers pressed for the public relations advantage during the conversion process, the administration moved quietly to ensure that institutional reforms were put in place for the country's civilian sectors, such as non-profit universities and profit-seeking industry, which adjusted to absorb military scientists, resources, and related material from the Biological Warfare Program.

Privatization in the name of national security

One of the ways the Nixon administration accomplished these reforms and ensured a continuing tight grip over the conversion process included the decision to hire Roy L. Ash, president of Litton Industries and future director of the Office of Management and Budget (OMB), to chair a committee charged with reorganizing the executive branch thoroughly.[12] Significantly, Litton had been an industry leader in the government's Biological Warfare Program in the 1960s, during which time it received the second largest number of government contracts of any U.S. company (Wampler—d). Furthermore, once Ash was director of OMB, Litton Industries' Bionetics Research Laboratories received a "research program contract" in 1972 to run the new National Cancer Institute at Fort Detrick (Frank 1974: 161). Despite these obvious conflicts of interest, the Ash Council, as it was called, proposed detailed plans to maximize oversight of the conversion process by centralizing authority and decision making of federal science policy in the White House.

In order to carry out this institutional change, the Ash Council dealt directly with the structure of science advising in the Executive Office of the President.[13] According to the *New York Times*, "The Nixon Administration is moving to make the hydra-headed Federal science and technology apparatus more responsive to the nation's needs" (Lyons 1970: 1). The Ash Council's assignment was to provide key White House officials with proposals for providing the president with more leverage over the nation's R&D enterprise. The Ash Council's report, which was never made public, argued that the entire White House science advisory apparatus that had been erected in the wake of WWII should be replaced.[14] Nixon administration officials also believed that firmer executive branch control over federal science policy would increase its capacity to persuade Americans' of science and technology's benefits rather than harms. DuBridge informed the president:

> In the past the pluralism of support by many agencies has been a healthy development, both for the agencies concerned and for the strength of American science. If a transition away from this pluralism is deemed desirable, we should plan it with great care through building up the National Science Foundation budget which Congress has never been enthusiastic about supporting.[15]

The National Science Foundation garnered increased attention during the conversion process because it served to position the majority of federal science funding in a civilian agency rather than a military one. It also gave the executive branch considerably more control over the direction of federal science policy. By moving a large share of the Pentagon's basic science funding to a civilian agency, the administration hoped to quell student and scientist protests regarding military research on university campuses.

By January 1973, Nixon announced his Reorganization Plan No. 1, abolishing the science advisory apparatus in the White House, which included the position of science advisor, the Office of Science and Technology Policy, and the Presidential Science Advisory Committee.[16] This radical departure from the postwar science advising practice fulfilled the Ash Council plan of concentrating federal science policy within the White House. At the time, President Nixon appointed H. Guyford Stever to serve as director of the NSF, a position, which now also included serving as science advisor to the White House. In Nixon's official message to Congress about his Reorganization Plan, he argued that reforms to the NSF were part of his ambitious goals for "Streamlining the Federal Science Establishment" (Nixon 1973). Specifically, he said, "The National Science Foundation has broadened from its earlier concentration on basic research support to take on a significant role in applied research as well. It has matured in its ability to play a coordinating and evaluative role within the Government and between the public and private sectors." By 1975, historian Toby Appel notes that the NSF "incorporate[d] an entirely new element, namely NSF's relation to the growth of new industrial biotechnology" (Appel 2000: 269). In other words, by placing a civilian agency at the forefront of biological R&D during the early phase of the conversion process, the administration centralized oversight of the nation's R&D enterprise and fostered closer university–industry collaboration.

Not only did Nixon administration officials seek to reorient the nation's R&D enterprise toward a heavier reliance on the private sector, but the military officials also supported the change, especially those involved in the sensitive, yet strategic, conversion process. Military officials recognized that the civilian and commercial sectors needed to be integrated into a national effort of fortifying the country's dual-use capabilities in the biological sciences. In one such indication of these views, Leonard J. Goldberg, research physicist at the Naval Biomedical Research Laboratory in Oakland, California, wrote a letter to Kissinger, recommending ways to retain the country's defensive capabilities in the biological sciences without violating President Nixon's new disarmament posture.[17] Goldberg argued rather forcefully that his 23 years of experience at the laboratory led him to "conclude that basic 'War Research' should be directly integrated into carefully selected peacetime requirements, i.e., the goals of 'War Research' should be kept broad, encompassing peacetime goals as well as maintaining a cognizance of the possible uses which can occur when this research is directed towards a 'Weapons System.'" Goldberg lamented that exclusive "military funding" at Fort Detrick in the past had precluded the opportunity to "integrat[e] scientists into a peacetime role which maintains a broad awareness of our total needs." Therefore, Goldberg advocated, "What is needed is funding of basic and applied research which will quietly serve as a reservoir of military strength."

In order to provide a pertinent example of government-business relations for such a purpose, Goldberg mentioned "our present chemical insecticide industry." According to Goldberg, this industry "serves as an excellent deterrent against chemical warfare." Goldberg's letter concludes by:

> respectfully suggest[ing ...] that we direct a portion of our nation's resources into a microbial war against insects, thus clearly demonstrating our desire for peace, but at the same time maintaining our technological strength in an area which has unlimited military potential. This in no way negates the Presidential pronouncement on B.W. but does maintain a body of technology which can become immediately available when required in answer to a military challenge.

Apparently, Kissinger took Goldberg's recommendations very seriously. He wrote to Goldberg on August 1, 1970 thanking him for his letter "on the role and funding of biological research relative to the broad needs of the United States."[18] Kissinger assured Goldberg that he found his letter "most interesting and I have taken the liberty of sharing it with my staff and have forwarded a copy to Dr. DuBridge."

In light of Goldberg's historical analogy of the chemical industry's serving as a reservoir for the national security and defense, it is interesting, and likely significant, that Monsanto, one of the country's largest chemical industries at the time, became the first corporation to partner with a university in pursuit of molecular biology's industrial potential. In 1974 Monsanto spent $23 million over a 12-year period to enter into the *first ever* industry–university partnership agreement with Harvard University.[19] This agreement received a great deal of attention at the time because it vested patent ownership rights for any discoveries made at the university with Monsanto rather than with Harvard. In order for Harvard to accommodate the terms of this new patent agreement with a firm, it changed university policy in June 1974, making "it permissible, under certain ground rules, for the university to assign patents to industry." After conducting negotiations for a year and a half to iron out the terms of this agreement, *Science* then described this establishment as "unprecedented in the annals of academic-business affairs." For reasons that were never fully explained, Monsanto and Harvard refused to reveal complete information on this agreement. Monte C. Throdahl, group vice-president for technology at Monsanto, mentioned to *Science* that "at about the same time" the company became increasingly interested in biological research to complement its research in agricultural chemicals. Monsanto's long-standing role in the nation's defense-industrial base throughout the 20th century suggests policymakers viewed the company as a vital component of the country's "reservoir of military strength."

In 2012, Milton Leitenberg and Raymond A. Zilinskas, two experts on the history of biological warfare, wrote a major book on the Soviet Union's Biological Weapons Program in the 20th century (Leitenberg and Zilinskas 2012). The book deals at length with the period under investigation in this chapter because one of the supposedly great historical puzzles surrounding the period deals with the Soviet Union's decision to accelerate dramatically its development of biological weapons *after* it signed and ratified the Biological Weapons Convention of 1972. As a result of their extensive research of Soviet archives and interviews, the authors discuss several possible hypotheses for this outcome. One of the hypotheses that they find persuasive stems from firsthand knowledge that Raymond L. Garthoff, former CIA and State Department official from the 1950s through the 1970s, wrote about and shared with them, claiming the Soviets succumbed to an elaborate U.S. disinformation campaign. According to Garthoff, the U.S. deceived the Soviet Union and the world when it announced its disarmament decision while actually continuing it all along in secret.[20] Garthoff argues that the ramifications of this "successful" disinformation campaign weighed heavily on U.S.-Soviet relations for the remainder of the Cold War and undercut trust in the newly established arms control agreement. Nevertheless, for the purposes of this chapter, it is important to highlight Soviet perceptions of the Nixon administration's actions in carrying out this scheme while gaining domestic and international credit for arms control. According to Leitenberg and Zilinskas, Colonel General Yefim Ivanovich Smirnov, who ran the Main Military Medical Directorate of the Red Army, and was "the most important military decision maker in the Soviet BW program" between 1954 to 1985, became convinced that the Soviets would be left further behind their American scientific counterparts unless they made every effort to keep up with and surpass the U.S. in biotechnology's military potential (2012). Leitenberg and Zilinskas note that Smirnov lobbied Soviet officials to continue and expand the country's BW program dramatically. In so doing, he made the following claims to his superiors:

> In briefings to BW workers in subsequent years, he repeated one particular message again and again, namely, that when the United States had publicized closing down its offensive BW program in 1969, it had lied. What the Pentagon actually did, he said, was to transfer the program from the Department of Defense's laboratories to private companies and university laboratories that were then responsible for the R&D required to develop new biological weapons.
>
> (Leitenberg and Zilinskas 2012)

While Smirnov's claims may seem far fetched, as Leitenberg and Zilinskas suggest, one of the principals involved in the conversion process during détente and BW arms control negotiations in the early 1970s was H. Guyford Stever. In 1980, Stever reflected upon his time in the Nixon and Ford administrations, noting the delicate negotiations under détente when the U.S. and U.S.S.R. established the Science and Technology Exchange Program. Stever notes that this program served as "the first specific agreement to be signed," following the initiation of détente with the Soviet Union in 1972 (Stever 1980: 71–72). He explains how senior policymakers were keenly aware that the exchanges involved extraordinary sensitivity over national security secrets; hence, Stever recalls how the exchanges:

> did not create a threatening leak in the vast science and technology information banks of the country, for we were careful to choose the fields of cooperation in areas where we both had something to gain. On this latter point, I am sure that the Soviets were disappointed, because they had hoped that this exchange would open wide to them the flow of the science and technology of our private industry; there were often difficulties on this point.

Hence, Stever seems to acknowledge the national security role private industry played in these exchanges. With the private sector off limits to the Soviet military and scientists who wanted to participate in the exchanges, it is not a surprise or a stretch to see why they became convinced by the disinformation campaign's claims. This section shows where the national security lessons of privatization and secrecy meet, highlighting the domestic and geopolitical stakes of the molecular biology revolution as well as of the legitimacy crisis.

Centralization of political authority and power over federal science policy

The United States finally ratified the Biological Weapons Convention of 1972 in February 1975 and the treaty went into effect in 1976. The lengthy period between Nixon's conversion decision in November 1969 and the U.S. government's compliance with the BWC in 1976 enabled senior policymakers to unwind the conversion process in a slow and orderly manner, ensuring that the institutional, legal, and regulatory reforms were completed. During this seven-year process, the Nixon and Ford administrations as well as Congress and the military managed to produce two seemingly contradictory outcomes in federal science policy by 1976. On the one hand, the U.S. government pursued a deregulatory regime by institutionalizing the new National Institutes of Health Guidelines for Research Involving Recombinant DNA Molecules (NIH Guidelines). On the other hand, the U.S. government established a centralized mechanism for overseeing and directing the biological sciences in the new omnibus legislation known as P.L. 94–282, the National Science and Technology Policy, Organization and Priorities Act. These twin outcomes fortified a novel approach to addressing the opportunities and risks posed by the molecular biology revolution. This section evaluates the national security rationales that underlay them both.

Deregulation to enhance national security interests in molecular biology

The historiography of molecular biology almost universally describes 1973 as the starting point of debates surrounding the potential health and environmental dangers posed by genetic engineering.[21] These influential narratives tell a riveting story of brave scientists making an unexpected discovery with genetic engineering in the early 1970s, followed by public outcries over the dangers of the new discoveries, whereupon these same scientists responded by heroically and voluntarily imposing a moratorium on their research in this controversial area to alleviate public fears and ensure the safety of their scientific endeavors. While these narratives capture part of the drama that surrounded widespread public attention to recombinant DNA techniques in the early 1970s, they do not capture the political strategizing involved behind the scenes in forging one particular, narrow story line over another. Furthermore, these narratives do not capture the military's interest in ending the scientists' moratorium as soon as possible to ensure the resumption of R&D in the fertile area of molecular biology.

The real challenge for the scientific community, which depended heavily on federal funding for its lifeblood, recognized the imperative of dissociating molecular biology with militarism and warfare in order to reassure a fearful public that the new science of genetic engineering would not unleash uncontrollable horrors. As historian Susan Wright has documented, several months before the Asilomar Conference proceedings in February 1975, an "early draft of the [Paul] Berg committee's letter" expressed concerns about the "military use of genetic engineering technology" but these critical issues were "later excised" from the final draft (Wright 1994: 137–138). Wright compelling argues, "The final version of the letter, published in July 1974 in the *Proceedings of the National Academy of Sciences, Science,* and *Nature,* constituted a crucial move in reducing and restricting discourse concerning issues surrounding genetic engineering as well as defining mechanisms for its resolution." This crucial move centered on gaining widespread public support for recombinant DNA techniques to ensure Americans would focus on the benefits of molecular biology rather than its risks.

In order to accomplish this political objective, the lawmakers and scientists joined forces in a concerted elite counterattack to construct the NIH Guidelines in response to the Asilomar Conference. Even though these famous guidelines are commonly viewed as a regulatory framework, they are in fact just guidelines that contain no regulatory requirements for researchers in the public and private sectors whatsoever. Donald S. Fredrickson, director of the NIH in the Ford and Carter administrations, concedes that a "crucial distinction" exists "between Federal guidelines and regulations," with only the latter embodying "the force of law" (Frederickson 1974: 152). Hence, the NIH Guidelines should be seen as part of a continuing public relations campaign that enabled government officials to ease the public's fears while simultaneously opening the floodgates of R&D in genetic engineering by relaxing regulatory oversight.

Almost immediately after the NIH Guidelines were issued on June 23, 1976, major criticisms of their weakness erupted into open debate. For instance, on July 19, 1976 senators Jacob J. Javits (R-NY) and Edward M.

Kennedy (D-MA) wrote President Ford about their concern that the NIH Guidelines were too narrow since they did not cover research in the private sector as well as research abroad.[22] In other words, the NIH Guidelines were confined exclusively to laboratory work conducted in the public sector. The senators' letter stressed:

> We are gravely concerned that these relatively stringent guidelines may not be implemented in all sectors of the domestic and international research communities and that the public will therefore be subjected to undue risks. The National Institutes of Health has the authority to require adherence to the guidelines as a condition of their grants and contracts for research, but they cannot enforce the guidelines with respect to other Federal agencies, with respect to research in the private sector in this country, and with respect to research done in other nations.

Significantly, David Mathews, Secretary of the Department of Health, Education and Welfare, shared the senators' view that the NIH Guidelines were too weak and ineffective since they failed to cover research conducted across the public and private sectors. Mathews wrote to President Ford on June 18, a week before the Guidelines were issued, to argue for stronger and more comprehensive guidelines "in light of the great public concern" about recombinant DNA experiments.[23]

Congress held hearings in September of 1976 on the breadth and effectiveness of the guidelines, making "clear that if industrial companies fail to comply with the NIH guidelines voluntarily, [Senator Kennedy] will make them do so by law" (Wade 1976: 304). Among expressed concerns about the reach of the NIH Guidelines impact on the private sector, Director Fredrickson also fielded questions about the Central Intelligence Agency's compliance with the guidelines. This particular line of questioning generated a significant amount of consternation in Ford's White House, considering the Church Committee hearings recently found that the CIA had been blatantly violating Nixon's biological weapons ban by holding onto shellfish toxin and other crucial items from the nation's former Biological Warfare Program's arsenal.[24]

In September 1976 James Cannon, White House staff, wrote to National Security Advisor Brent Scowcroft about his view that the administration needed to draft "an appropriate Administration response" to the questions raised about CIA's genetics research.[25] Interestingly, the same memo mentions that the National Security Council was in the process of "developing appropriate legislation with other department and agency representatives" to ensure DOD implemented the Biological Weapons Convention of 1972. Cannon's memo to Scowcroft said that the "DOD considers the Biological Weapons Convention as prohibiting its involvement in this research area at the present time." Cannon goes on to point out that the NIH guidelines would not bear on the DOD's research on molecular biology because the Office of the

General Counsel of the Arms Control and Disarmament Agency says that the BWC already "prohibit[s] production of recombinant DNA molecules for purposes of constructing biological weapons."

Even though the BWC prohibited the military from conducting genetic engineering research "at the present time," it did not alter DOD's interest in this rapidly evolving area of R&D since the Pentagon wanted to ensure it could stave off technological surprise. In fact, Congress asserted in a 1976 report, "There is no evidence available at this time that there are any restrictions on DNA recombinant research in the Soviet Union," which necessarily concerned U.S. military officials.[26] Consequently, Malcolm R. Currie, director of Defense Research and Engineering, wrote Director Fredrickson in September in response to his inquiry about DOD's research on recombinant DNA and whether the department had reviewed the NIH Guidelines.[27] Currie assured Fredrickson that DOD had reviewed the guidelines and found them "acceptable" if and when the military decided to resume research in this area. The letter went on to stress that even though DOD was currently refraining from conducting research in this area, "the DOD remains vitally interested that research and technology development in this area be continued by the civil sector to assure its availability to DOD for use in meeting any military surprise which might arise from a nation or group." Currie argued, "Any further delay in the resumption of this research to permit refinement of the guidelines is judged counterproductive in meeting our defensive role." Hence, the U.S. military advocated for the NIH Guidelines to be issued as soon as possible since the new policy would end the scientists' moratorium on research in molecular biology.

While the NIH Guidelines provided much needed political cover with the public, there were still heated battles raging over whether to extend them to all government agencies and to the private sector. These debates were even more politically fraught in a presidential election year. Hence, on September 22, 1976, President Ford made in effect a non-decision, providing him with precious political cover, by taking the path of least resistance. Therein, he issued a Memorandum for the Heads of Departments and Agencies to inform them that Secretary Mathews would convene "an interagency committee to review Federal policies on the conduct of research involving recombinant DNA."[28] Ford said he "expect[ed] the full cooperation of each department and agency conducting or supporting recombinant DNA experiments" to assist Mathews in his review efforts. On the same day, Ford finally wrote a response letter to senators Javits and Kennedy about their "grave concern" that the Guidelines did not cover all government agencies and the private sector. He assured them that his administration shared their view that "The application of these Guidelines beyond the NIH to the public and private sectors merits further consideration."[29] In support of this view, he pointed toward his recent support of Secretary Mathews' "proposed committee." With this non-decision, Ford successfully punted this controversial issue to the next administration where it languished in obscurity.

What's at stake in the privatization debate? 119

Implementing centralization over nation's scientific enterprise

During the years these voluntary guidelines were being debated and established to loosen the reigns of government regulatory oversight and ensure the privatization of molecular biology experiments, another policy development emerged concurrently wherein an entirely new federal science policy apparatus was created to centralize oversight of the nation's R&D system. These centrifugal forces sought to maximize the American state's capacity to channel the conversion process toward industrial as well as national security ends.

Despite the controversies surrounding President Nixon's abolition of the White House science advisory apparatus and the vesting of more authority in the NSF, astute observers soon realized that the new scientific arrangement based within the NSF appeared successful. Nevertheless, the geopolitical stakes of the conversion process in the midst of the molecular biology revolution did not change. Hence, the Ford administration and Congress moved beyond the modest centralization activities that vested greater resources and authority in the NSF by instead proposing a sweeping overall of the entire federal science policy apparatus. The omnibus piece of legislation known as P. L. 94–282, the National Science and Technology Policy, Organization and Priorities Act of 1976 (S.32) accomplished this goal.[30] When signing the landmark bill, President Ford proclaimed that it "outlines a comprehensive policy for achievement of our national objectives through the effective utilization of science and technology."[31] According to the legislative history of the act, the bill "establishes an institutional capability at the Federal level" for carrying out these efforts.[32] With the passage of this legislation, the centralization of federal science policy began. This major reform existed alongside the deregulatory and privatization regime that emerged with the NIH Guidelines. Hence, by 1976 policymakers and military officials had succeeded in resolving the conversion process in such a way that the American state increased its capacity to reap the benefits of the biological revolution for national security ends as well as industrial ones. All the while, the American public came to associate molecular biology with a beneficent future, eschewing its military past.

Conclusion

This chapter examined two pivotal moments in the 1970s, surrounding President Nixon's decision to convert the nation's Biological Warfare Program into the Biological Research Program in 1969, to provide an illustrative example the origins and evolution of *hybrid rule* as state strategy. These two moments expose three national security lessons that form the basis of *hybrid rule*: secrecy, privatization, and centralization. The patterns of public–private partnerships that blossomed during WWII took on a new hue in the wake of Nixon's conversion decision, becoming embedded in altered institutional, regulatory and legal changes that shaped state–society relations in the

American polity and beyond. As the definition of *hybrid rule* asserts, political elites created a set of practices that rely on the private sector to shield national security activities by expanding state power while constraining democratic accountability. Hence, the change in public–private relations that emerged in the early 1970s addressed the legitimacy crisis, in part, through the deployment of federal science policy.

The implications of this historical case study for understanding American state power and world politics centers on how the practices and patterns of *hybrid rule* that were developed in the 1970s have come full circle in the massive post-Cold War and post-9/11 biodefense buildup that the country is experiencing today. The nearly twenty-year national emergency covering the proliferation of WMDs places extraordinary strain on the scientific community in upholding its professional duties in a transparent manner to produce the best possible outcomes and build public trust. This challenge to the scientific community's mission can be seen in two recent developments. First, the CIA released a report in 2003, proclaiming that the "US life sciences research community was more or less 'over its Vietnam-era distrust' of the national security establishment and would be open to more collaboration" (Central intelligence Agency 2003). Second, 758 life scientists sent a petition to the director of the National Institutes of Health in 2005, protesting the "shift of tens of millions of dollars in federal research money" since 2001 away from pathogens that cause major public health problems to obscure germs the government fears might be used in a bioterrorist attack" (Shane 2005). Finally, Joby Warrick of *The Washington Post* recently revealed the practical impact of the U.S. government's growing "secretive fight against bioterror" (Warrick 2006: A. 1.) Therein, Warrick notes that the National Biodefense Analysis and Countermeasures Center (NBACC), a new lab at Fort Detrick, MD, is shrouded in unprecedented secrecy. Apparently, in what Warrick describes as "an unusual arrangement, the building itself will be classified as highly restricted space, from the reception desk to the lab benches to the cages where animals are kept. Few federal facilities, including nuclear labs, operate with such stealth." This evident conflict within the life sciences community becomes concealed once the government increasingly delegates biodefense responsibilities to the private sector in the name of protecting national security at all costs both at home and abroad. Hence, what's at stake in the privatization debate is democratic participation and accountability.

Notes

1 The author warmly thanks Ronnie D. Lipschutz for his patience and perseverance as well as for being a great debate partner. The author also thanks all of the contributors to the volume for inspiring and pushing the lines of debate.
2 Central Intelligence Agency, "The Darker Bioweapons Future," unclassified (November 3, 2003): http://fas.org/irp/cia/product/bw1103.pdf.
3 See Polyani 1944.

4 Harry S. Truman: Proclamation 2914—Proclaiming the Existence of a National Emergency," December 16, 1950, *The American Presidency Project*, 13684. I note that a 2007 Congressional Research Service report mentions that the National Emergencies Act of 1976 (P.L. 94–112) "rendered ineffective Truman's Proclamation. Nevertheless, the CRS notes that the 1976 legislation "did not cancel" Truman's 1950 Proclamation. In my own research, I have found that President Carter cancelled the Proclamation in 1979. See Relyea (2007).
5 This near-singular focus defies the empirical evidence on the ground. For instance, on Thursday, August 29, 2013 *The Washington Post* released so-called "black budget" intelligence information obtained by Edward Snowden that showed non-proliferation of WMD's as one of five primary missions within the intelligence community. See Gellman and Miller (2013).
6 For a more thorough treatment of this topic, please see Hurt (2010); Hurt in Block and Keller (2011: 31–56).
7 For a few representative examples, please see Roland (1985); Wang (1998); Westwick (2003); Hogan (2000).
8 For an excellent representation of this literature, please see Russell (2001).
9 Osgood made the following comments during a presentation of his book at the Miller Center of Public Affairs at the University of Virginia on May 2, 2006. The transcript and video of his comments can be found at: http://millercenter.org/scripps/digitalarchive/forumDetail/1942.
10 Reprinted in Melman (1970: 134–231).
11 Memorandum: Peter M. Flanigan to President re: "Meeting With Dr. DuBridge," March 14, 1970, White House Special Files, White House Central Files, Confidential Files, folder [no title], Box 15, Declassified by Executive Order 12958, Sec. 3.6, March 4, 1998, *Nixon Materials*.
12 The official name of the council Roy L. Ash chaired was called the President's Advisory Council on Executive Reorganization.
13 Memorandum: Peter Flanigan to Staff Secretary, January 30, 1970, White House Special Files, White House Central Files, Confidential Files, folder EOP, Box 13, *Nixon Materials*.
14 Memorandum: Roy L. Ash to President, Subject: "Report on Selected Activities in the Executive Office of the President," January 20, 1970, "Administratively confidential," White House Special Files, White House Central Files, Confidential Files, folder EOP, Box 13, *Nixon Materials*.
15 Memorandum: DuBridge to President, Subject: "Agenda for Meeting December 11–11:45 AM," December 10, 1969, White House Central Files, Subject Files Science, folder 12-6-68 to 12-30-70, Box 2 of 5, *Nixon Materials*.
16 Nixon's controversial decision to abolish the science advisory apparatus in the White House continues to define much of the historiography on his administration and American science policy in the latter half of the twentieth century. The conventional wisdom about this decision insists it represented a downgrading of science in the Federal government and represented another indication of Nixon's hostility toward the scientific community. These views are mistaken. See Smith (1990: 91) for support of my perspective.
17 The next two paragraphs cite this letter at length. Letter: Leonard J. Goldberg to Dr. Henry A. Kissinger, July 22, 1970, White House Central Files, AG, folder GEN AG 5-1 Pest Control [1969–70], Box 9, *Nixon Materials*.
18 Letter: Kissinger to Goldberg, August 1, 1970, White House central Files, AG, folder GEN AG 5-1 Pest Control [1969–70], Box 9, *Nixon Materials*.
19 Most of the material in this paragraph draws heavily from Culliton (1977: 759–763).
20 For a riveting portrayal of Garthoff's claims, see Garthoff (2000: 37–40).
21 This history is well known. For the most thorough analysis, see Wright (1994); Wright (1990: 76–96).

22 Letter: Senator Javits and Senator Kennedy to President, July 19, 1976, White House Central Files, Subject Files #9, folder: HE8 Research, Gerald R. Ford Presidential Library and Museum, Ann Arbor, Michigan (hereafter cited as *Ford Library* only).
23 Memorandum: Secretary David Mathews for the President, June 18, 1976, White House central Files, Subject Files #9, folder: HE8 Research, Ford Library.
24 See, Hearing before the Select Committee to Study Governmental Operations with Respect to Intelligence Activities of the United States Senate, *Intelligence Activities, Senate Resolution 21*, Ninety-Fourth Congress, First Session, Volume I: Unauthorized Storage of Toxic Agents, September 16, 17, and 18, 1975 (Washington, DC: U.S. Government Printing Office: 1976).
25 Memorandum: James Cannon to Brent Scowcroft, September 29, 1976, Subject: Congressional Inquiries Concerning CIA Involvement in Genetics Research, White House Central Files, Subject Files #9, folder: HE8 Research, *Ford Library*.
26 See the report prepared for the subcommittee on Science, Research and Technology of the committee on Science and Technology, *Genetic Engineering, Human Genetics, and Cell Biology: Evolution of a Technological Issue—DNA Recombinant Molecule Research (Supplemental Report II)*, House of Representatives, Ninety-Fourth Congress, Second Session, December 1976 (Washington, DC: The U.S. Government Printing Office, 1976): 59.
27 Letter: Malcolm R. Currie to Dr. Fredrickson, September 21, 1976, White House Central Files, Subject Files #9, folder: HE8 Research, *Ford Library*.
28 This memorandum is available on the Gerald R. Ford Library website. www.ford.utexas.edu/library/speeches/760801.htm.
29 Letter: President Ford to Mr. Chairman, September 22, 1976. White House Central Files, Subject Files #9, folder: HE8 Research, *Ford Library*.
30 For a recounting of the history of this legislation, see U.S. Congress, Committee on Commerce, Science and Transportation, 1977: *A Legislative History of the National Science and Technology Policy, Organization and Priorities Act of 1976.* April. However, the legislative history covered in this document begins with S. 32, the Conversion Research, Education and Assistance Act of 1971, and not S. 4241.
31 For a recounting of the history of this legislation, see U.S. Congress, Committee on Commerce, Science and Transportation, 1977: *A Legislative History of the National Science and Technology Policy, Organization and Priorities Act of 1976*, April.
32 Ibid.

6 Sovereign wealth funds and varieties of hybridization

Herman M. Schwartz[1]

Introduction

The sudden and spectacular increase in the size and number of sovereign wealth funds (SWFs) in the late 2000s seems to run against the trends regarding more hybrid public–private forms of governance analyzed in the rest of this volume. Indeed, some analysts (Bremmer 2010) saw the rise of large SWFs not just as a simple reversal of prior trends towards privatization but also as the return of state capitalism as the dominant form of industrial organization. Hybridization occurred as the state delegated tasks to private entities or deregulated private activity. By contrast, states used SWFs as an instrument to expand their ownership of and control over private entities rather than delegating authority to private entities. What does the (re)emergence of SWFs tell us about the current relationship between states and markets, the boundaries between public and private actors, and the nature of the hybrid state?

Three problems diminish the utility of most current analyses of SWFs with respect to understanding state formation and hybridization: data deficiencies, faulty framing, and conceptual confusion. First, many SWFs conceal their holdings, investment strategies and behaviors. Secrecy in itself is informative— what is there to hide?—but it also subtracts enough information to render any conclusions tentative. Second, as with most social phenomena, initial analyses of SWFs framed the issue in terms of some 'usual suspects.' Here the usual suspect issue was SWFs' salience for U.S. international economic policy and power. This orientation turned these analyses into pragmatic policy exercises lacking any grounding in a theoretical perspective and obscuring all the most interesting things about SWFs.[2] Finally, conceptually, the label 'sovereign wealth fund' obscured rather than illuminated the social phenomena it was supposed to represent. SWF is a portmanteau label that confusingly conflates three distinct patterns of on-going state formation and thus does not always signify hybridization. A SWF is not a SWF is not a SWF—the label covers a heterogeneous not a homogenous phenomenon.

This chapter places the analysis of SWFs on firmer ground by approaching it from the perspective of hybridization. It identifies three different kinds of

124 *Herman M. Schwartz*

SWFs based on divergent state building processes and forms of hybridization. Some SWFs constrain actors' current spending and thus buffer resource economies against price volatility or secure pension income for the future. These are closest to the hybrid phenomenon explored in the rest of the book A second set of SWFs are largely an instance of Max Weber's political capitalism, in which actors make profits on the basis of special deals with political authorities (Love 1986). In the best case this makes them useful vehicles for development. In the worst case they create the third and final group of SWFs, which encompass personal investment vehicles for politically powerful actors in patrimonial regimes.

What are SWFs?

The famous social scientist Thomas Pynchon (1973: 251) once said, "If they can get you asking the wrong questions, they don't have to worry about the answers." Conventional analyses of SWFs ask the wrong questions. They start with a nominal definition of SWFs: SWFs are state-owned financial institutions that invest the state's own savings offshore. They arise from overt state intervention in the economy—otherwise how could the state accumulate savings—and thus are deleterious from the point of view of those ideologically committed to a neo-liberal understanding of the proper boundaries around state action. They thus trouble those concerned about maintaining U.S. global economic power because of the potential that states might use their SWFs to exercise control in global and local markets (Truman 2008). These analyses inadvertently homogenize SWFs, diverting analytic attention to the fact of state ownership and interests rather than asking what SWFs actually do. This misplaced focus obscures the origins, behavior and consequences of SWFs.

The nominal definition identifies between 40 and 100 major SWFs depending on one's decisions about how to label public pension funds or other state entities that are also active global investors.[3] The modern definition of SWF links them to oil surpluses or capitalized (as opposed to PAYGO) public pension plans. With a few exceptions, like Botswana's 1966 diamond-funded SWF, oil revenues funded the efflorescence of SWFs in the 1970s and 1980s. After a lull, the next big rush came from 1998 to 2008, when 23 funds came into existence, again mostly on the strength of rising oil prices. The concentration of oil revenues and other export surpluses with countries that were cool to U.S. foreign policy preference triggered the moral panic around SWFs.

This moral panic reflected quantity rather than quality. The conventional definition points to Kuwait's Investment Authority, founded in 1953, as the first SWF—but no one much cared about SWFs until the mid-2000s' oil shock swelled SWF revenues to reach previously unimaginable heights.[4] In addition, Asian and above all Chinese export surpluses rested on massive state intervention in foreign exchange markets, which also ran counter to expressed U.S. policy preferences. Finally, using a more expansive definition, many of the newer SWFs also capture local wages as a form of forced pension savings. Singapore's public pension fund, the Central Provident Fund, for example, captures about 32 percent of wages.

Secrecy, particularly on the part of the Gulf State SWFs, makes a precise accounting of SWF holdings impossible, but estimates made before the 2008 financial crisis ranged from $1.5 trillion to $3 trillion (Johnson 2007; U.S. Treasury 2007). This made SWFs as large as the global hedge fund industry at that time, but considerably smaller than the $16 trillion global pension industry (albeit, obviously, with some overlap). Estimates current in mid-2013 placed SWF holdings in the range of $5.5 trillion, giving SWFs somewhere in the region of 10 percent of marketable securities globally, with Norway's government pension fund—Global, or GPF-G—alone holding about 1 percent of global equities.[5] At that time global pension assets amounted to roughly $30 trillion. High volatility in both the numerators and denominators here makes these estimates particularly unreliable.

The contemporary 'SWF' label creates conceptual confusion by obscuring earlier organizations that also accumulated export revenues and/or fiscal surpluses. But we could and should consider the marketing boards used by European imperial powers in Australia, Africa and elsewhere as proto-SWFs, because they performed the same functions as many modern SWFs, and indeed they persisted well past decolonization. From a naïve or functionalist economic point of view, SWFs (including these earlier versions) in principle can and should perform three natural and benign functions for economies that are highly dependent on raw materials exports. They could buffer economies from the high price and volume volatility (beta) characterizing those exports. They could help diversify the economy. They could help prevent Dutch disease by sterilizing sudden increases in export revenues.

But the naïve view misses the point. All of these functions are public goods and, as such, neither come into existence without political will and a legitimating ideology nor persist without the support of organized social groups. SWFs and marketing boards are inherently political creatures. Politics is about power, and different SWFs are manifestations of efforts to create or maintain different forms of power. The state's power comes from its ability to define and redefine property rights and to thereby structure the routine behavior of market actors. Property rights set the boundary between public and private arenas and incentivize behavior. The hybrid turn described in Chapter 1 shifted the public–private line in ways that freed the state from social obligations and from political pressures around those obligations (Schwartz 2001). This shift undercut the basis for popular collective action (Schwartz 1994).

Considering SWFs in this light permits us to see three different processes of on-going state formation and hybridization that are inadvertently homogenized under the label of 'SWF.' One set of SWFs is mainly about hybridization: these SWFs are efforts at governmentality, in which the state constrains its population—including politicians—from individually rational behaviors that are collectively irrational, and from internal time inconsistency. A second set of SWFs mainly re-packages the classic developmental state fusion of public and private interest in accumulation and industrialization. As with the earlier fusion, the state's interest in creating an (industrial) bourgeoisie is paramount; hybridization cannot occur until some counter-party exists. These SWFs make hybridization possible rather than manifesting hybridization per se. A third set of SWFs mainly inverts the hybridization discussed in much of this volume. In this set, social actors are colonizing the state and using the state as a vehicle for their particular, rather than collective, interests. This group exhibits pure political capitalism as described by Max Weber. The following sections deal with each type in turn.

Type 1: collective investment funds and rational capitalism

> I don't like disturbances in my place. Either lay off politics or get out.
>
> Rick

Collective investment funds look like rational economic responses to the opportunity created by the gradual liberalization of international capital flows after the 1970s. These collective investment funds use offshore investment to resolve the economic risks associated with raw materials exports and a small economy. They smooth out long-term consumption for economies whose raw materials export receipts are quite volatile. They remove voters' temptation to yield to time-inconsistent preferences favoring immediate consumption, and politicians' consistent preference to maximize short-run electoral gains. Both voters and politicians consider non-renewable raw materials as a form of income rather than as an asset. Finally, these investment funds also reduce the risks associated with concentrating long-term savings into the asset markets of a relatively small economy. So, in principle these collective investment funds could be understood as rational 'Beckerian' efforts to diversify and protect life-cycle income at a national level. Funds that most resemble this ideal type are the Alaska Permanent Fund, the Alberta Heritage Fund, the Australian Future Fund, the New Zealand Superannuation Fund, and, especially, the Norwegian government pension fund—Global (GPF-G). The Singaporean Central Provident Fund (and government investment fund) and the Chilean Economic and Social Stabilization Fund and Pension Reserve Fund in some respects also conform to this type. Norway's GPF-G is the acknowledged champion of this type, and it will serve as the major empirical example later.

Economies based on raw materials exports face very high price and volume volatility; they have high 'beta.' The average annual price change for all agricultural exports from LDCs, 1955–81, was about 7 percent (Talbott 1995). Oil is even more volatile, with an annual average price change of 35 percent 1994–2009, and copper only slightly less so at 28 percent (Lipsky

2009). This creates obvious macro-economic risks for countries that rely mostly on raw materials exports.

Second, raw materials exports create a situation that is the reverse of the usual Beckerian hypothesis with respect to lifetime income. In Becker's model, households smooth lifetime consumption by borrowing against expected future income on the assumption that income rises with age. Exporters of exhaustible raw materials (and slowly renewing ones like forestry) face exactly the opposite problem. Non-renewable raw materials are in principle an illiquid asset (figuratively for oil, literally for most of the rest). Once harvested, they no longer provide income, so future income is likely to be lower than current income. Thus illiquid assets should be transformed into more liquid and hopefully higher-yielding assets. This would smooth national and individual consumption into the future, if actors could commit to draw only on the permanent income stream the asset generated and not the asset principal itself. But capturing and banking the income from raw materials sales requires individuals and their state to exhibit extremely high levels of discipline.

Many agricultural countries tried to buffer against volatility by using state-run marketing boards. These boards theoretically maximized export receipts by withholding surpluses from world markets and releasing them during periods of low supply and by confronting the big buyers of agricultural outputs with an oligopsonist. Thus, the government of São Paulo and later Brazil set up a valorization scheme in the early 1900s in which the state borrowed abroad to buy up surplus coffee and then repaid the loans by releasing coffee into world markets in lean years. The Australian Wool Realisation Commission and the New Zealand Dairy Board (and their predecessors/successors) performed similar functions, buying up entire crops and then reselling them to end users in world markets. With global market shares ranging from 15 to 80 percent, these various organizations potentially could stabilize volumes and prices. It is notable that these boards mostly arose out of colonial or wartime marketing arrangements in which states enjoyed a higher than normal autonomy from social groups and could unilaterally create these boards, compel sales by producers to marketing boards, and dictate prices to producers.

Similarly, something like a marketing board or a dedicated recipient of royalty receipts can assure that illiquid assets become liquid, rather than being consumed. If these boards were allowed to operate without political interference they might actually work to reduce price volatility and accomplish the asset transformation. But the waning of wartime exigency and state autonomy exposed marketing boards to the time inconsistency of producers, voters, and politicians. Thus royalty payments tend to be diverted directly into state budgets (or politicians' pockets).

Farmers (producers), voters, and politicians all exhibited high inter-temporal inconsistency of preferences and an alarming degree of fiscal illusion. They pressured marketing boards to release newly liquefied assets as current income, and to treat cyclical peak prices as if they were the normal baseline for determining how much income to release to producers. Farmers in particular tended to endogenize temporarily high prices as permanent extra consumption. Politicians likewise succumbed to the temptation to build high boom-time revenues into their baseline budgets. Both groups regarded high prices as 'normal,' and thus pressured marketing boards to pay out too much income during periods of high prices rather than releasing commodity surpluses to drive down those prices to the actual cyclical mean. Meanwhile, incomes for workers—voters—in the secondary and tertiary sectors also ultimately rely on raw materials exports in these economies. Here too, the average individual is strongly tempted to build above trend boom-time income into their baseline expectations about consumption. This is why the 'break-even budget price' for many contemporary oil exporters has inexorably risen, with some countries like Nigeria, Iran, and Russia typically having break-even points above the average price of oil in 2013.

Finally, a third consideration apparently motivates the choice for holding assets *offshore* rather than simply holding assets. Most of the countries with SWFs are relatively small and reliant on a relatively narrow range of exports. Coal and iron ore account for nearly two-fifths of Australia's exports; oil for three-fifths of Norway's exports; dairy and meat for one-third of New Zealand's exports. While Singapore—two-fifths electronics—has a much more diversified export base, it is essentially a city-state. Additionally, New Zealand sits on top of one of the world's most active geological fault lines and can anticipate more Christchurch-scale earthquakes at any time. In these circumstances investing locally appears to put too many eggs in one basket.

Collective investment SWFs appear to resolve all three problems described above at once. They diversify a country's income sources outside of that country and away from concentrated local risks, they disconnect income streams from peak prices, and they potentially reduce political and social pressure to 'un-smooth' consumption by bringing too much consumption into the present. The Norwegian GPF-G appears to provide the best example of this rational outcome.[6] But a close look shows a hybridization logic at work beneath the apparent Beckerian rationality.

The GFP-G emerged from a politics stressing the *responsible* use of oil revenues—a rhetoric very appealing to Scandinavian sensibilities—that emanated from the usual Norwegian corporatist politics. Political elites in Norway manufactured a strong consensus around the appropriate use of oil revenues, using the usual Norwegian tool of public commissions staffed by the usual corporatist actors and academics. Early in the build-out of oil capacity, a 1983 report already signaled the possibility of using a government fund to sequester oil revenues (NOU 1983: 27). Sequestration had two purposes matching the problems above. With the inflationary 1970s as a backdrop, elites did not want to add more demand to an economy with relatively rigid labor markets and low unemployment. Norwegian inflation (CPI) averaged 9.1 percent from 1970 through 1983. Second, elites feared that a rapid increase in oil extraction would cause the 'Dutch disease,' in which raw materials exports create an overvalued currency that in turn displaces manufactured exports and employment in favor of the non-renewable export sector. Dutch disease exacerbates the inverse Beckerian consumption problem described above by eliminating alternative and more durable sources of future income.

Slightly later, in 1988, a major review of Norwegian economic stabilization policy further strengthened the conceptual basis for a fund by arguing strongly that oil should be thought of as an asset, not current income (NOU 1988: 21). Viewing oil as an asset, the report argued that oil revenues should be shunted into savings, and only the income from those new savings should be spent. While it is always hard to judge how much influence ideas exert on policy, one indicator of the degree to which the 'oil is an asset' meme traveled can be found in the career of Jens Stoltenberg. In the 1980s his economics MA thesis dealt with the optimal rate of oil extraction from a financial point of view and the degree to which oil could generate national income. Stoltenberg became finance minister in the 1990s, then prime minister of successive Labour Party-led coalition governments in the 2000s.

The Norwegian government thus created the predecessor of the GPF-G in 1990. Low oil prices in the 1990s meant the fund filled slowly. But as oil prices boomed in the late 1990s and 2000s, the fund began to generate serious income. By 2013 the fund owned a bit more than 1 percent of global equities by value, which is about 20 times Norway's share of global population. The questions of the decade thus were: Should this income be spent? And on what? And how fast? Once again organized interests negotiated a deal. The major parties agreed that the fund's income could be used to supplement the government budget, but only up to a cyclically adjusted deficit equal to 4 percent of the fund's assets. Instead, elites positioned the fund as a supplement to the Norwegian pension system (National Insurance Scheme) to help cushion the demographic transition to an older society. By contrast, the (as yet) un-coalitionable Progress Party saw export revenue as current income rather than as an asset, and called—ineffectually—for more rapid disbursement of funds directly to citizens.[7]

Despite this dissent, the GPF-G presents us with a specific form of ongoing state formation à la Hibou's chapter. This project of governmentality started in the 1980s (Burchell, Gordon and Miller 1991; see also the discussion of ordo- and opto-liberalism in Lipschutz' chapter). GPF-G's disciplined behavior reflects and reinforces a process in which Norwegian society and its state build citizens who are incapable of making and taking decisions that are not good for the long term and not good for everyone.[8] State regulation and the practices embodied in its welfare state tightly control Norwegian society, and in turn social norms tightly constrain both state actors and social behavior. The ethos of the Norwegian welfare state is the repression of individually rational behaviors that are collectively irrational, and the suppression of economically irrational behaviors arising from time-inconsistency of preferences and cognitive biases (Ervik 2005). The implicit ethic here is that people should save for their retirement and should accept health care at a level that is societally determined even if they might prefer to spend and enjoy more now, and might prefer levels of health care at the end of life that the entire society could not afford. GFP-G is a modality for forcing long-term saving.

This is more than an abstract ethic. It is also a structure of power that locks individuals into self-reinforcing patterns of behavior, continuing earlier patterns set in Norway's welfare state. Where farmers were generally successfully pressuring marketing boards in ways that prevented boards from adequately balancing income over the cycle, the GPF-G has moved oil revenues offshore and strictly limited temptations for the public and the political class to spend this money on current consumption. Moving money offshore removes it from immediate parliamentary supervision. Linking the GPF-G to pensions makes it easier for the average person to make the difficult cognitive leap of conceiving of oil revenues as an asset rather than current income. This cognitive leap is what makes possible the inverse Beckerian behavior of saving now in anticipation of falling (per capita) income in the future. The GPF-G is thus not a manifestation of some hyper-rational reaction to the fragility of oil revenues on the part of the average Norwegian citizen or politician. Instead, this behavior emerges from prior patterns of state building in Norway that have become compelling logics of appropriateness favoring collective solutions around life-risks. Everything else about the GPF-G—its transparency, its unwillingness to take positions in firms over 10 percent of the free float of any given company's shares, its geographical diversification, and its occasional ethical stand—stems from and reinforces prior Norwegian collectivist norms.

Other offshore public pension funds present even more robust examples of current political processes shifting risk onto individuals, and removing obligations from the state and high-income taxpayers. Individualization started in the 1980s with efforts to marketize the provision of public services and to impose market or market-like disciplines on public sector producers (Schwartz 1994). In its extreme version, this politics sought to place all social welfare on an individual basis, making people save for their own pension and health care. Offshore pension funds are one way to delink future pension spending from the main revenue base.

Here too, a plausible economic rationale exists. Today's demographic considerations reinforce the need to manage current income prudently so as to assure future consumption. All of the advanced industrial economies must find some way to finance the retirement of the baby boom cohorts out of the production of smaller baby bust cohorts. The issue is how? One way is transformation of the assets locked up in non-renewable raw materials into offshore financial assets, while another is diversion of current tax revenues into similar assets. But it is equally plausible that raw materials royalties or surplus revenues could be transformed into local infrastructure or human capital that yields the same level of future income. Why put funds offshore?

Over the past two decades right-wing parties and think tanks in the OECD countries have mounted a sustained campaign to promote the idea by that pensions represent an unfunded liability for the state, and thus that public debt levels are both much larger than they appear and also ultimately unsustainable. The explicit discourse around the SWFs that connects them to pensions suggests that SWFs' assets—whose value is ultimately limited by the export income or fiscal surplus diverted into them—constitute the only assets that offset the unfunded pension liability on the state's balance sheet. This is a sleight of hand. The exaggerated claims about public debt levels come from capitalizing on-going pension liabilities as if the state were going into the market today to purchase an annuity for its pensionable citizens. But the same exercise is not done for the stream of income represented by a state's ability to tax GDP, which is also a flow, not a stock. (Moreover, in almost all scenarios GDP per capita will continue to grow, although not necessarily in nominal terms.) Capitalizing tax income creates the 'asset' that offsets the otherwise unfunded pension 'liability.'

Instead, the sleight of hand that connects off-shore assets to on-shore pension liabilities limits the state's political capacity to capture current income for publicly defined purposes other than funding the SWF. This sleight of hand matters because people's perception of what is justly due to them motivates their political action. Creating the idea that people only have a claim on offshore assets rather than on-shore tax revenues weakens claims to that revenue for this purpose, just as the explicit tax contribution for the American Social Security program creates an explicit moral link to social security income for most American workers.[9] It also limits alternative uses of the money that might achieve the same purpose. On-shore investment that increased productivity in the local economy would increase the resources available for future pension payments.[10] But this would require some state-controlled investment targeting. Offshore investment reinforces an ideology that says that states are inherently less able to generate returns than private markets.

The other sleight of hand motivating the creation of SWFs is to reduce claims on current budget surpluses. Robust economic growth in the 1990s and 2000s in the OECD economies characterized by American-style housing finance markets led to budget surpluses. Surpluses create demands to increase spending (as well as demands to cut taxes), even though, to return to the example of marketing boards, these surpluses merely offset prior and expected deficits over the whole cycle. Legislation that mandated parking surpluses in a SWF removed voters' and politicians' control over that money.

These processes are visible in Australia, New Zealand, and Norway. Australia has mandatory personal, funded, defined contribution second-tier pensions for the private sector. But the Australian Future Fund was explicitly set up to offset the liability created by the defined benefit pensions owed to Australia's federal civil service. These would otherwise be a claim on future federal tax revenues (Clark 2009: 13). New Zealand's state similarly set up an offshore pension fund. As Littlewood (2010) points out, the New Zealand Treasury argued that "pre-funding may provide greater fiscal discipline on government than debt repayment or a general accumulation of assets, as it ensures some of the future costs of provision for retirement are taken into account in current fiscal decisions" (New Zealand Treasury 2000). However Littlewood (2010), disagrees, noting that the appearance of greater security for offshore assets might induce less private pension saving and thus greater fiscal stress. Finally, even the GFP-G provides us with a 'least likely' example of these processes, as Scandinavian social democracies have strong normative and institutional commitments to collective provisioning against life-cycle risks. Indeed, Norway has not gone down the road of total privatization, nor has it created quasi-individual second tier accounts like Sweden. Yet the GPF-G nevertheless is a manifestation of efforts to liberate the state from the fiscal burden of pensions, and thus ultimately to liberate higher income taxpayers from obligations to lower income retirees. Why?

On the recipient's side, the pension is now calculated on the basis of the number of years of employment and a percentage of the actual wages earned. This moves the second-tier pension away from a pure defined benefit pension and towards a defined contribution pension. Pensioners no longer have an unlimited right to share in growth in national income above and beyond their original contributions. On the state's side, the funding basis for pensions now rests on as much on the GPF-G and the income it generates as it does on the general tax capacity of the state. This also limits pensioners' potential for an unlimited right to share in future national income. Similarly, the explicit structuring of the GPF-G (and the parallel Australian Future and New Zealand Superannuation Funds) as pension funds is as much a political exercise as an exercise in economic rationality.

The SWFs that act as offshore pension funds thus originate from quite reasonable economic rationales. But this does not mean that they are devoid of political origins and consequences. They constitute a Thaler-Sunstein (2008) type 'nudge' in the direction of limiting pension claims on state revenues. In this respect they continue the politics of the 1990s and 2000s, which steadily shifted socialized burdens and risks back onto individuals. By doing so, this politics steadily liberated states from collective claims and undermined the basis for collective action. This politics aims at increasing state autonomy (Schwartz 1994). These SWFs present a hybrid in which the state attains greater autonomy by hiving responsibilities onto para-public organizations subject to market disciplines.

Type 2: developmental states, SWFs and the missing bourgeoisie

> I am by no means an admirer of the bourgeoisie; its crudeness, its prosaic vulgarity offend me as much as anyone else; but for me it is facts that count ... my sympathy is undoubtedly on the side of the workers as the downtrodden class. And yet I cannot help adding –
> God grant us such a bourgeoisie!
>
> V. I. Botkin 1839[11]

Botkin's lament reflects an enduring problem in economic development, namely that states in backward economies need to intervene to provide the pre-requisites for industrialization. The line of argument running from Alexander Gerschenkron (1966) to Alice Amsden (1989, 2001) focuses on the absence of adequate capital, capitalists, managers, appropriately skilled workers, and a domestic market to validate investment. In these arguments, greater economic backwardness requires greater state intervention to create the preconditions for industrialization. Just as the need to reduce volatility and smooth consumption appears to call our first type of SWF into being, the functional need to concentrate and allocate capital in the absence of a bourgeoisie apparently calls our second type of SWF into being. But as with our first type, this functional or rational need conceals a specific process of state building and hybridization of state–social relations.

Here state building has two different components. First, the very process of creating a bourgeoisie is a process of state formation. States cannot function efficiently through direct control of the economy. Second, very few late-developing societies actually lack a mercantile class with capital or experience in managing manufacturing. What they lack is a mercantile class that is ethnically isomorphic with state elites. Existing state elites aim their SWFs at both problems. SWFs are a mechanism for indirect control through which state elites can nurture a local and ethnically 'correct' bourgeoisie. Here the exemplary cases are the array of Singaporean funds: Temasek, the Government Investment Corporation, and, in principle, the Central Provident Fund. Developmentalist SWFs are the latest manifestation of state efforts to construct a counterpart bourgeoisie that is intertwined with the state, complicit in nation-building efforts (and not just economy building), and relatively immobile geographically. In short, the represent an effort to build a social counterpart for the state that permits hybridization to occur.

Economic development in the world economy is neither automatic nor unproblematic (Schwartz 2007). The continual expansion of demand in the most advanced parts of the world economy creates an opportunity for new or expanded economic activity in relatively backward parts. Yet areas that lack social institutions appropriate for the production of commodity in global demand or that possess relatively less effective institutions than their competitors can take only limited advantage of those opportunities. Most of these social institutions provide public goods that enable production and enhance both profits rates and volumes. Moreover, even areas with the appropriate institutions find themselves constrained by world market pressures. In the absence of state efforts to shape development outcomes, world market signals will sort production zones into areas of lower and higher value added production, and thus also consign populations to lower and higher levels of per capita income. Participation in world markets guarantees neither development nor long-term growth.

Gerschenkron noted the relative and sometimes absolute lack of the public goods, particularly investable capital and capitalists, which are prerequisites for growth. Gerschenkron's states generated novel institutional solutions to overcome the problem of concentrating and allocating capital into industry. SWFs are an updated version of these institutions. While a well-to-do family or an existing but pre-industrial textiles producer might be able to capitalize mechanization of textiles production, capitalizing railroads and metals production was out of their reach. Moreover, rail and metals production required long-term investments at a time when most savings were in short-term deposits. Gerschenkron's successful late industrializers confronted this problem with a range of increasingly larger and more comprehensive efforts at mobilizing and intermediating capital. Thus, the French state (unsuccessfully) supported the Péreire brothers' *Crédit Mobilier*, the Prussian imperial state supported the emergence of the four big *D-banken*, and the Russian state used state-owned banks to back new industry. Gerschenkron did not consider the Brazilian or Korean experiences, but there too state-owned banks provided the lion's share of long-term capital to industry, much of which was state owned in Brazil.

On this view, SWFs dress up the old development banks in modern clothing. In addition to concentrating and capitalizing local industry, they also facilitate penetration of foreign markets, transfer technology through the acquisition of foreign firms or espionage, and gain political access to protected markets. Consider Singapore's Temasek. In the domestic economy it has capitalized major infrastructure industries like Singapore Airlines, power generation and gas systems, telecommunications, shipping, and heavy engineering firms. Externally it has considerable stakes in Indonesian, Korean, Chinese, and Indian financial firms. Temasek thus boosts Singapore's prospects as a regional headquarters for foreign firms and the expansion of Singaporean and MNC firms into those other economies. Temasek thus updates the old Prussian *Seehandlungsgesellschaft* (Overseas Trading Company), a state bank and trading company founded by Frederick the Great. The *Seehandlung*'s job was to maximize Prussian exports, provide finance for new firms, modernize those firms, and acquire—by any means—the technologies behind the British industrial revolution. The *Seehandlung*'s role diminished as a new local industrial bourgeoisie emerged.

While this view of SWFs as developmental agonists is in many ways accurate, it also obscures another important state-building phenomena, just as the income-smoothing view of pension SWFs obscures on-going disciplining of the population. State-owned enterprise is to a functioning bourgeoisie as despotic power is to infrastructural power. As Kiren Aziz Chaudhry (1993) has forcefully argued, the high level of state economic involvement in developing economies reveals state weakness rather than state strength. The fact that the state cannot delegate direct management of economic activity not only shows the absence of an industrial (or modern) bourgeoisie, but also that the state cannot cheaply mobilize economic information and bodies. Developing economies often lack a civil society that can serve as a counterpart to the state. But the absence of a civil society does not always arise from the absolute absence of a bourgeoisie. As Chaudhry points out, many late developers have an extant and competent bourgeoisie from minority ethnic or religious groups. But it is intrinsically harder for the state to hybridize with or delegate tasks to these deviant groups, particularly when development requires compliance with projects that run against short-run market signals.

The absence of a counterpart for hybridization or delegation also creates a political problem. States' ability to provide public goods is a function of their ability to mobilize social groups behind simultaneous state, economy and nation-building projects. Those projects require a moral justification of short-term sacrifices in the name of long-term benefits, what Friedrich List called the 'price of the industrial training of the country.' These sacrifices are easier to accept when one is part of the nation that is being built, as with the ethnically Japanese merchant houses that formed the nascent *zaibatsu* after the Meiji restoration. Some sacrifice of short-term gains can plausibly be understood as the price of social and political acceptance, as with the German Jewish merchants that formed the core of three of the four big *D-Banken*, although their compliance with the state's development goals required years of negotiation and cultivation by Bismarck (Stern 1977). Sacrifices are harder to accept when the nation being built explicitly excludes that minority bourgeoisie, as with Greeks and Armenians in the late Ottoman Empire and then post-1919 Turkey, or the Chinese in most Southeast Asian polities.

In this light, developmentalist SWFs serve at least three more purposes. They create firms that can later be privatized to ethnically/nationally correct groups, thus providing the state with a social base. They also serve as a counterweight to local bourgeoisies that are ethnically or religiously indigestible from the point of view of the majoritarian state. And SWFs can help states take control over the levers of power in a modern society. Singapore provides examples of each process.

Singapore's core political problem since independence has been to maximize employment in a resource-less speck of land, peopled by a heterogeneous (though majority Chinese) population, whose largely expatriate bourgeoisie ranged from large-scale British firms through highly mobile and medium-scale Chinese family firms, down to a variety of small firms owned by Muslim, Hindu, and Baghdadi Jewish Indians. Immediately post-independence, unemployment was very high. The People's Action Party (ideologically nominally social democratic but in practice Leninist) emerged dominant from a series of political conflicts. PAP immediately sought to lower unemployment by attracting foreign capital, and to maximize local savings and lock it into illiquid infrastructure investments. This strategy generated average annual growth rates of around 8 percent for 40 years.

PAP used a range of government-owned firms to build and manage Singapore's politics and economy. The Economic Development Board enticed foreign direct investment; the Housing and Development Board built and managed public housing and land development; the Development Bank of

Singapore funded future state-owned firms. In addition, the Central Provident Fund (founded 1955) handled retirement, medical savings accounts and housing related savings, while the much later Government Investment Corporation (founded 1981) invested the fiscal surplus. These firms and their related infrastructure successfully lured foreign electronics firms to Singapore in the 1960s and early 1970s. They also constructed a set of state-owned firms in ship and aircraft building, harbor services, and telecommunications. PAP created Temasek in 1974 to gather ownership control over these firms under one roof and supervise their future expansion.

Temasek nurtured a class of domestic managers/entrepreneurs that could serve as a domestic counterpart to the Singaporean state. These firms and manager/entrepreneurs provided an economic counterweight to the otherwise overwhelming presence of multinational manufacturing firms operating in Singapore. Those foreign firms, whose attachment to the Singaporean project cannot be taken for granted, generated the bulk of industrial employment and exports for Singapore. Only constant upgrading of Singapore's workforce and infrastructure made Singapore a continuously attractive location for both high-value-added production and regional headquarters, validating PAP rule through continued employment and rising wages. Temasek directly controlled the production of attractive infrastructure, while also providing a domestic counterweight to the foreign firms.

Yet Temasek was also a powerful vehicle for political and social control. Through Temasek, the state—understood abstractly and also as an entity dominated by the Lee dynasty via the PAP—controlled virtually every mode of telecommunication and media. Temasek controls the fibre-optic and broadcasting systems that are the infrastructural backbone for information dissemination in Singapore. It controls a comprehensive array of TV and radio channels, as well as Singapore's major newspapers and journals. It subsidiary MediaCorp also produces feature length content for its distribution channels. Temasek's majority-owned subsidiary SingTel operates the land and mobile phone system as well as the internet. In short, the state can exert considerable influence over much of the information circulating it. By controlling domestic political debates and outcomes, Temasek is a powerful tool for social control and state building. It has helped to mold compliant citizens whose well-being is tied to a wide range of government-owned firms.

Like pension fund SWFs, developmental SWFs have a plausible economic rationale. Yet developmental SWFs simultaneously are a vehicle through which the state can create a parallel civil society by fusing state interests with select segments of society. They present a different form of hybridization to that found in pension SWFs.

Type 3: personal ownership, political capitalism, and the (potential) shift from patrimonial to legal-rational authority

> Talk about centralization! The credit system, which has its focus in the so-called national banks and the big money-lenders and usurers surrounding them, constitutes enormous centralization, and gives this class of parasites the fabulous power, not only to periodically despoil industrial capitalists, but also to interfere in actual production in a most dangerous manner—and this gang knows nothing about production and has nothing to do with it.
> (Marx 1981, *Capital*, vol. 3, Chapter 33, "The medium of circulation in the credit system": 544–5)

Our final group of SWFs contains personal vehicles for capital accumulation whose investment strategy is marked by what Max Weber called 'political capitalism' (or 'politically oriented capitalism'), in contrast to 'rational capitalism.' Political capitalism runs counter to the hybridization phenomenon found in developmental SWFs—it erodes the potential emergence of a counterparty for the state and thus prevents effective delegation. These SWFs are largely found among the oil exporters, and in particular the Arabian oil exporters with states built on patrimonial rather than legal-rational lines. While domestic patrimonial authority and political capitalism appear to go hand in hand here (as do legal-rational authority and rational capitalism), this is an elective affinity rather than a strict causal or mutually constituting relationship. Indeed, Diwan (2009) argues that some Saudi elites are trying to use their SWF to build something closer to a legal-rational, albeit corporatist state from the existing patrimonial state.

As noted above, pension SWFs could be understood as an effort at a hyper-rational capitalism in which actors consciously craft structures to cure themselves of time-inconsistency and other irrationalities that stand in the way of maximum life-cycle consumption and fiscal balance. This is Max Weber's 'rational capitalism,' in which enterprises continuously produce goods to exchange them in free markets in an effort to obtain continuous and rising profits (Weber 1978: 913–21). Although these markets are marked by a struggle over price, actors have power by virtue of their capital rather than interference by political actors. Developmental SWFs could be understood as an effort to maximize state power relative to other states through the pursuit of relative economic gain and the creation of infrastructural power in Michael Mann's (1984) sense. Developmentalism tends towards rational capitalism as an outcome—the state wants to create firms capable of surviving on their own in global markets—but in effect could be seen as a form of Weberian value rationality.

By contrast, patrimonial SWFs maximize particular economic gains using political capitalism. In political capitalism actors are oriented toward profit, but seek large and irregular profits through discontinuous political events and favors. These profits can arise from predation, from direct use of force and from special deals—"privileges from the political authority [*politischen*

Gewalt]" (Love 1986). The last of these is more typical of the patrimonial SWF, while the former two are typical of the large joint stock enterprises that engineered European colonial empires in earlier centuries. While patrimonial SWFs appear to be state owned, their links to their respective states are tenuous precisely because of the low level of institutionalization of those states. Rather, notables who have captured state offices use those offices to generate deals in which they capture resource rents. Their ability to continue to capture those rents is a function of their political power relative to internal rivals, and thus also their ability to offer political goods to external actors. Unsurprisingly the investment strategies and internal organization of these SWFs are opaque, oversight is limited, and the purposes of investment remain murky. Dubai's *Istithmar*, for example, owns the ocean liner Queen Elizabeth II.

Saudi Arabia's proposed SWF is not archetypical here but, given the absence of public information on SWFs marked by pure political capitalism, like *Istithmar* or *Mubadala*, has to serve as the best available case. The proposed Saudi SWF, *Sanabel*, which will be built on the earlier Public Investment Fund, and the Saudi Arabia Monetary Authority (SAMA—a proto-SWF) both deviate from the pure type of patrimonial SWF. But by looking at the intended purposes of these Saudi SWFs we can infer what the current status quo looks like. The Saudi state intends that its SWF constructs modern social groups and organizations out of what would otherwise be tribally based affinity groups (Diwan 2009). As with developmental SWFs, this new organization could create the firms and organizations that will eventually make hybrid governance possible. The Saudi SWF is thus part of a strategy to transform patrimonial authority/legitimacy into rational legal authority. This strategy has an economic logic behind it—as with our first type it might help avoid Dutch disease and the other pathologies of the rentier state. But it also has a dual political logic—formal bureaucracy is impossible if ministries are considered the property of specific princes and tribes, and a modern economy cannot be built if commoners are debarred from both politics and significant roles in the state apparatus. These SWFs aspire to be developmentalist SWFs, but their efforts reveal in negative the problems with patrimonial authority.

Up until the late 1990s, the Saudi state was an incoherent aggregate of ministries with overlapping functions and behaviors and the state lacked any substantial counterpart in civil society (Hertog 2004, 2007). Individual princes in the al-Saud family treated ministries like their own private property, with occasional subcontracting to commoners acting as agents for those princes (Hertog 2007). Princes used their ministries to line their pockets and those of their clients. Bureaucratic appointment was not meritocratic, despite some calls pockets of efficiency (Geddes 1994; Hertog 2007: 544–5, 552). Saudi elite politics thus operated through an institutionalized struggle over ministries and state revenue flows, while elite–mass politics operated through direct patronage and personal appeals to elites. This flowed over into Saudi holdings of foreign assets. Overall, about two-thirds of Saudi external assets are held by private entities rather than public ones, which is the reverse of the

Sovereign wealth funds and hybridization 139

pattern for the other petro-states (Diwan 2009: 353). And as many as 50 different public agencies—each naturally linked to some ministry or power-holder—serve as conduits for individuals seeking to transform local revenue into substantial foreign asset positions (Diwan 2009: 354).

In this situation, SAMA operated as the only institutional arena in which collective interests could find expression. SAMA functioned as a quasi-central bank, as the locus of efforts to manage relations with the United States and as an investment agent for some princely wealth. SAMA accumulated assets of nearly $300 billion by 2009, and parked most of it in U.S. Treasury bonds. This hoard is the physical manifestation of the political exchange of Saudi support for the U.S. dollar and U.S. military protection for the Saudi regime (Spiro 1999). It also acts as a blanket concealing the personal offshore investments of various princes. In the absence of SAMA, both domestic corruption and income inequalities would be much more visible. Instead, SAMA shields the princes from internal and external scrutiny. Only a few princes, like the $19 billion man al-Waleed bin Talal, were visibly global investors.

The continuing degree of fragmentation can also be seen in efforts to build new, more stable institutions in Saudi Arabia. The wake-up call for Saudi elites came at the end of the 1990s. While Saudi Arabia had accumulated a huge net international asset position in the 1970s and 1980s, rising consumption and domestic welfare commitments at a time of low oil prices steadily reduced this net position in the 1990s. In 1998 Abu Dhabi had to rescue the Saudi state with a loan, and after 2001/2 Saudi Arabia briefly became a net international debtor. It ran budget deficits until 2004 and came close in 2008, when the oil price briefly dropped to around $30 per barrel (Setser 2008; Ziemba 2008). Saudi princes needed some agency to impose collective discipline on themselves by channeling oil rents into sustainable development, and new forms for channeling domestic political claims into manageable venues.

SAMA and the proposed *Sanabel* play a role in both areas. SAMA supported the Saudi Arabian General Investment Authority (SAGIA) and *Sanabel*'s ventures in petrochemicals, on- and offshore agricultural investment, and increased education. These new roles reflected King Abdullah's determination to centralize and rationalize economic decision-making (Diwan 2009: 355–6). Yet this is a far cry from what Singapore's collection of SWFs and SOEs had been doing for the prior 40 years. The crucial difference appears to be that Singapore inherited a formal bureaucracy intact from the old colonial state, while Saudi Arabia built one helter-skelter as oil revenues flowed in. The Saudi state remains relatively uninstitutionalized and fragmented. Its quasi-patrimonial SWFs reflect this fragmentation. The other oil SWFs undoubtedly exhibit even more fragmentation. The much smaller United Arab Emirates have at least six different SWFs, for example, reflecting the UAE's political fragmentation. The Saudi SWFs aspire to developmentalism and a future hybrid state, but the fact of aspiration rather than realization signals the degree to which they and similar Gulf SWFs actually impede the emergence of a hybrid state.

Conclusions

Bremmer (2010) and others herald SWFs as a sign of the resurgence of state capitalism and a reversal of the general trend towards privatization that characterized the 1990s. They thus seem to run counter to the hybridization trends analyzed in the rest of this book. Yet that conclusion is misleading for at least two reasons. First, SWFs are not a uniform phenomenon. I have identified three different ideal types of state formation and power that motivate the behaviors hiding behind the misleading collective label of 'SWF.' Each reflects a different kind of institutionalized power in different societies, and thus each reflects a different hybrid or the absence of hybridization. Pension and developmental SWFs clearly manifest continued state power and construction of a specific form of society. Pension SWFs and other collective saving manifest Weber's rational capitalism and Foucault's capillary power via collectively held capital. They seek to balance the economy over the business cycle or inter-generationally, and also free states from claims on tax revenues. They permit state control over society at a distance. Developmental SWFs are vehicles by which the state seeks to create its counterpart bourgeoisie and civil society in order to subordinate other domestic rivals, permit hybridization, and bridge the developmental gap between itself and its external rivals. Patrimonial SWFs manifest a reversal of hybridization in which social interests colonize the state. They manifest of what Weber calls political capitalism, in which personal capital is valorized via privileges from the political authority.

All three SWFs are for the most part an expression of on-going processes of state formation, although, as we have seen in the third type, this does not mean that the state in formation necessarily is institutionalized or bureaucratized. Given that state formation differs across societies, so too do SWFs in terms of their origins, behaviour, and effects. Naturally, any given fund may blend aspects of all three phenomena, and indeed most do.

Second, more generally, as Hibou argues here and elsewhere (Hibou 2004), and as I have argued with respect to welfare states (Schwartz 1994), the dichotomy between public and private is arbitrary and misleading. Privatization or the delegation of tasks to the private sector is a way for the state to regain autonomy and create a social base of support for itself. By the same token, increased state control over investment—which anyway is occurring in locales different from those most affected by deregulation and privatization—does not necessarily represent an increase in state power or evidence of state power in general. Pension SWFs' concentration of control over (future) consumption signals states power to shape and domesticate their populations. Yet even there, organized interests dominate politics, and most pension SWFs are carefully barred from the accumulation of a controlling share of a given firm's equities. Ostensibly this is about prudence, but equally so it restricts these funds from taking an active management stance. These funds end up reinforcing the current political dominance of financial capital in the advanced economies.

Similarly, developmental SWFs do not manifest a uniform and generic trend towards greater or lesser state power. State capitalism of Bremmer's (2010) sort will face the same limitations and advantages it historically always has. State control over investment via developmental SWFs signals the absence of state infrastructural power. The state cannot rely on organized social groups and in particular a competent bourgeoisie to carry out management of the economy. Consequently these states try to construct a counterpart bourgeoisie. The limits of that phenomenon can be seen in the inability of Russian firms to craft durable deals with their counterparts in joint ventures. Patrimonial SWFs, of course, exhibit behaviors at odds with any argument about rising state power (or economic prowess, as Dubai World's disastrous Palm Islands project shows). And surely, overt interference in markets by developmental and patrimonial SWFs will provoke a similar response by currently more market-oriented states.

SWFs are thus mostly neither a totally new phenomenon nor clearly exhibit the same Weberian ethic. Instead they combine existing modalities for governance and well-known tropes from the repertoire of legitimations for a given social distribution of income. As with past structures of power, they blend direct and indirect modes of rule. Each deserves to be analyzed on its own terms, because each contains a different and specific configuration of power. Some of these are what Chapter 1 calls hybrids, and others are not. The relevant criteria for discerning the differences lie in the degree to which these SWFs represent a delegation of power and the motivations for that delegation.

Notes

1 The author thanks Brian Easton, Michael Littlewood, Anne Peters, and Bent Sofus Tranøy for comment and criticism and/or help with sources. Errors remain mine.
2 The Oxford SWF Project (http://oxfordswfproject.com/) represents a salient exception to this pattern.
3 The labeling problem can be seen immediately if one considers the New Zealand Accident Compensation Corporation, which combines workers compensation with other injury compensation (e.g. automobile accidents). The NZACC invests part of the insurance premia it levies on firms and drivers offshore. Sovereign wealth fund or (state-owned) insurance company?
4 That said, Iranian and Kuwaiti SWFs' efforts to buy into the German steel and automobile industries in the 1970s did provoke a German backlash and a negotiated entry into German capital markets. But there was no generic panic akin to that in the late 2000s.
5 www.swfinstitute.org/fund-rankings/. 8 August 2013.
6 My thanks to Bent Sofus Tranøy for help with this section.

7 At the time of writing, the Progress Party (Fremskrittspartiet) appeared to finally become part of a governing coalition. Unfortunately, it is too early to tell what this means for the oil fund.
8 This should not imply that Norwegians never act selfishly or for the short term, or that the state is totalitarian. For an example of self-regarding, short-term behavior, see the discussion of the privatization of the gains from rising prices for apartments in housing co-ops in Tranøy (2009).
9 Note that my point here is not that people *should* have such an unlimited right (at least, not until I am of pension age), but that this connection is neither natural nor automatic. Political discourses create this connection.
10 I am indebted to Brian Easton for this point.
11 Quoted in Kingston-Mann (2003: 93–117).

7 Seen and unseen
Hybrid rule in international security

Anna Leander[1]

Introduction

In February, 2012, *The New York Times* reported that "More civilian contractors working for American companies than American soldiers died in Afghanistan last year for the first time during the war." And, continued the article:

> American employers here are under no obligation to publicly report the deaths of their employees and frequently do not. While the military announces the names of all its war dead, private companies routinely notify only family members. Most of the contractors die unheralded and uncounted.
>
> (Norland 2012)

What is startling about such intelligence is the dearth of commentary on it. Everyone knows that private contractors have played major roles in America's three wars during the first decade of this century and, for anyone wishing to learn more, a veritable truckload of commentary has been published on the subject.[2] The transformation and commercialization of security provision can be seen by anyone interested in it. Yet at the same time, the transformation, particularly as it pertains to the transformation of politics, paradoxically remains unseen. While there is considerable commentary on the economics and regulation of security contracting, relatively little has appeared about how the politics of security is being transformed as a result (Leander 2013a). As with news about contractor deaths, there is a dearth of commentary. This chapter explores why this is so and how security politics has been transformed. I analyze why it seems so difficult to analyze seriously the politics of commercializing security, how it is possible that hybrid security can remain seen *and* unseen and what the consequences of this paradoxical status are.

In the chapter, I advance a two-pronged argument. I suggest that security can remain seen *and* unseen precisely because of its hybridity and that hybridity is core to the normalization, expansion and grip of hybrid security on the politics of security. I make this argument by suggesting that the current

144 *Anna Leander*

transformation of security has generated hybridity and hybrid rule, but not privatization (first section). I then show that hybridity has been integral to the normalization of military markets. It has been reproduced in three moves that are at the heart of this normalization: the presentation of markets as a historical necessity (second section) and the delinking of markets and mercenarism to which they had traditionally been attached (fourth section) and the missing of the politics of the markets (fifth section). I conclude by insisting on the most immediate practical implications of the argument. I point out that, like the mythological goat, lion and snake Chimera of antiquity, hybrid security markets reproduces a power that derives from being elusive, seen and unseen and therefore difficult to capture and resist. I therefore also insist on the importance of tackling hybridity head on, of looking at the hybrid as hybrid. Only by doing this is it possible to turn it into something that can be grasped—that is, into something seen but no longer unseen.

Security markets: hybrid *not* private

States and markets or public and private are usually positioned against each other. Contemporary security markets do not fit this pattern. Indeed, security markets have been encouraged, regulated and developed under the auspices of states. More than this, markets have bolstered rather than undermined states where security is concerned (Leander 2009a: 151–170). In debates over the role of markets in security, one of the rare widely agreed-on truths is that the public and private are deeply intertwined. This exchange is ill captured through metaphors of "revolving doors" between the public and the private spheres. A better description is "enmeshed spheres"(Leander 2011: 1–16). In truly hybrid fashion, individuals, companies and security services are frequently, and at the same time, *both* private and public. Such hybridization and enmeshment is captured in the expression "SOBEL"—the fusion of SOldier and reBEL—used in Sierra Leone. But enmeshed hybridization is by no means restricted to that context: a soldier on leave from the South African Defense Forces working as a contractor is *both* South African soldier and contractor. Similarly, civilian technicians assisting in the collection of surveillance data during operations missions, civilian maintainers providing battlefield maintenance of a TOW missile, the M1A1, the Bradley, or the Patriot missile as well as contractors supporting the gathering and interpreting of data from the Joint Air Forces Control Centre and feeding intelligence and targeting information to weapons operators are *both* contractors on the battlefield and integral to activities of the public armed forces. Either the private sector has migrated into the heat of battle or war has diffused into the realm of civil society and the market. Or both. "Everyone in the sector is an exsomething from the armed forces" has become one of the many established truths about military markets (Singer 2001/2: 186–220). Indeed, most accounts of military markets offer some version of the statement that "the public/private dichotomy is itself illusory … . [I have noted] the emergence of various forms of public–private interface and hybrid institutional forms" (Dupont 2005). Professionals in the sector are increasingly prone to describe the spheres as thoroughly interlinked, too. When the EU attempted to establish a private–public security partnership, "most consultees argued for a 'trusted forum' in which security professionals would trade their knowledge and expertise, rather than 'representing' specific private firms or state agencies" (Dorn and Levi 2009: 302–16).

Hybridity has become a feature of international security. Those active in security "governance" have integrated it into their own world, practices and discourses. Security professionals regard the two spheres as largely integrated, as exhibited in *The Circuit*, the telling title of a book whose author, a former member of the British SAS, reflects on how the creation of the security market has altered his career —and more generally the lives and trajectories of security professionals who move in and out of public service. Instead of retiring as a bodyguard, the author has travelled across the world, in the service of security companies, to Afghanistan, Iraq, the West Bank, Gaza and other places. From his perspective, he has never left "The Circuit" (in singular!) of security professionals like himself (Shepherd 2008). In both politics and public opinion hybridity is recognized. A study of U.S. public opinion shows that reactions to the fate of private contractors differ only marginally from reactions to the fate of soldiers (Avant and Siegelman 2012: 230–265). Finally, lawyers are acutely aware of hybridity, whether they are working to defend human rights or dealing with contractual issues. They have been involved in an intense discussion—a "mad scramble," according to Ian Kierpaul (2008: 407–435)—about making legal categories more applicable and useful for dealing with the category of activities and actors generated by security markets that span the public–private divide (Zamparelli 1999: 1–17; Heaton 2005: 157–208; ICRC 2008).

Paradoxically, the widespread consensus that the market is a hybrid, that roles are hybrid and that the lines between public and private are entirely "blurred," has not triggered a commensurate shift in vocabulary; "public" and "private" continue to be used as if they were unproblematic points of departure. Questions are still often posed in terms of a public state outsourcing, contracting with a private market or manipulating it.[3] If the market is a hybrid, however, such a distinction makes little sense and is directly counterproductive for the understanding of—and (hence) for efforts to shape—the *hybrid* "state-market." For example, established legal and political terminologies see the market through a public–private divide; as a consequence, they break up hybridity. This conventional legal move of seeing the world "as if" makes it possible to work with law, although in the process it evacuates that which does not fit, especially that which is directly spanning of categories. If security markets are as hybrid as the consensus has it, this amounts to evacuating them. Even though everyone "sees" them, security markets therefore also remain "unseen"; they are state-markets. The public–private categories through which these hybrid state-markets are viewed make them invisible as hybrids.

That hybrid security actors and activities are both seen *and* unseen is closely related to the form the normalization of military markets has taken. There is nothing natural about markets; they must be fabricated, as Polanyi or Bourdieu would remind us (Polanyi 2001; Bourdieu 2005). The creation of markets presupposes the emergence of a market imaginary, a *homo oecomonicus*, and a set of institutions and practices that reproduce markets and make them appear natural and normal. Such creation also presupposes a theorization and rule-making laying down market boundaries and governing their operations (MacKenzie 2006; Callon 1998). The rest of this chapter analyzes how the specifically hybrid form of military market we now have was fabricated. More specifically, it traces three related moves that have played a fundamental role in this fabrication: the move of turning military markets into a historical necessity, the move de-linking them from mercenarism, and the move missing the politics entailed by and in markets. The chapter follows the traces of these three moves, insisting that they were facilitated by the very hybridity they entrench.

Making markets a historical necessity

Beginning in the mid-nineteenth century, states have taken an increasingly restrictive approach to markets and market actors (Thompson 1994). Indeed, the space for markets was in steady decline in functional, spatial and geographical terms—until the end of the Cold War (Shaw 2000; Leander 2006). At that point, markets and market actors had a very restricted independent space for dealing in military related services and goods, being either under strict state control or operating in a grey or illegal zone. Treaties, trade regulations, production subsidies and informal pressures kept commercial military "market" actors within the remit of states, who sometimes used them for their own "dirty work'. Reflecting on these conditions, Janice Thompson argued that "the twentieth century has ushered in another stage in which these practices [private uses of force] are not only prohibited but have become unthinkable" (1994). A specific interpretation of history underpinned this view on appropriate limits to markets, and the normalization of military markets therefore required a re-interpretation of history, (re-)opening space for military markets. While the developments in the late 1960s and early 1970s described in the introduction to this volume were crucial in laying the ground for this reinterpretation, the feat was accomplished by the "liberation" of military markets as the only possible response to the historical conditions prevailing at the end of the Cold War.

The first element in this story was the idea that the end of the Cold War created a "gap" between the demand for security and the supply; a gap that could only be filled by market actors.[4] The promise of a "peace dividend" inspired cuts in military budgets, subsidies and procurement, even as countries with an international military presence pulled back their forces and were less and less willing to provide allies with military-related support and credits (Klare 1996: 39–53; Shearer 1998). Firms specializing in the military sector saw demand dwindle and were encouraged to develop "dual-use" technologies or entirely convert their activities to the civilian sector (Kaldor 1998: 3–33). Public armed forces were reduced in size (Schméder 1998: 11–35). These changes were especially rapid and drastic in the Soviet Union/Russia and South Africa, where the end of the Cold War coincided with the fall of the *ancien régimes* (O'Brien 2000). But, with variations in speed and style, these changes touched most countries. The consequence was, as observers so often and so rightly pointed out, the emergence of a global "security" market in which firms, people and countries struggled to find buyers for their products and skills, with sellers providing support and services no longer being supplied by state allies. Even as the peace dividend remained illusionary and elusive, the policies it inspired ushered in military markets.

This "historical necessity" was confirmed by the second element: a reading of markets as increasingly central in response to the post-Cold War "threat picture" marked by the de-statization of wars, the growing role of non-state actors and diminished state control over violence as a result of "globalization." This proposition was articulated most vividly in Robert Kaplan's well-known and influential "coming anarchy" (1994). Markets were seen increasingly as indispensable for providing the security services no longer provided by states yet desired by everyone (states, firms, NGOs, journalists and ordinary citizens, as well as rebels, insurgents and even terrorists). Under this logic, firms and markets were not threats to order; rather, they were indispensable for upholding it. They were helping to "shore up fragile state structures"(Coker 1999: 95–113). To fit this account, it became increasingly common to underline the role of markets in the maintenance of peace (Brooks 2000: 33–35). In fact, eventually an entire segment of the security industry rebranded itself as the "peace and stability industry."[5] The linking of such markets to the "new" threat picture clearly confirmed markets as a logical and necessary response to a historical context. A third element of the story was provided by the linking of markets to the technological "revolution in military affairs" (RMA) (Latham 2002: 231–266). The RMA was a result of the radically increasing technological sophistication of the military which required very substantial organizational changes at all levels. One of the things that came with technology was a growing reliance on markets. It became vital for the military to access civilian markets and the firms selling technologies and the related services (Edmonds 1998: 114–129; Susman and O'Keefe 1998). Ideas about the pivotal role of strategic alliances and network-based organization for technological development were taken on board and reflected in defense strategies prioritizing "dual-use", "off-the-shelf" technologies (Albrecht 2000: 120–146; Adams 1998). Moreover, simulation programs developed in and with the market were increasingly used for military training of various types. For example, the U.S. Air Force deployed Marine Doom,

Falcon 4 and MEU 2000, all three slightly modified versions of games sold on the open market (Lenoir 2000: 289–335; Der Derian 1987: 91–110). The belief that markets were necessary to military technologies turned into a self-fulfilling prophecy. By the early 2000s, armed forces across the world had become thoroughly reliant on market providers of technology and on contractors for training and operations. The development of military markets had also become a historical necessity for "keeping up with the technology."

Finally, the private market was presented as a historical necessity in order to meet the personnel needs of armed forces, in particular those upholding and defending the "new world order." The United States maintained a global "security" mission even as resources diminished. The end of the Cold War had not spelled the end of military operations. On the contrary, U.S. forces became engaged in an ever-widening range of deployments, including a "war against drugs" that involved military training and consultancy, "humanitarian interventions" and the wars in Yugoslavia, Iraq and Afghanistan. It was also heavily involved in arming and training of military forces of its allies. In the United States, advocates of an increased role for the private security industry argued that a logical response to the resulting "overstretch" of armed forces and budgets was a turn to markets—which would surely cost less (Brooks 2004). Even critics of the private security industry quickly came to see its rapid growth as linked to military manpower needs and the political goal of masking the costs of military operations, their casualty toll on the U.S. armed forces and their expansive nature. Markets thus became the necessary underpinning of America's international engagements, whether read positively as the expression of responsible foreign policy (Spearin 2001: 20–43) or negatively as expression of a "new unilateralism" (Tiefer 2007: 1–56).

This framing of "military markets" as a historical necessity has required substantial and systematic eliding and forgetting of alternative interpretations and views. Manpower needs did not have to be provided through markets; a new draft was an alternative. Military technology could have been supplied through firms controlled or even owned by the state, states could have chosen to continue supplying security, to limit reductions in their security budgets and/or to control commercialization of the security sector. The idea that markets were a "historical necessity" linked to the specific conjuncture at the end of the Cold War became dominant. It provided the grounds for ignoring dissenting views and for seeing the (hybrid) military markets as both normal and necessary. Such normalization would, however, have remained fragile if it had not also been linked to a revision of the link between military markets and mercenarism.

Delinking markets from mercenarism

Mercenaries are the "whores of war" (Burchett and Roebuck 1977) and, to Niccolo Machiavelli's way of thinking, "useless and dangerous" (2004 [1532]). His imprint on political imaginaries has been far reaching: Mercenarism is a negative reference to illicit and illegitimate uses of force, out of state remit. It is a term of condemnation and rejection. Yet, there is no practical definition of mercenary or mercenarism. As Sarah Percy shows, there is a "strong" norm against mercenaries. She also persuasively argues that international law is weak precisely because of this. States wished to preserve their liberty to define as "mercenary" any use of force they condemned. They could therefore not fix the meaning of the term. According to Percy, "the reason states pursued a clear yet unworkable definition is because that definition reflected and publicized exactly what they felt to be problematic about mercenaries" (2007: 367–397). This stance became exceedingly problematic for the normalization of security markets, as mercenarism and "private" military markets had long been regarded rough equivalents. Revising this linkage was, therefore, a necessary condition of possibility for the fabrication of normal, legitimate military markets. This took place in the 1990s, through two partly contradictory moves. The first involved a reversal of the connotations of mercenarism, while preserving the links to the market. The second was a move to sever the linkage between markets and mercenarism completely.

First, the revalorization of mercenaries involved underscoring the historical normality of mercenarism and especially its close symbiotic relation to the state and state policies. We are routinely told things such as: "War is most certainly as old as mankind itself—and as warfare evolved, so did the profession of soldiering for hire" (Lanning 2005), and "the sovereign's resort to mercenaries is as old as history itself" (Milliard 2003: 1–95). Such historical continuity is rehearsed, elaborated and proven in various forms and places, while condemnation of mercenarism is said to rest on historical short-sightedness—"myopia" in Major Todd Milliard's words—reflecting judgments made about a historically exceptional period. For Milliard, such views are merely a reflection of the narrow, and now anachronistic, concerns of decolonialization. For others, condemnation mirrors a more general neglect of a transhistorical phenomenon, reflecting an exceptionally statist and time-bounded era. The emphasis on the historicity of mercenaries serves to normalize them and makes their present appearance less spectacular.

Along similar lines, it became common in the 1990s to assert that mercenaries had been positively viewed in history, making a more "moral" form of war possible. Reflecting utilitarian criticisms of public civil servants elsewhere, the emphasis was on the virtue of self-interests that combine to result in the best possible outcome—a military version of Smith's Invisible Hand, in other words. In the case of mercenaries, advocates argued that self-interests make for more ethical and professional soldiers. For example, one line of reasoning was that the purely pecuniary motivation of mercenaries makes them less prone to commit atrocities. Nationalist, ethnic or other ideological motivations for killing an enemy or acting inhumanely become irrelevant. A rereading of Albert Hirschmann's arguments in *The Passions and the Interests* underscores that these arguments have a long history (1977). In the wake of the Cold War, they were remobilized to reverse the negative connotations of mercenarism. As one observer argues, "in a mercenary context there may well be less killing motives around ... the moral economy of a mercenarist world would appear to be preferable to that of the Statist societies I currently inhabit" (Lynch and Walsh 2000: 133–153).

Lastly, in the vein of revalorizing mercenarism, it has been suggested that mercenaries have pecuniary motives to *save* lives, inasmuch as they are paid for live captives, not dead ones: "the ethics of market motivated protectors may actually be more humane as they are not fighting for a principle but for money and are more prone to take ransom but less to ethnic cleansing or massacres" (Tabarrok 2007: 565–577). Another way of establishing the superiority of mercenaries emphasizes not their superior conduct but the significance of results: self-interest promotes professionalism and a capacity to "get the job done." Assuming this to be true, utilitarian thinkers follow a consequentialist logic and argue that, if mercenaries can halt massive human rights violations, as they had purportedly done in Sierra Leone and Angola, they should be welcomed. Who could possibly reject forces that might prevent or stop the next Rwanda or even end war in general (Brooks 2000: 129–144)? Even Michael Walzer, as non-utilitarian, finds it difficult to dispute such arguments (Walzer 2008).

Such revalorizations of mercenaries have not convinced everyone and, in most contexts, the term remains an essentially negative and condemning one. Even if soldiers for hire often call themselves "mercenaries," as revealed by a glance at *Soldier of Fortune* magazine, security firms do not advertise themselves as "mercenary firms" and resist being associated with mercenaries, in recognition that armed forces, governments, businesses and non-governmental organizations will not contract with security companies or rely on military services that present themselves as "mercenaries" (Brooks 2007; Leander 2013b: 147–113). That being said, revalorization of mercenaries has unsettled the clear sense of the word. Its negative connotation can no longer be taken for granted. Revalorization arguments can therefore be draw upon by those defending market. Max Boot of the U.S. Council on Foreign Relations for example tried to persuade activists from Code Pink, protesting against Blackwater, with the argument that "it is easy to ignore the long and distinguished history of mercenaries, and their legitimate uses down to the present day" (Boot 2009). Such unsettling of the meaning and connotations of mercenarism is one way to normalize military markets.

A second (and more common and straightforward) route is to sever the link between military markets and mercenarism by insisting that markets have no relationship to mercenarism. The argument is that the two are historically distinct phenomena. Historical lessons about mercenaries are, on this account, inapplicable, and today's military service providers must be evaluated by different standards and judged by different laws than those applied to mercenaries. This effort to sever the links to mercenarism is most strongly expressed in efforts to rename the private military services sector by those wishing to promote and/or regulate it. Former Lt. Colonel Tim Spicer,[6] for instance, launched and promoted the term "private military company" in academic seminars and debates, interviews and his ghost-written memoirs precisely to sever the links to mercenarism (according to himself) (ICIJ 2002; Spicer 1998, 1999). Analogously, activists and lawyers have promoted alternative naming and classification, distinguishing contemporary private military companies from mercenaries in order to promote and develop workable regulation (Leander 2012: 91–119). Whether among lawyers/activists or market advocates, three themes recur in these efforts to de-link contemporary military market actors from mercenaries.

The first is the close tie between states and contemporary market actors, by contrast with the looser ties between historical mercenaries and sovereigns. Juan Carlos Zarate, for example, has suggested that "security companies have become a type of state agent linked to their home state by tacit or licensed approval of their activities and enlisted as contractors for the employing country" and that, consequently, "the customary international law banning the use of mercenaries should not apply" (1998: 75–162). Such ties are also used to underline the extent to which contemporary private market actors are welcomed and used by states, thereby making it ineffective to equate them with the mercenaries outlawed by customary law. Worse, such an equation may be counterproductive, it is argued, as it prevents the development of effective accountability (Rakowsky 2007: 366–397; Leander 2010c: 467–490).

A second recurring theme involves the corporate nature of contemporary military service providers, with supporters pointing out that many are large corporations organized "first and foremost as private firms"(Frye 2005: 2607–2664; Kinsey 2006) concerned about their image and traded on stock markets. The language of contracting, public–private partnerships, entrepreneurship and service provision gives these firms a respectability that distances them from mercenaries of the past. Suit-clad representatives of (legitimate) private military companies can be contrasted to rogue mercenaries with a decidedly bad reputation, such as Bob Denard or Wild Mike Hoare (Silverstein 2000). Even more directly, insistence on the corporate nature of contemporary private market actors does make a tangible difference in terms of international law, which defines mercenaries as individuals.

Finally, the de-linking is made by an insistence that the nature of the activities undertaken by contemporary military market actors fundamentally differs from those of the mercenaries of the past and present. Avoidance of "offensive" activities is held up to underscore this difference. Whereas mercenaries fought wars for their employers, the majority of contemporary military service providers "do not engage in offensive activities." Instead, they provide back-up activities of various kinds, such as logistics, training and intelligence (Calaguas 2006: 58–81; Shearer 1998: 80–94). These specialized professional services indispensable to and requested by armed forces and states. To be sure, such services do sometimes place contractors on the battlefield. However, they are not there in an independent offensive role but as an integral part of operations led by a *public* military (Heaton 2005). Moreover, contemporary military service providers enhance the capacity of public forces and are more akin to "force multipliers" or even "weapon systems" than the mercenaries of the past (Michaels 1999: 14–17).

These three themes, through which distance is created between contemporary military market actors and mercenaries, are not repeated here as accurate representations of real-world practice. They are introduced because of what they *do*: because of the way they contribute to the fabrication of military markets. Indeed, for such markets to be possible it has been necessary to remove the connotation of mercenarism, that is, of illicit and illegitimate activity. While this connotation was still strong in the early 1990s, by the end of the decade, the established truth in most quarters was that military markets and mercenarism had little or no relation. Even the UN working group overseeing the UN Convention against the finance and use of mercenaries had come to defend this view. According to its 2002 report:

> the conclusion arrived at by the Special Rapporteur ... is that such [private military] companies need not be banned, but that domestic and international law must deal with the issue so that there are oversight, regulation and monitoring mechanisms that clearly differentiate military consultancy services from participation in armed conflicts and from anything that could be considered intervention in matters of public order and security that are the exclusive responsibility of the State
>
> (UN 2002)

As this underlines, as long as they are working under the auspices of a state, regulated markets are legitimate and even welcome. Not only have they become a historical necessity, they are also freed from the connotation of mercenarism, working in the service of states. As long as they are infused by the state, working as genuine hybrids, military markets can be considered as normal as other markets. Yet, a third and final move was necessary, playing a core role in completing and consolidating this normalization story: evasion of the politics of the military markets.

Missing the politics of military markets

Dwight D. Eisenhower's "military industrial complex" has long held the potential of robbing the military markets of their normality. As Eisenhower put it in his Farewell Address:

> the conjunction of an immense military establishment and a large arms industry [... whose] total influence—economic, political, even spiritual— is felt in every city, every State house, every office of the Federal government [... has] grave implications. Our toil, resources and livelihood are all involved; so is the very structure of our society.
>
> (Eisenhower 1961)

If military markets are believed to have an analogous deforming influence, delinking them from mercenarism and seeing them as historical necessities has little normalizing power. In the world of the military-industrial complex, hybridity is no guarantee of normality; rather, it is a worrisome sign of the opposite. Therefore, a final element crucial to normalization of military markets is the degree to which they are constructed as non-political and the extent to which hybridity therefore either ignored or presented as non-political; as if the presence of the state in the market and the market in the state were devoid of political significance. Two sets of intertwined constructs play a crucial role in making this counter-intuitive idea of apolitical hybrids viable. The first is the construction of the market as if it were there to provide efficient technical solutions to pre-existing problems posed by states. The second is the construction of accountability as residing either with the market or the state, and hence removing it from the hybrid *qua* hybrid.[7] These two constructs both contain politics in a public/state sphere neatly separated from the private/market sphere. In the process of breaking the hybrid into its constitutive parts, these two constructs not only miss the politics of markets, they reinforce the paradoxical status of the hybrid security market as both seen and unseen. The constitutive parts are seen but the hybrid whole is not. The result is that worries about the influence of a military-industrial complex seem irrelevant while the normality of the hybrid market is preserved. Hybrid security markets have been introduced and justified in a broader context, marked by a neo-liberal faith in markets as quintessential governance techniques with "risk" as a core preoccupation. Markets have become sites for generating efficient, technical solutions. This presentation of military markets has been an integral part of the self-presentation and perception of private military force (Leander 2006: 333–355; Schneiker and Joachim 2012: 495–512). Companies consistently portray themselves as promoting *technical solutions* for mitigating risk and dealing with pressing security challenges and problems (Leander 2011: 1–16). This understanding of markets masks the politics folded into these supposedly technical and efficient solutions. It obscures the political choices embedded in the processes by which risks are identified and insecurity created. Markets are assumed to provide solutions to pre-given problems, not to problems produced in and by the processes through which companies assist their (public or private) clients in identifying risks and providing suggestions for how to mitigate them.

This understanding of hybrid markets evacuates politics. The political context in which problems appear, risks are defined and solutions devised slides out of view, as do the practices involved in handling them. For example, private security firms can help corporations, foreign services, or journalists mitigate the risk of kidnapping in Bogota. All involved will agree that neither the market nor the company providing the protection service has created the risk of kidnapping in Bogota nor, unless we are speaking of a mafia-like protection racket (Gambetta 1993), did they impose their services on anyone. Similarly, logistics companies offering protection to convoys, aid organizations, embassies and bases in Afghanistan will insist that they do not create the threats against which they are offering protection. Such insistence on the provision of "solutions" to pre-given problems is powerful and so commonsensical: who would claim that the companies or the markets are responsible for the kidnapping risk in Bogota or the insecurity of aid workers in Afghanistan?

Yet common sense is sometimes a poor guide to politics, leaving out a range of fundamental questions about the political import of markets and particularly about their impact on the processes that make (specific) private security companies appear as the only solutions to predefined (and undeniable) problems. Such questions include: What role do markets play in defining the risks and threats and in obscuring alternative risks/threat definitions? How do firms influence the practices that create the problems they purport to solve? And finally, what alternative ways of approaching the threats and risks are made (in)visible through recourse to markets? These are questions about politics; about the processes that make us nod and embrace the idea that markets are merely solving given problems. Still, they must be answered in context and not in the abstract, and in the absence of such answers, it is impossible to know whether or not the commonsensical view is justified. When ArmorGroup escorts a convoy in Afghanistan or Control Risks provides Kidnap and Ransom services in Bogota, are they merely responding to a pre-given demand for a security service or are they fashioning not only the demand, but also the context which generates it and the kind of security practices involved in responding to it?

The heated discussion among humanitarian aid workers—many of whom are critical of private security companies—is a sign that the politics involved is less straightforward than common sense might suggest (Cockayne 2006; Spearin 2008). This sign is reinforced by the growing debate regarding how companies—including very respectable and unspectacular ones such as Control Risks (Leander 2013b: 97–113)—shape the conflict context through their relations with the local context and role in fashioning overall security approaches (Leander and Christopher 2013: 202–218). Contestable or not, the widespread view that markets solve predefined problems is powerful in perpetuating the illusion that military markets are apolitical and have no implications for how security is defined and practiced. The result is a silencing of the public debate surrounding the politics of security and a focus on security *management* through markets, often with expressed intention of bolstering this "industry" as any other sector of employment and growth. As Lucia Zedner comments on the discussion in the UK context: "instead of debating what security is for, for whom it must be secured and by what means, the emphasis of governmental regulation is upon ensuring the health and profitability of the industry" (2006: 267–288).

Current trends in the academy have done little to undermine this counterintuitive image of hybrid military markets as apolitical. Security studies and international relations—including most "critical" security studies—remain squarely focused on state practices and are prone to see military markets as separate from the state, possibly used by states, but for ends defined inside the state. Markets have no agency and do not transform the state; rather, states use markets.[8] At the same time, with few exceptions, scholars of "international political economy" (Dombrowski 2005; Kirshner 1998: 64–91) have long been uninterested in security issues and continue to be happy to restrict their labors and inquiry to finance and trade. As the editor of *Review of International Political Economy*, one of the area's main journals, told me after publication of a review essay (sic) covering security markets: "I have already published an article on this now. I don't think I will want any more on this topic for the foreseeable future."[9] A glance at subsequent tables of contents confirms his commitment to this position. As a result, scholars in both IPE and IR/security studies accept and reproduce the assumption that "security" is about high politics and handled primarily by states, and that even beginning to contemplate the role of markets is superfluous. In security, the hybridity of markets and states can somehow be neatly separated and broken up, and politics contained in the public sphere, very much by contradistinction from how most IR/IPE scholars would see the situation in trade or in finance.

Paradoxically perhaps, "critical" political discussions of the military markets also do little to counter the tendency to split hybridity and re-establish neatly separated public and private spheres. Such discussions are generally aimed at pinning down accountability and improving accountability, rather than focused on politics let alone the politics of language. Critique is therefore framed in and reproducing the (exceedingly political) language that assumes neat distinctions between market/state, civilian/military, private/public, security/military, or inside/outside. Such language is productive; it produces roles, rights, duties, responsibilities and impunities. It is therefore not surprising to find language of public and private constantly used also in critical discussions. Critique is most clear and persuasive precisely when it is formulated in this straightforward and accessible language. However, at the same time this reinstatement of prevailing language and the divisions in it, also reproduces and consolidates the difficulty of capturing the hybridity of the security markets spanning these divides and hence allows precisely for the "sphere-shifting" that makes critique (let alone accountability) so difficult.

This pattern is identifiable in any specific attempt to criticize military markets and pin down responsibility. For example, critics of CACI's implication in the Abu Ghraib prisoner torture scandal have struggled with a constant sphere-shifting.[10] CACI responds that they were hired and directed by the responsible military officials. Responsibility, therefore, lies in the public sphere (London 2008). The public sphere has responded that it cannot take responsibility for the non-contracted activities of a private company. This sphere-shifting thus makes accountability impossible. More than this, it reinstates and reinforces an impunity engendered by the public–private lines along which the accountability debate is constructed. By the same token it consolidates the invisibility of the politics of markets. The constant breaking up of hybridity, the re-affirmation that the hybrid should be understood through its constitutive parts, makes hybridity appear conventional and harmless. In sum, the splitting of the hybrid into its constitutive parts conspires with the picture of military markets providing a "supply" of services in response to a given "demand" to allow the politics of hybridity to escape attention. But there is no reason to believe that such evasion will be successful in the long run, as there are many well- established traditions that would permit a chopping away at its underpinnings. These range from classical economics (Jean-Baptiste Say's law) to contemporary feminist theorizing (Donna Haraway's market power). For the time being, however, such traditions have had only limited impact on the debate about military markets. Instead, the discussion has effectively marginalized the politics of hybridity and ensured that Eisenhower's ghost can be comfortably interred in the historical past of a geographically specific place: the U.S. of the late 1950s and early 1960s. The normalization of military markets is safe: they are a historical necessity, they are de-linked from mercenarism and they do not pose any fundamental political questions.

Conclusion: recognizing hybrid rule moving the seen and unseen

In this chapter, I have traced the normalization of military markets over the decade following the end of the Cold War. The idea of such normalization would have appeared alien to observers in early 1990s, when the end of the Cold War seemed to be holding the promise of a "peace dividend... an opportunity to reorient resources freed up by the cessation of hostilities, towards human and economic development" (Markusen, DiGiovanna and Leary 2003). Two decades later, military markets are expanding exponentially. We are told they are indispensable for states and security policies and that there is no way they can or will or will be allowed to disappear. As I have insisted throughout this chapter, such normalization was possible precisely because the military markets are *hybrid* markets, in which public and private, the state and the commercial, are not merely interacting but *enmeshed*. Hybridity was necessary to construct markets as historical necessities, as de-linked from conventional mercenarism and as a-political. Hybridity was so significant because it allowed military markets to be seen *and* unseen simultaneously. Precisely because of the enmeshment of the state, hybrid markets could be *seen* as answering historical needs, as different from mercenaries and as providing neatly separated efficient and technical solutions. For the same reason, their role in marginalizing historical alternatives, in illicit uses of force (that is in mercenarism) and in the formulation and doing of politics could remain invisible and unseen.

By way of conclusion, I wish to insist on the core implication of this argument that is on the importance of tackling these seen-unseen dynamics head on and paying direct attention to hybridity and hybrid rule. Hybridity is redrawing the boundaries of security. Resources and understandings are being reshuffled not only within and among military/security institutions professionals but also between these and other institutions and professions (Leander 2005: 803–836). Hybrid markets are likely to reorder priorities and reclassify issues. As military markets expand they are also placing a growing grip on other areas. Walking through airports, making phone calls, sending e-mails have moved from being activities with weak links to security to becoming activities that are partly governed by it (see Lipschutz' chapter in this volume). The development of hybrid military markets *may* well be part of the explanation for this transformation. As with all markets, military markets are indeed likely to be prone to "market imperialism," that is, to cover an ever-wider range of things (Radin 1996; Walzer 1983). As Habermas expressed it, the instrumental rationality of markets is prone to "colonize" increasing portions of the life-world (1989 [1962]). The violence and "harm" entailed in the process of turning things into commodities can be resisted through what Margaret Jane Rudin terms "rehabilitating counter discourses" (1996) reversing commodification. The trouble is that such discourses are prone to remain so inarticulate and weak that they are hardly heard at all. They are emanating from weaker positions with fewer symbolic and material resources to draw upon than those undergirding commodification. Radin therefore suggests that special legal regimes are required for commodities in situations in which commodification is contested and contentious. She suggests that, to limit discursive harm, such regimes should, for example, restrict entrepreneurship, recruitment, advertising, free speech and brokerage.[11]

In some areas, such a special legal regime does exist. In relation to military markets, it does not. More specifically, while such regulation exists and continues to weigh on the statement of public security professionals, there is no equivalent for private ones. There are formal and informal rules limiting the role of public military and intelligence officials in politics (Leander 2007: 49–64), but for the private sector, marketing, advertising, lobbying, brokerage and employment are legitimate activities. This is unlikely to change. Not only do the potential "rehabilitating discourses" have to face the enormous resources of a multibillion-dollar industry, for which the symbolic are no doubt the most significant, the normalization of military markets outlined in this chapter makes unlikely any counter move in this direction. Military markets have become "normalized" to the extent that they can be presented as on par with "Christmas tree decoration."[12] They are not only accepted but encouraged in most quarters. Markets have become integral to the security management. Perhaps most significantly, the quarters from which regulation might emanate that is the public and the state, are all profoundly enmeshed in the market, too.

Arguably, the most potent effect of hybridity is that it obstructs interrogation of these processes. The urge to return to the safety of the public/private divide blocks any focus on processes that are neither market nor state but generated by the enmeshment of the two. As Bourdieu points out, "hyperbolical suspicion" of the state is always warranted but also always exceedingly difficult (1994). The consequences of such obstacles to interrogation are momentous. They drive the regulatory discussion to implement more regulation, along existing public–private lines and hence to draw these lines ever more firmly. Yet, this accentuates the elusiveness of hybridity and the seen *and* unseen nature of security. In other words, not facing hybridity leaves regulators in a double bind. More regulation consolidates the elusive hybridity of military state-markets and by the same token weakens the grip of the regulation.[13] The scarcity of attempts to grapple with this fundamental double bind is one of the most immediate consequences of allowing the public–private divide—rather than hybridity—to frame thinking and discussion. It is therefore of fundamental importance to explore, as this volume does, "hybrid rule." Indeed, as argued here, such explorations are a precondition for understanding politics and thinking about resistance and accountability. Making the essentially linguistic move to hybridity is a precondition for moving beyond the present seen and unseen stalemate in our approaches to markets of international security.

Notes

1 This chapter has benefited from extensive review and editing by Ronnie Lipschutz, for which I am very grateful. I also wish to thank all those who have commented on and inspired the final version of this chapter in the workshops held in relation to this project.
2 There are exceptions to this sweeping generalization including work by scholars such as Louise Amoore, Rita Abrahamsen, Paul Higate or Elke Krahmann. For an overview see Leander (2009b: 200–210); Leander in Burgess (2010a: 208–216).
3 We need not look far to identify this separation of public/state and private/market. In their introduction to this volume the editors argue that "hybrid rule results from a set of practices deployed by political elites that rely on the private sector […] to safeguard the state's legitimacy through valorization of the market as a primary mechanism in pursuit of myriad political objectives'. This chapter suggest "enmeshment"is at the core characteristic of the hybrid and hybrid rule is the enmeshed form government and it re-produces. As this chapter argues in detail the power of this kind of hybrid and hybrid rule is precisely that it eludes the idea that there are clearly separable "political elites", "private sectors", "states" and "markets".
4 Formulated most clearly by Mandel (2001: 129–151).
5 There is an industry association euphemistically called the International Peace and Stability Operations Association. See www.stability-operations.org.
6 At the time, he was working for Sandline but was subsequently a key figure in the industry including through his involvement with Aegis.
7 As seen in the recent revelations regarding the NSA's metadata collecting activities.
8 For a chapter length exposition of this also pointing to the current indications of change see Leander in Ougaard and Leander (2010b: 57–78).
9 Personal conversation with one of the editors of the *Review of International Political Economy* in August 2008. He was referring to Abrahamsen and Williams (2007: 131–146).
10 CACI (originally referring to "Consolidated Analysis Center, Incorporated') is indeed a private company, which among many other things offers a "range of force

protection and critical infrastructure protection expertise." See http://caci.com/about/profile.shtml (accessed 18 June 2013). It was mentioned along with TITAN as directly implicated in the abuse in the internal report of the U.S. Armed Forces; the so called "Taguba Report."
11 As she argues with respect to prostitution "to check the domino effect [of market expansion] I believe I should prohibit the free-market entrepreneurship that would otherwise accompany de-criminalization and could operate to create and organized market ... such regulation would include for example, such deviations from laissez-faire as banning brokerage (pimping) and worker training (recruitment) ... an incomplete commodification regime might also include banning advertisement" (135–136).
12 The analogy was used in an interview I carried out with Brintley Zalsmann responsible for the ethics program of the AeroSpace and Defense Industries Association in the UK (15 June 2013).
13 This is a high price to pay for (a potential) legal accountability. Moreover, it is a price that may not be worth paying. As in other areas, it may do more to entrench invisibility and hence impunity than to further accountability. See e.g. Johns (1994: 893–923); Cutler (2003).

8 World war infinity
Security through economy, economy through security

Ronnie D. Lipschutz

> We know roughly who you are, roughly what you care about, roughly who your friends are … . The power of individual targeting—the technology will be so good it will be very hard for people to watch or consume something that has not in some sense been tailored for them … . I actually think most people don't want Google to answer their questions … . They want Google to tell them what they should be doing next
>
> (Eric Schmidt, CEO of Google, quoted in Jenkins 2010)

> On a remote edge of Utah's dry and arid high desert, where temperatures often zoom past 100 degrees, hard-hatted construction workers with top-secret clearances are preparing to build what may become America's equivalent of Jorge Luis Borges's "Library of Babel," a place where the collection of information is both infinite and at the same time monstrous, where the entire world's knowledge is stored, but not a single word is understood. At a million square feet, the mammoth $2 billion structure will be one-third larger than the US Capitol and will use the same amount of energy as every house in Salt Lake City combined. It's being built by the ultra-secret National Security Agency—which is primarily responsible for "signals intelligence," the collection and analysis of various forms of communication—to house trillions of phone calls, e-mail messages, and data trails: Web searches, parking receipts, bookstore visits, and other digital "pocket litter"
>
> (Bamford 2009)

Introduction

The world is at war. It is at war against you and me. Against us. This is not a classical "world war," with bombs and bullets or national armies facing each other on fields of battle. It is not even the Global War on Terrorism, brought to life by George W. Bush in 2001 and buried by Barack Obama in 2009. Rather, this world war is a *hybrid* that merges economy and security and utilizes the data—or "pocket litter"—that individuals generate as they go about their daily activities. Increasingly, these data are being used to screen friend from foe, to control and contain individuals and to disarm them. As such, it is a war with no foreseeable end, a world war infinity (WWInf).

In WWInf (and notwithstanding the stealth occupation of Crimea by Russia), it is not states that are threats to each other, it is their dangerous citizens and their citizens' unruly bodies, those that threaten the existing order and the status quo. Most of these dangerous people are neither terrorists nor militants nor home-grown radicals nor lone wolves [sic]. Instead, they are ordinary individuals going about their ordinary lives. Edward Snowden's data dump of the U.S. National Security Administration's secrets only serves to confirm this, as well as suspicions that big data are the new "super weapon" in WWInf.

Are these claims merely hyperbole? I think not. In WWInf, growing numbers of the world's civilians are being enlisted—often unwittingly—in a total (izing) war in which everyone is a plausible enemy and everyone a potential target (Priest 2010; Mazzeti & Schmitt 2014). This war is waged not only through labor contributed to the war effort but also incorporation of the private sector into the statist project of "total information awareness" and "battlefield dominance." If there ever were any purely civilian or private–personal sectors in the world's capitalist societies, these have now have now been merged with the world's military, police and intelligence systems.[1] WWINF is a *hybrid* war, one that is going on everywhere, even between our ears (Jennings 2006) where, as we shall see below, valuable data reside.

To be sure, state-instigated warfare has been hybridized for many centuries, as citizens and capital were pressed into serving, defending and producing weapons for the Mother/Father/Home-land. But the impressment of the private sector industry into serving the nation's defense in World War One and Two and the Cold War involved the sale of goods and services to the state, or perhaps nationalization until the end of hostilities. Present practice, by contrast, involves private parties participating directly in the prosecution of WWInf and even military action in place of armed forces (Thompson 1994; Owens 2008) and civil society revealing its innermost secrets in place of intelligence agencies. The goal of WWInf is the securing of a social order deeply embedded in the global economy and the process of capital accumulation. Mobilization in WWInf comes via what David Levi-Faur (2009) calls "regulatory capitalism" and through what I call the "bio-opticon." These seek to enlist citizen-consumers in the "long twilight struggle" against social disorder and to guard against their own disloyalty and defection from the social order (Lipschutz 2008). As the second epigraph to this chapter, regarding the NSA's new data-collecting installation in Utah, seems to indicate, this enlistment takes place through close reading of the pocket litter[2] that individuals deposit in cyberspace. What we shall see, in this chapter, is how economy and security have been yoked together in the service of hybrid rule and WWInf.

I begin with a discussion of "social securitization," that is, how the widespread accumulation of personal data via public and private channels serves to enmesh individuals in a reflexive bio-opticon that rests on self-discipline and self-government. Can the thoughts and intentions of dangerous people be detected in the accumulated masses of personal information and pocket litter? How might they be discovered and neutralized, quietly and efficiently, before they can act against the public good? And who better to engage in such activities: government intelligence agencies or corporate data-mining offices, or both? The comments by the CEO of Google (first epigraph) seem to suggest that, by tracking and analyzing the behaviors and practices that give rise to such personal data, it also becomes possible to nudge, direct or even coerce subjects to behave in particular ways and desired directions and to pre-empt those who might be contemplating actions against the public welfare. In the second section, I scrutinize more closely this bio-opticon, the process of "data mining" and the role of intelligence collection in hybrid rule. How are personal data collected and by whom? What do they do with it? And does analysis of such data actually stop threats to society and social order before they materialize? I ask next: who owns such personal information? Is it the property of its originators or those who do the collecting, processing, analysis and judgment? This is not as simple a question as one might imagine: as Locke argued, the labor of his servant belonged to him, but what about personal data "pocket litter?" I argue, in the conclusion, that the struggle over the ownership of personal data lies at the core of both hybrid rule and WWInf.

Life and death in the bio-opticon

There is no need to recapitulate here the scale and scope of the contemporary global information network, or the extent to which individual engagement with the extraordinary range of on-line applications leaves behind masses of data and pocket litter associated with his or her activities and communications (see, e.g., Pugliese 2010; Angwin 2014). In today's cyber-regime, each consumer-producer "exists" not only as corporeal being but also in the form of a "data doppelgänger" (DD) (Janssen 2012; Slee 2012). An individual's personal bits and bytes are stored in many different computer memories and servers but can be reassembled into an individualized electronic representation of desires, preferences, beliefs, practices, even thoughts.[3] We tend to regard such personal data as proprietary, as our individual property. Just as an individual's labor is her private property, to be alienated as she wishes (Stanley 2008), so it would appear that our personal data are the product of *our* effort and work, to be used or disseminated with care, consent and as we see fit.

The DD, however, can be constructed without such explicit consent or consideration and, moreover, it can be appropriated in the name of both commercial opportunity *and* security concerns. The DD does not belong to the corporeal being from whom it is expropriated and it cannot be erased. In effect, the DD is a hostage of the matrix, enslaved, as it were, to work for others. Appropriation of this personal data represents a new form of property and a new property regime, one that is central to hybrid rule. I leave until later in this chapter further consideration of property rights to personal data and who or what gains power from its appropriation.

How does such appropriation take place? Via everyday life. As the U.S. National Academy of Sciences has pointed out:

> Everyone leaves personal digital tracks in these [electronic] systems whenever he or she makes a purchase, takes a trip, uses a bank account, makes a phone call, walks past a security camera, obtains a prescription, sends or receives a package, files income tax forms, applies for a loan, e-mails a friend, sends a fax, rents a video, or engages in just about any other activity. The proliferation of security cameras and means of tagging and tracking people and objects increases the scope and nature of available data. Law-abiding citizens leave extensive digital tracks, and so do criminals and terrorists.
> (National Research Council 2008: 3)

Haggerty and Ericson make a similar observation:

> Instead of being subject to disciplinary surveillance or simple repression, the population is increasingly constituted as consumers and seduced into the market economy... monitoring for market consumption is more concerned with attempts to limit access to places and information, or to allow for the production of consumer profiles through the *ex post facto* reconstructions of a person's behaviour, habits and actions. In those situations where individuals monitor their behaviour in light of the thresholds established by such surveillance systems, they are often involved in efforts to maintain or augment various social perks such as preferential credit ratings, computer services, or rapid movement through customs. (See also Angwin 2014).
> (Haggerty and Ericson 2000: 615, citing Bauman 1992: 51)

In this respect, we are all "open (face)books," inasmuch as it is virtually impossible to leave no litter behind in cyberspace (Duhigg 2009). Although today's consumer-producers willingly consent to provision of personal information to all manner of enterprises and collectors, they do so without much recourse, inasmuch as the contractual terms for most paper and electronic transactions and platforms make clear that such data are subject to use, transfer and even limited confidentiality (not to mention hackers and intelligence agencies). Not withstanding constant promises that personal information is collected and stored in secure, encrypted form and not shared with "unauthorized" parties, these data are arguably available for both commercial and intelligence-gathering purposes, accumulated in vast and near-comprehensive databases and treated as commodities. For the right price, almost all personal secrets can be purchased (Sahadi 2005). A refusal to agree to the "terms of service" means a refusal of service. Few opt out.

Is there anything new about this? "Personal" information, whether incriminating or not, has long been subject to appropriation, examination and distribution by a broad range of state authorities, police departments, military agencies, social welfare bureaucrats and tax system employees, among others (Nakashima 2008). We also know that, with the help of HUMINT (human intelligence)—often, fellow citizens (see, e.g., Anderson 2008)—secret and security agencies in both East and West assiduously compiled dossiers about those deemed to be threats to the body politic and the state (even as the information accumulated was often absurd and incorrect). There exists a long tradition of states relying on informants to infiltrate groups and organizations suspected of planning or engaging in subversion and violence. In most such cases, however, the information was neither openly nor willingly provided by the targets of investigation, and such materials were rarely analyzed with the purpose of inferring beliefs and intentions of individuals in groups or among the masses (subversive intent was generally assumed before the fact). Much of this data was collected after the fact, when individuals were believed to have committed crimes or sedition against the state. Finally, acquiring such data was no easy task, insofar as it existed primarily in paper form or transcripts of verbal statements stored in many different and often widely separated locations (Revillo Arango 1968).

When such surveillance and data mining were launched in earnest, in 2001, the program was named "Total Information Awareness" (TIA), although this was quickly dropped after widespread public and Congressional criticism and concern that TIA might be used to spy and inform on civilians (Clymer 2002). Nevertheless, many elements of the program have continued under other names. According to a recent law journal article:

> The TIA program itself was the "systems-level" program of the IAO [Information Awareness Office] that "aim[ed] to integrate information technologies into a prototype to provide tools to better detect, classify, and identify potential foreign terrorists [with the goal] to increase the probability that authorized agencies of the United States [could] preempt adverse actions." As a systems-level program, "TIA [was] a program of programs whose goal [was] the creation of a counterterrorism information architecture" by integrating technologies from other IAO programs (and elsewhere, as appropriate).
>
> (Taipale 2003: 46, citing IAO 2010)

The actions of ex-NSA subcontractor employee Edward Snowden, reported on extensively by Glenn Greenwald (2013) and others in the British newspaper *The Guardian*, have provided a much clearer picture of the kinds of TIA-type activities underway. Much of these data are vacuumed up daily by the National Security Agency, from the myriad electronic networks that comprise the world's telecommunication system (Lichtblau & Risen 2005; Ackerman 2013), to be stored in servers at the new Utah facility described earlier.

Such data collection extends far beyond telecommunications: All sorts of entities, such as governments, corporations and non-profits routinely collect personal data for commercial, security, educational, health and fundraising purposes, assuring privacy but retaining the right to use the information for commercial purposes (Duhigg 2012; Angwin 2014). For example, as reported in *The Wall Street Journal*:

> According to current and former intelligence officials, the spy agency [NSA] now monitors huge volumes of records of domestic emails and Internet searches as well as bank transfers, credit-card transactions, travel and telephone records. The NSA receives this so-called "transactional" data from other agencies or private companies, and its sophisticated software programs analyze the various transactions for suspicious patterns.
>
> (Gorman 2008)

It is not legal today to eavesdrop on the conversations and emails of *American* citizens but, as of this writing, the NSA is permitted to collect "meta-data" that record when and to whom calls are being made and emails sent. Much of these data are also being accumulated by private parties, at some cost to themselves (MacAskill 2013), for the apparent use of public authorities in the effort to identify potentially unruly bodies (and those parties apparently are permitted to read customers' emails).[4] Notwithstanding these informational treasure troves, there is some dispute over whether such surveillance has prevented any terrorist activities (Hirsh 2006; Savage 2013; Watt 2013).

More recently, some of the larger private data collecting entities, such as Google and Facebook, have raised objections to the NSA's surveillance and accumulation activities, for fear that users, especially those outside of the United States, will move to platforms that are less vulnerable to intelligence agency snooping. Given the architecture of the Internet, many of whose primary circuits run through the United States, it seems unlikely that these protests will bear much fruit. In an effort to calm both sides in this struggle, Barack Obama has recently accepted a proposal by his President's Review Group on Intelligence and Communications Technologies that:

> legislation should be enacted that terminates the storage of bulk telephony meta-data by the government ... and transitions as soon as reasonably possible to a system in which such meta-data is held instead either by private providers or by a private third party.
>
> (President's Review Group on Intelligence and Communications Technologies 2013: 25)

Any agency seeking access to such data would be required to request permission from the Foreign Intelligence Surveillance Court. In those cases where the court's decisions have been made public, however, it has shown a high degree of reluctance to forbid such access. And Obama refused to accept most of his review group's recommendations, thus ensuring that surveillance will continue.

An underlying premise behind the collection of personal data is that skilled and knowledgeable individuals have the ability to sow havoc and disorder across society, whether with bombs or bytes (if anyone is unintentionally caught up in the dragnet, too bad). At one level, there is nothing new about such capabilities, either: bomb-throwing anarchists were considered as disruptive in the 19th century as they are today. What appears to have changed, perhaps, is the potential for individuals and small groups to inflict very high levels of death and destruction on populations, and to do so with clear intention, as evident in large numbers of car, truck and suicide bombings, as well as the events of 9/11, 7/7 and other dates. More to the point is the claim that the capabilities required to wreak such havoc are now within the grasp of every person with scientific training or even access to the internet (see, e.g., Falkenrath, Newman and Thayer 1998).

How are such individuals and groups to be detected, disarmed and detained before they are able to act or, better yet, before their project can even be launched?[5] And how can significant wheat be separated from irrelevant chaff? Returning to the discussion above, the personal data accumulated in a myriad of commercial and other databases might prove a treasure trove of clues to threatening evils and intentions. It is at this point that pocket litter meets "data mining"; as the U.S. Congressional Research Service defines it:

> Data mining involves the use of sophisticated data analysis tools to discover previously unknown, valid patterns and relationships in large data sets. These tools can include statistical models, mathematical algorithms, and machine learning methods (algorithms that improve their performance automatically through experience, such as neural networks or decision trees). Consequently, data mining consists of more than collecting and managing data; it also includes analysis and prediction.
>
> (Seifert 2004)

Those with data mining capabilities can then assess individuals' capabilities, behaviors and intentions, compare activities associated with electronic trails to algorithmic templates of notional dangers and threats, and seek language and behavioral patterns that might reveal concealed activities and hidden motivations and intentions. As the National Targeting Center of the U.S. Customs and Border Protection Agency reports on its website:

> Like modern-day archeologists, the personnel at U.S. Customs and Border Protection's National Targeting Center (NTC) sift through information looking for miniscule pieces of evidence. Except that the targeters, a term coined for the data analysts who work at the NTC,

aren't sifting through the sand of ancient tombs. Instead, NTC targeters are filtering through advance information on people and products looking for potential terrorists or terrorist weapons.
(U.S. Customs and Border Protection Agency 2005)

In other words, pocket litter is "dual use": it can as easily be used to sell goods and services to consumers as to rationalize the surveillance of individuals and targeting activities of public agencies

While much of this analysis is unobtrusive, with individuals unaware that they are or can be tracked and watched (but see Braun 2014), knowledge that such tracking takes place shapes and nudges consumer-producers toward "proper" behavior, becoming an important shaper of individual subjectivity and normative practice (Jones, Pykett & Whitehead 2011). As producers of pocket litter, each individual is sensitized to behaviors or patterns of activity that might fall outside templates of "normative behavior" and subject him or her to scrutiny, penalty, interrogation and even arrest. Who among the readers of this volume, for example, has not experienced a blocked credit card while travelling? Who has not received a phone call inquiry about "unusual purchases," followed by an interrogation in order to reassure the card issuers, all in the name of "identity security?" And after such experiences, who has failed subsequently to notify those that need to know about such travel or has not been more cautious with card and purchases?

These and other security/economy techniques reflect the social securitization of daily life, life in the bio-opticon, as the private and personal become part of the "public" record and as producer-consumers in civil society come to participate actively and eagerly not only in sustaining the mechanisms of co-production of rule, regulation and self-discipline but also the very operation of the "surveillant assemblage" that watches them and in which they have been embedded (Wood 2013; Braun 2014).[6] All of this may sound similar to Bentham's panopticon, but it reflects a more complex environment, what I call the "bio-opticon." The prisoner in the panopticon self-regulates in the knowledge that s/he is being watched; the prisoner does not, however, reveal his inner thoughts or intentions, in ways that might be deployed to pre-empt future behaviors. In the bio-opticon, not only thoughts and intentions come under scrutiny, so do the very contents of individual bodies (Hester 2014).

But the story does not end there: Within this surveillant assemblage, and exposed to it on a daily basis, each individual is also charged with the "security" of all, in terms of civil behavior, order and "seeing something, saying something." Those in both physical and virtual motion within this assemblage are told and warned repeatedly to be watchful and cautious, to report suspicious items, people and events (without those ever being fully defined), and to fear those who do not comport themselves in a "proper" fashion (again without specific definition). We are each thus engaged in self-regulation, self-surveillance, self-discipline and self-garrisoning, even as our individual behaviors are subject to constant surveillance, scrutiny and assessment by others, mechanical, electronic and flesh (Lipschutz 2008; Lipschutz & Turcotte 2005; Lipschutz & Hester 2014).

Pocket litter as property

The idea that "private parties" should hold accumulated personal data for potential use by the state highlights a central element of hybrid rule: "To whom does pocket litter belong?" Who holds title to it? Is pocket litter private and personal as many would argue (and as would be the contents of our pockets) and therefore the property of its creator? Or is it open for appropriation by whoever has the capability to do so? The answer to these questions says something about the status of the individual under hybrid rule (see Hester chapter in this volume).

In liberal society, we believe that the personal and private are distinct from the public, the market and, most of all, the state. This includes what we think about life, how we think about things, people, institutions and practices, and even contemplation of potentially dangerous actions. What actually constitutes the "private" sphere is not, however, so self-evident. In the past, "private papers" were exactly that: not to be seen by anyone except those granted permission by the author or her heirs and executors. The same rules were thought to apply to many other personal materials. Not any longer. The emergence of international intellectual property rights (IPR) law and regulation has had significant impacts on the very nature of the public and private domains and the distinctions between them (Drahos with Brainthwaite 2002).

If we draw parallels to the individual's ownership of her labor, the individual producer-consumer should be proprietor over the products of her bodily intellectual "work." As John Locke wrote in the *Second Treatise of Civil Government*, "every Man has a *Property* in his own *Person*. This no Body has any Right to but himself. The *Labour* of his Body, and the *Work* of his hands, we may say, are properly his."[7] Locke then argues that:

> the Grass my Horse has bit; the Turfs my Servant has cut; and the Ore I have digg'd in any place where I have a right to them in common with others, become my *Property,* without the assignation or consent of any body. The *labour* that was mine, removing them out of that common state they were in, hath *fixed* my *Property* in them.
>
> (Locke 1698: Ch. V, §28)

When we dig and sow in the fields of cyberspace, then, are we planting our seeds in a commons or in someone's field? Is cyberspace a domain that we are sharecropping? Having paid "rent" to the domain owner, do we not have legal ownership of the produce that grows there, even if we are not freeholders?

The law remains vague on this point. U.S. courts have ruled, for example, that medical and biological innovations and products derived from organs taken from a patient are not the property of said patient (Skloot 2010; Zimmer 2013) although, a recent U.S. Supreme Court ruling appears to be eroding this principle (see SCOTUSblog 2014). That is, anything deemed to be "natural" and unaltered cannot be subject to private property claims. Certain types of life form developed in labs can be patented, as can pharmaceuticals derived from plants removed from public properties and commons. Copyright is available to those willing to commit the time and energy to ensure that the "products" of their minds are protected against illegal public appropriation and dissemination (although the question of copyright and patent ownership is always a subject of dispute). If we consent to the small print in electronic contracts and give the data gatherer exclusive use of our personal information, are we transferring ownership? Is pocket litter a work-for-hire? What is not clear is whether such off-the-cuff creations are the property of their creator or, like waters flowing in a public river, subject to capture on such bases as "prior appropriation" or "common use" (Drahos with Braithwaite 2002; Smith 2008; Arrow 1996). Arguably, in the absence of digital intermediaries able to motivate creation of the data and to collect them, neither electronic pocket litter nor the property rights question exist.

The literature on the ownership of "intelligence information" is somewhat equivocal. A 2007 RAND study of counterinsurgency tactics makes the rather startling argument that:

> The United States and its allies can dominate the digital domain of COIN [counterinsurgency], but only by embracing the principles by which information is shared and used in society at large. The first step toward this goal is for the U.S. military, intelligence, and diplomatic establishments to stop treating information as the property of those who originate it and start treating it as a vital resource of those who need to use it.
>
> (Gompert and Gordon 2008: xxli)

This argument does not, of course, suggest sharing that information with the publics; it extends only as far as other Executive agencies. It does seem to stand in diametric opposition to the U.S. government's position on intellectual property. A more recent law review article (Sales 2010), addressing "ownership" of information collected and generated by U.S. intelligence agencies, makes the following observations (Sales 2010: n. 271; emphasis added) in a footnote:

1 "The former Vice-Chairman of the 9/11 Commission has faulted intelligence agencies for viewing information 'as their property, rather than the property of the entire government, and the property of the American people'";
2 "the Commission on the Intelligence Capabilities of the U.S. Regarding Weapons of Mass Destruction rejects 'the (incorrect) notion that

information is the property of individual intelligence agencies, rather than of the government as a whole'; and
3 the Third Report of the Markle Foundation Task Force states that '[T]here should ... be an explicit statement of policy that *originators or producers do not own or control the information they produce*.'"

In another, rather lengthy footnote, reproduced here in full, Sales writes that:

> Finished intelligence assessments may be thought of, in copyright terms, as original works that "possess at least some minimal degree of creativity." The creative element here consists of intelligence analysts assembling, synthesizing, and interpreting raw information, thereby yielding an entirely new work. The assessments also could be thought of, in patent terms, as "inventions" or "discoveries," though the analogy is less exact. An intelligence analyst typically discovers new realities about enemy intentions (al Qaeda plans to attack within the month), not new processes for use in producing assessments. (A more precise patent analogy would be an agency launching a new satellite capable of vacuuming up an unprecedented volume of international telephone calls, or placing a new spy whose reports offer exceptionally clear insights into the target's plans.) *Unprocessed information doesn't fit as neatly into an established IP category; "facts are not copyrightable." Yet these raw, unadorned facts resemble other types of information that enjoy what are known as sui generis IP protections.* For instance, they are similar to "hot news," first recognized in International News Service v. Associated Press, 248 U.S. 215, 235–39 (1918). Like hot news, an intelligence agency gathers raw facts "at a cost," the data "is time sensitive" (an indication that a terrorist attack is imminent isn't much use after the bomb goes off), the agency directly competes against rivals that might free ride on its efforts, and such free riding might reduce or even eliminate the incentives to produce assessments. *Raw facts also resemble the bulk information that, in Europe, is subject to a new type of IP protection known as "database right". That right protects firms that make a "substantial investment" in preparing the contents of a database against commercial rivals who "extract" or "reutilize" database information for their own operations.* Whatever the appropriate IP analogies, the basic point is simple: finished assessments and raw data both should be protected under a *hybrid* system (citations can be found in the original article).
>
> (Sales 2010: n. 274; emphasis added)

None of this—except, perhaps, the EU directive—makes ownership any clearer. Arguably, personal data have little economic or security significance until they are organized into an intelligible form by analysts and others (much in the way that an individual's labor must be organized in a socially legible and productive way to generate social value). If the means of production are owned by the worker, she is owner of whatever she produces; if the means of "production" are owned by others, the product is their property—but does the NSA own the infrastructure from which they glean information. Aren't they stealing data?

Perhaps the definition of "private property" is the problem here (see Munzer 1990; Rose 1994; Davies 2007). Generally speaking, private property is understood as a thing possessed or controlled by an individual holding title (Macpherson 1978: 2–4). But it may be more accurate to say that private property is (1) a relationship between owner and owned that is recognized by society and law as legitimate; and (2) a notional grant to the owner of *political* regulatory authority over that to which s/he holds recognized title (Wood 1995: 36–44). It is this political authority that is subject to limits and constraints imposed by society, custom, practice and law. In theory, "rights in the body" ought to convey political authority to an individual over her/his body and at least some forms of ownership (Macpherson 1962; Davies and Naffine 2001). Inasmuch as intellectual property law grants individual copyright to music, words on paper and various forms of body movement, it is difficult to see why, except for its presumably minimal market value if unprocessed, pocket litter should be excluded.

In any event, thus arises the paradox that personal information may be used to sell consumer goods to those individuals whose consuming practices indicate an interest in or preference for said goods. This is commonly rationalized as "providing a service" to the customer and "increasing efficiency"; it is *never* described as a form of exploitation or "identity theft." Instead, it would appear, the accumulation of personal information in proprietary databases fundamentally transforms it, with the data doppelganger being a wholly new expression that could never be created by the original creator-producer of that data, acting individually; therefore, it *must* be the private property of those who have assembled the databases. This is not a conclusion that will sit well with those concerned about individual privacy.

The critical question then becomes whether the collection and appropriation of individuals' personal data in commercial and intelligence databases constitute a significant change in the Lockean property regime of self-possession and proprietorship (Macpherson 1962), and are evidence of a larger displacement of one system of property relations and market exchange by another, as theorized by Randall Collins, an historical macro-sociologist.

War by other means?

Randall Collins, an historical macro-sociologist, has written (1999: 199) that "At their outermost sweep … crises [of market systems] are the turning points of history that bring an end to one system of property exchange and replace it with another." Often, such "turning points" are coincident with wars, because these new systems of property exchange and rights almost invariably threaten (and often achieve) dispossession of many who were dominant under the old regime (Halperin 2004). Is the world at such a turning point? Is there a new market system taking hold?

Arguably, the answer is yes: under hybrid rule, *contra* Locke, individuals no longer hold full property rights in their own persons (if they ever did). Fordism was based on full labor rights in the body and the sale of labor to capital; post-Fordism is based on appropriation of information, as property, from a knowledge commons, which extends to the individual body. This transition is accompanied by struggles to sustain the old order and instantiate the new one, and it is not a peaceful or orderly process (just as transitions in the past have been accompanied by large-scale violence). World War Infinity is a consequence of this struggle—not the cause—predicated in part on the principle that those who threaten society must be known and defended against. While WWInf sometimes breaks out into open violence, much of it takes place out of sight and out of mind. In the effort to sustain order so that markets remain stable and orderly, there can be no individual private secrets. Personal data is hybridized, becoming the shared possession of both security and economy whose agencies and corporations seek such data for purposes of both state security and market expansion.

From this perspective, then, the struggle began not in 2001, as commonly believed, but, rather, in the initial crisis of accumulation of the 1970s and the long rise of neoliberalism, aided and abetted by high individualism, and the proliferation of knowledge-based means of production, in biology, electronics and financialization. The crisis of Fordism and declining demand pushed producers of goods and services to design and sell to ever more specific consumer tastes and preferences. Ultimately, these could only be identified through tracking increasingly individualized patterns of consumption and behavior, a project that has reached fruition through global electronic networks (a product of the U.S. defense sector). But the same technologies that facilitate exchange of goods and money also permit exchange of threatening ideas and plans. The collaboration of economy and security, and the prosperity and safety of society, has come to depend on hybrid rule and hybrid war: World War Infinity.

Some readers will have noted that the yoking of security and economy in hybrid rule is nothing less than Michel Foucault's (2003: 244) concept of governmentality, in which "the principle form of knowledge [is] political economy" and the "essential technical means apparatuses of security." In the first instance, "political economy" involves regulation of social relations and practices relating to production and reproduction, and not just exchange in the market. In the second, "apparatuses of security" are those instruments and mechanisms that ensure this order, including surveillance of attitudes, behaviors and practices, and not just threats or force applied by the military and police. This particular form of governmentality is premised on the deployment and manipulation of knowledge as the means of exercising control over both the tastes and actions of individual bodies, and to shape preferences and behaviors (Pykett 2012). Indeed, it is not far-fetched to imagine that, in the future, as Eric Schmidt seems to hope, we will be advised by our personal electronic devices on what to do next or what not to do, who to meet and who not, and what to buy and what to avoid. Those devices will also report to databases somewhere what we have done or failed to do. And, if what we have done, or not done, does not comport with some sort of approved or individually tailored profile or program, we will be gently reminded by our device and nudged toward the "correct" behavior. In other words, as long as we can receive the signal, we will be *governed* through the tools and good graces of data-driven governmentality, which will keep watch and ensure order.

I do not want to read into all of this any kind of clear intentionality or project. It is tempting to think that, somewhere, there exists a master plan, perhaps cobbled together by Dick Cheney and his minions, with the objective of keeping tabs on everyone (Braun 2014). With the capacity to collect and process almost infinite quantities of data, intentionality is almost beside the point: *government by bio-opticon* becomes an end that no one foresaw, that no one desired and that no one controls. What is done in the service of economy and security is being done because it can be done, by those whose jobs it is to collect, mine, analyze, process and manage, and not because there is some cabal in charge.

So, what we have is *government(ality)* through endless, infinite war, without politics, people, states or corporations. Government that seeks order by shaping and managing behaviors. Government whose reach depends more on server farms than legislatures. Government whose existence and activities are almost invisible, except when someone like Edward Snowden reminds us that it is there. Government that is most assuredly *worldwide*. Think of government as a steel web with eyes and ears, that makes us secure even as it limits our freedom and that watches over us even as it imprisons us, with the mission of peace through war. As Barry Buzan (1991: 37) once wrote, "There is a cruel irony in [one] meaning of *secure* which is '*unable to escape*.'"

Notes

1 The New York Police Department has its own international intelligence division (see, e.g., Worth 2005; NYPD, n.d.).
2 "For example, a piece of paper with a list found on a suspected terrorist—known in the field as "pocket litter"—could turn out to be a grocery list or a coded roster of associates. It takes an analyst trained in what to look for to tell the difference" (McConnell 2007: 53).
3 See "The Human Face of Big Data App," at: http://humanfaceofbigdata.com/about/ (accessed Feb. 23, 2014).
4 "Select TSA [U.S. Transportation Security Agency] employees will be trained to identify suspicious individuals who raise red flags by exhibiting unusual or anxious behavior, which can be as simple as changes in mannerisms, excessive sweating on a cool day, or changes in the pitch of a person's voice" (Donnelly 2006).
5 Entrapment has become increasingly popular in seeking out putative terrorists (Anderson 2008; Anderson 2010; Glaberson 2010; Weiser 2013).

6 The term "assemblage" comes from Deleuze and Guattari 1987. Here, I rely on the modified definition offered in Haggerty and Ericson 2000: 608, citing Patton 1994: 158: "'Assemblages' consist of a 'multiplicity of heterogeneous objects, whose unity comes solely from the fact that these items function together, that they "work" together as a functional entity.'"
7 "Whatsoever then he removes out of the State that Nature hath provided, and left it in, he hath mixed his *Labour* with, and joyned to it something that is his own, and thereby makes it his *Property*. It being by him removed from the common state Nature placed it in, it hath by this *labour* something annexed to it, that excludes the common right of other Men. For this *Labour* being the unquestionable Property of the Labourer, no Man but he can have a right to what that is once joyned to, at least where there is enough, and as good left in common for others." (Locke 1698: Ch. V, §27).

9 Biology as opportunity
Hybrid rule from a molecular point of view

Rebecca J. Hester

Biology is no longer destiny but opportunity.[1]

Introduction: biology as opportunity

Between 1932 and 1972, the U.S. Public Health Service conducted a medical experiment on human beings, one that was, in many respects, little different from those experiments inflicted by Nazis on concentration camp inmates (Mellanby 1947). In the Tuskegee Syphilis Experiment, a group of poor, rural black men with syphilis were denied treatment in exchange for free medical care, meals and burial insurance from the U.S. government so that the natural course of the infection could be studied.[2] What had been deemed a war crime during World War Two was found to be perfectly legal under U.S. law, with any "inventions" resulting from the experiment being the "sole property of the United States" (Roy 1995: 65). Moreover, as part of the Clinical Cooperative Study under the League of Nations, the Tuskegee study was deemed an "international agreement" which, according to a 1920 Supreme Court decision (*Missouri v Holland* 252 US 416), put it under the executive authority of the United States rather than the U.S. constitution, thus putting it beyond the reach of constitutional questions or interpretation. While Tuskegee was certainly not the first example of public–private hybridization, for its time it was exceptional. According to Benjamin Roy, and contrary to arguments made by the study's proponents, the central issue at stake in the experiments was not scientific understanding but property in the body (1995). Claiming that the Public Health Service (PHS) engaged in "clinical subterfuge" to obscure its political objectives, Roy maintains that the Tuskegee Syphilis Study had to do with "the economic exploitation of humans as a natural resource of a disease that could not be cultivated in culture or animals in order to establish and sustain American superiority in patented commercial biotechnology" (1995: 56). More to the point, he argues that, once removed from the body, tissue and body fluids ceased to be considered the property of the Tuskegee subjects, and instead became the property of the PHS.

One physician involved with the research illuminated the grave implications of such biological exploitation when he proclaimed that the Tuskegee study was a "never-to-be-repeated opportunity" (Faden and Beauchamp 1986, cited in Angell 1997: 847). The "opportunity" at hand was twofold. On the one hand, it was economic as the commercialization potential became clear. On the other, it was political. The study facilitated U.S. global dominance over Germany in syphilis serology—at the time, the latter was ahead in the field—while also contributing to a superior role for the United States in the World Health Organization (Roy 1995). In addition, it exploited a domestic population that, in a racist society such as the United States, has historically been seen as less than human and, therefore, of little social value.

The most insidious facet of the study was that it permitted the U.S. state to effectively exercise ownership over the bodies of vulnerable subjects under the guise of health and for the purposes of increasing political and economic power. The fact that treatment existed to cure the research subjects but those subjects were actively prevented from accessing it (Brandt 1978) supports the idea that the goal of the study was not to cure the black male syphilitics of their disease but, rather, to utilize these men as human incubators of the bacterium that causes syphilis in order to develop new, more reliable and profitable tests for syphilis (Washington 2006). In his critique of the experiments, Roy compares the Tuskegee study to slavery, asserting that "the generative ability of the body made the Tuskegee subjects real property and gave untreated syphilis and the sera of the Tuskegee subject's immense commercial value" (1995: 56).

In hindsight it has become clear that, far from being a one-time opportunity, under neoliberalism the biological exploitation of human subjects for political and commercial profit has only increased in recent decades. As public and private objectives merge and converge on human biology, bodies are regularly converted into data sources to be mined and manipulated at the molecular level. Despite an increase in human subjects' protections and the rise of bioethics, individuals and populations are often unaware of the uses to which their tissues, blood, and genetics are put. This is the case because hybrid rule, in which the public sphere colonizes the private sphere—from industries to individuals—in order to extract and exploit human biology for profit and power, is obscured both from the theoretical level, as scholars focus on the mutual imbrications of capital and biology while ignoring the role of the state in provoking those entanglements, and on the empirical level, as public health, scientific research, and national security are increasingly privatized thereby masking the role of the state in regulating and managing the privatization process.

In this chapter, I examine hybrid rule from a molecular perspective and argue that the emphasis on the economic gains of biological extraction, storage, and manipulation largely ignores the political imperatives and effects of such activities. The way that the state has used the private sector to create what this volume calls "hybrid rule" has provided an opportunity to exercise a kind of unprecedented "biological control" (Franklin 2003), through which it is now possible for the state "to control, manage, engineer, reshape and modulate the very vital capacities of human beings as living creatures" (Franklin 2003) while minimizing mechanisms to understand and contest such political control. My argument challenges the privileging of capitalism as the reason for the rise in biotechnology (Rajan 2006) and takes issue with explanations of neoliberalism that suggest that the state has been rendered weaker. The focus on the biotechnology industry as the next stage in contemporary capitalism forecloses the question of what both the U.S. state and the country's population have to gain from supporting biotechnology beyond the projected yet largely elusive gains for the national economy (Nightingale and Martin 2004). Certainly, as Susan Wright (1994) has argued, had biotechnology not provided the basis for a new form of industrial production, the scientific community's rationales for deregulation of biological research might have been met with greater skepticism. Yet, this industry did not emerge simply as a result of scientific progress and certainly would not have been sustained had there not been political reasons to capitalize on its gains.

The reliance on private actors—whether scientific entrepreneurs working in privately funded public laboratories, venture capitalists willing to take a financial risk, or human subjects used to advance scientific research—to move this industry forward is by political design. Cases such as those of John Moore (discussed below) and Henrietta Lacks (Skloot 2010)—cases in which the U.S. state prioritized science over humans—reveal the political investment in molecular biology. A closer analysis of the state's historic and contemporary role in molecular science also refocuses our gaze from the economic consequences to the political potential for engineering, controlling, and managing human biology in the past, present and into the future. Given its central role, we can no longer conclude that the U.S. state has retrenched, downsized or ceded power to private corporations as a result of neoliberalism. Instead, I suggest that the state has been reconfigured and its power aggrandized as its reach extends, via the private sector, into and over the most micro aspects of human life.

Much like the research subjects in Tuskegee, the American public has largely signed onto the state's molecular agenda because genetic engineering is perceived and presented as a way to protect and optimize human health. Consequently, in exchange for promises of a better, longer, and more secure life for all, the more insidious and invasive political and economic consequences of molecular science, namely the ability to alter, order, manipulate, and control biological organisms and living systems and to privatize and generate income from these activities, are largely overlooked or elided. Within such promises, health and security become synonymous and political and economic projects are collapsed together.

In what follows, I briefly outline the history of advances in molecular biology and attendant changes in federal science policy, patent legislation, and science funding, beginning with further comments on the Tuskegee experiments and their implications for the United States. I then turn to a brief history of molecular biology and its politics prior to the 1970s. Although DNA was not discovered until the 1950s and the ability to move and recombine genes was developed only during the 1970s, there is a long record of political projects founded on eugenics that aimed to shape men biologically in order to "improve the stock" and weed out those deemed to be "unfit." In contrast to contemporary efforts, however, these projects were largely funded by private foundations which were nonetheless concerned with the composition of the national "stock." This is one feature that sets the current context apart from previous eras.

I then turn to the beginnings of the "molecular revolution" in the 1970s and the role of the Nixon administration in the commercialization of what had been, until then, largely under the purview of the country's biological weapons program (see the Hurt chapter in this volume). Drawing from Shelley Hurt's (2011) work on the dual-use origins of biotechnology, I argue that the American State has intentionally hybridized the field in order to minimize expenditures and visibility while maximizing control over human bodies and life itself. The vision of "making dollars out of DNA" (Smith Hughes 2001) loomed large in the eyes of the U.S. government but the fostering of a commercial biotechnology industry also meant that a whole host of molecular innovations could now be promoted by the state, ever mindful of their implications and uses for biosecurity. This historical overview is intended to address the question introduced in the first chapter of this volume: how and why did hybridization begin during the 1970s?

In the fourth part of the chapter, I address the relationship between capital accumulation and the State as it has played out through the reduction of the human body to its constituent molecules. Inasmuch as the dissemination of molecular control is effected more efficiently through the market than State-run public health and social welfare schemes, the expansion of anxieties about individual wellness and longevity offer endless opportunities to monitor, regulate and control bodies. I conclude that, in the twenty-first century, biological control has become increasingly important for all sectors of society as fears mount about bioweapons, pandemic flus and "every kind of biological danger" (Obama 2011). We are thus all entreated to join forces with the U.S. state to secure ourselves and society from every kind of embodied risk and danger emerging from the molecular world. Recent presidential health initiatives are but the latest in a long line of state-driven initiatives to achieve this end.

BioState and biocapital

Despite the *ex post facto* recognition that the Tuskegee experiments were unethical, and the fact that legal and ethical protections were subsequently put into place to protect human subjects in biomedical research, since the 1970s human biology has been increasingly exploited for social, political, and economic purposes.[3] In fact, over and against the not-too-distant memory of the Nazi medical experiments, and just as public criticism was being directed at the Public Health Service for its role in the Tuskegee study, an entire biotechnology industry emerged to extract, privatize, and commercialize biological material. Within this industry, cell lines can be patented and privatized, human tissues can be commercialized and globalized, and all forms of biological material can be mined, manipulated, and managed. In conjunction with these practices, governments are using biological information to track, trace, and surveil individuals, leading to what Bronwyn Parry (2012) calls "panoptical and dialectical biosurveillance." Meanwhile, a whole panoply of biodefense research has contributed to the development of more virulent and highly transmissible biological weapons (as seen, for example, in the recent creation of a highly contagious variant of avian influenza, funded by the U.S. National Institutes of Health; Gould and Connell 2008; McNeill 2012). In an interesting shift of sentiment, however, public criticism of biological control has declined as more and more people want to have their tissues sampled, their genes assessed, and their bodies intervened upon and optimized. While racial minorities continue to be targeted for particular kinds of biological exploitation and surveillance, in contemporary society, everyone's biology provides some form of political, social, or economic opportunity, either as a source of information, as raw material for a commercial product, or as a DNA "fingerprint" to be banked for a future use (Andrews and Nelkin 2001). What accounts for this dramatic shift? What role has the state played in this transformation?

The oft-told story of the emergence of the biotechnology industry is that it was spurred by a combination of technological progress in molecular science with venture capitalists eager to profit (see, for example, Kenney 1988). The state plays a "background role" (Kenney 1988: 241) in these narratives and matters only to the extent that it facilitated the emergence of the industry through legislative and policy changes. The emphasis in this origin story of advances in genetic engineering therefore focuses largely on the economic interests and imperatives of biotechnology companies, the scientific entrepreneurs who work for them, and the nations and universities that benefit. These accounts see biotechnology as the latest phase in the evolution of capitalism and focus on the commercialization of the life sciences (Kenney 1988; Sunder Rajan 2006) to the detriment of explanations that focus on the coincident politicization of biology.

According to Sunder Rajan, these changes in the life sciences represent a new face and a new phase of capitalism, one that is based on a "political economy of hype" (2006: 14), in which speculative capital and postgenomic life join together as defining forces in contemporary society. He calls this hybrid arrangement "biocapital." In a biocapitalist regime, researchers try to commercialize tissue without sharing profits with their sources of "raw materials" and "body parts are extracted like a mineral, harvested like a crop or mined like a resource." The economic language of supply and demand, contracts, exchange, and compensation is evident in contemporary discussions of molecular biology as cells, embryos, or tissue are frozen, banked, placed in libraries or repositories, marketed, patented, bought and sold. Using tissue engineering as an example, Linda Hogle argues that a new, hybrid form of economy is emerging:

> Although these techniques encompass elements of the 'boutique' style and 'just-in-time production methods characteristic of postmodern economies,' as David Harvey describes, a different calculus is at work. Tissue engineering is stratified and multiform production in which institutional forms, methods of manufacture, and ways of creating capital are neither old nor new but hybrid and emerging.
> (Hogle 2003: 77, citing Harvey 1989)

Indeed, the hybrid arrangements in biotechnology between the U.S. state and the private sector have led to a host of changes, including the development of new economic spaces (Kenney 1986), new economies of vitality (Rose 2007), and new forms of somatic expertise (Rose 2007), biocapital (Sunder Rajan 2006), biovalue (Waldby 2002) and biocommodities. It has also led to new forms of exploitation, as biopiracy becomes a global practice (Shiva 1997). Within this economy, pathologists routinely analyze tissue samples without obtaining anyone's consent and legal battles are fought in order to avoid physicians from viewing their patients as potential treasure troves (Ferrell 1990). In an article entitled "Whose body is it anyway? Disputes over body tissue in a biotechnology age," Andrews and Nelkin (1998: 54) cite Ernest Chargaff, a biologist, who warns that the increase in human tissue research may be a slippery slope to social disaster, "an Auschwitz in which valuable enzymes, hormones, and so on will be extracted instead of gold teeth."

Yet, the strong focus on capital accumulation, seen in much of the social science literature on biotechnology, shifts our gaze away from the political objectives and benefits that have resulted from aspirations to achieve biological control. It also obscures the ways in which sovereignty has been hybridized in conjunction with the private sector so as to recombine individual bodies and institutional relationships, rewrite legal frameworks, and regenerate life itself for political and economic purposes. From the molecular perspective, the market is both a means of and an end for political power, and is neither separate from the state nor dominant over it. Indeed, the state has "hybridized" and has itself been hybridized, encroaching on the private sphere to further its political objectives while at the same time furthering the economic objectives of the private sphere. When we focus on market forces alone and isolate the economic potential of biotechnology, the state is largely removed from scrutiny, or it is encouraged to take a more activist role, as if it had heretofore been passive and removed from political play. The state has not ceased, however, to take an active role in fostering domination and control over the very processes of life itself. Rather, it has adapted those forces to its needs while at the same time constraining avenues for individual and institutional contestation and resistance to this dynamic. This dynamic influences self-perceptions as individuals come to see themselves in biological terms. Nikolas Rose summarizes the changes:

> As human beings come to experience themselves in new ways as biological creatures, as biological selves, their vital existence becomes a focus of government, the target of novel forms of authority and expertise, a highly cathected field for knowledge, an expanded territory for bioeconomic exploitation, an organizing principle for ethics, and the stake in a molecular vital politics.
>
> (Rose 2007: 4)

Bruce Braun (2007) expands Rose's argument by bringing in the uses of molecular politics for security purposes. He argues that the molecularization of life has made our biological existence political in new ways as the "molecularized body" becomes the site of diverse political rationalities in which geopolitics, economics and biopolitics merge around the concept of security. Within this molecularized and securitized biopolitics, the government of life reveals itself to be intimately connected to the exercise and extension of sovereign power (2007: 8). Foucault (1978) outlined the biopolitical relationship between sovereignty, populations and individual bodies. With the advent of genetic engineering and biotechnology, this relationship increasingly operates at the molecular level.

Laying the groundwork: "The Science of Man"

Genetic engineering through selective breeding is a millennia-old practice, but the ability to alter a cell's genome by inserting or removing its DNA is a relatively recent technology. With precursors in the late nineteenth and early twentieth century, the modern history of this technology is most often traced (and attributed) to Watson and Crick's recognition of the double helix structure of DNA in 1953. This vital discovery allowed scientists to understand and alter the structure of DNA, and was followed in the 1970s by the work of Stanley Cohen (Stanford) and Herbert Boyer (UC San Francisco), who succeeded in moving genes among a number of organisms. The emergence of recombinant DNA in 1973 was widely celebrated as the "molecular revolution," a revolution whose premise was based on turning DNA into gold.

No revolution occurs without precursors, and this one had many. Foremost among them were the institutional collaborations between the public and the private sector much earlier in the twentieth century. In 1986, a science policy study (U.S. Congress 1986) on research support between 1940 and 1985, conducted for the U.S. House Committee on Science and Technology, observed that "the federal government was by no means the only major patron of scientific research prior to World War II." Private industry, private foundations, and universities were scientific sponsors as well; indeed, during the 1930s, industry supplied the largest share of funding for scientific development (U.S. Congress 1986). Private foundations were also key players in American science during this period, with the Rockefeller Foundation taking a central role in setting the ideological and intellectual agenda for the objectives and uses of molecular advances between the 1920s and the 1950s. This agenda, guided by mathematical physicist Warren Weaver, was driven by "the pursuit of an understanding of life" in largely reductionist terms, beginning with atoms and molecules and working upwards (Vettel 2008: 11).

In *The Molecular Vision of Life,* Lily E. Kay (1993) describes the political uses of molecular biology during the 1930s, as it emerged through the Rockefeller Foundation's "new science of man" agenda. By contrast with earlier models of eugenics, based on racial theories and promoting social control through selective breeding (i.e. through reproduction), the Rockefeller Foundation's "Science of Man" agenda sought to foster the study of simple biological systems and analyses of protein structure as "a surer, albeit much slower, way toward social planning based on sounder theories of eugenic selection" (Kay 1993: 9). The social goal promoted by the Rockefeller Foundation, and sanctioned and supported by many American scientific leaders in the first half of the twentieth century, took as its intellectual mission the technological control of life, with an emphasis on restructuring human relations in congruence with the social framework of industrial capitalism and "improving" the individual (rather than "weeding out" those thought weak or dangerous (Kay 1993: 8). By unleashing molecular biology from its links to medicine, the Rockefeller initiative directed molecular research toward amelioration of "social dysfunction," primarily among the poor and minorities, operationalizing a "molecular vision of life" (Kay 1993, 2008).

The Foundation's "agenda" was also meant to align the social goals of the private sector, including industry, foundations, and individual donors, with the research goals of the life sciences in higher education. One way to do this was through the peer-review system of project and program funding proposals. By targeting research funds to particular universities, such as Cal Tech, the Rockefeller Foundation was able to shape the research objectives and methodologies of university laboratories. Kay argues that, despite the fact that many life scientists at the time were unaware of their participation in the Science of Man agenda, a consensus emerged between private and public actors that there could be "an optimal match between technocratic visions of human engineering and representations of life grounded in technological intervention, a resonance between scientific imagination and social vision" (1993: 18). A reconfigured grant-making system, in which public and private resources were mingled to fund molecular tinkering and the rise of the research university in the 1940s to support wartime efforts, were central to making this vision a reality.

The post-war period saw the emergence of a new research arrangement: scientists and engineers were allowed to carry their wartime activities into civilian life, in settings as close as possible to their accustomed venues, the universities and industrial research laboratories (Atkinson and Blanpied 2008: 34). This blending of the public and private scientific sectors and laboratory spaces was funded through a peer-review grant system in which mutually beneficial scientific discoveries could be generated. Unlike the pre-war period, when private foundations largely supported molecular work, these new, postwar grants were distributed primarily through federal organizations, such as the newly created National Science Foundation and the National Institutes of Health, and were provided primarily for the purposes of developing and improving military technologies. Other federal agencies, such as the Office of Naval Research, the Atomic Energy Commission and several organizations in the Department of Defense also got into the business of funding basic research (Atkinson and Blanpied 2008: 36). This unprecedented era of federal science funding was the result of Cold War competition—even further increased after Sputnik—and several influential reports, notably *Science: The Endless Frontier,* written in 1945 by Vannevar Bush, President Roosevelt's science adviser, and the 1950 "Seaborg Report," *Scientific Progress, the Universities, and the Federal Government.* Both argued for the importance of conducting federally supported basic research in university settings. One of the remarkable features of this era (especially by contrast with the later rush to "privatization") was the rejection from within the scientific community of private funding for applied research, which was held to be the "domain of engineers, private industry, and political debates and influenced by popular opinion and commercial markets" (Vettel 2008: 20). During the Vietnam War, however, opinion shifted as social, economic, and political pressures came to bear on the harmful and supposedly disinterested uses of science. Such public pressure led to a transformation in science policy and spurred major shifts in scientific funding, political vision, and social relations.

The molecular revolution and its political and economic repercussions

As related in Chapter 1 in this volume, the 1960s witnessed a rapid erosion of confidence in the national institutions of the United States. This crisis of confidence was focused broadly, targeting the presidency, Congress, the courts, business, the military, the unions, the media, and the universities (Yankelovich 1974). According to pollster Daniel Yankelovich (ibid.: 1), the shift from post-war optimism to anxious unease was characterized by "a cynical, quasi-sophisticated public view of political and business leaders as dominated by a selfishness so widespread and corrupt as to pit [...] central institutions against their own constituencies." In addition to critiques of the political and economic elites, widespread criticism of science was heard for its role in war-making and its perceived inability to address the basic human needs of society. Growing numbers, responding to the thalidomide scare which caused deformities in children all over the world, the Cutter laboratory polio outbreak which caused vaccination-induced polio in hundreds of children, radioactive fallout from atmospheric testing, and Rachel Carson's warnings of permanent ecological damage as a result of excessive DDT applications, demanded that bioscience serve the people.

The so-called molecular revolution emerged against this backdrop, in the midst of a conflict between President Nixon and the science community. Citing the scientific community's frustrations with Nixon's policies, in 1973 *Time* described the near exile of the scientific establishment from Washington under Nixon (Time 1973). That same year, recombinant DNA was discovered in California. Herbert and Boyer's scientific breakthrough became an important catalyst for turning around public and private sentiments, marking as it did what has been touted as "the single pivotal event in the transformation of the 'basic' science of molecular biology into an industry" (Kenney 1988: 23). Yet, the rise of the bioeconomy was not an inevitable outcome of the evolution of capital; rather, "the U.S. biotech industry was actively fostered, promoted and brought into being from the top down by a series of quite deliberate legislative and institutional decisions" (Cooper 2008: 25). In *Biotechnology: The University-Industrial Complex*, Martin Kenney asserts that "numerous State interventions made the formation of the biotechnology industry possible," among which he lists federal funding of NIH and NSF research, minimal state regulation of corporate activities, and the state's role in validating new areas of the natural world as private property (Kenney 1988: 241–242). But why did the American state have such an interest in biotechnology?

In her chapter in this volume, Shelley Hurt offers us a more detailed account of the government's role in the rise of this industry. In her work on the dual-use origins of American biotechnology, Hurt argues that the commercialization of advances in molecular biology was part of an explicit government plan to disassociate biological research from biological warfare and link it to peace, progress, and economic growth. There were four reasons behind this move: to advance molecular research, centralize federal science policy, jumpstart the economy, and restore political legitimacy (especially to science). The conversion process was undertaken during the Nixon administration, involving a move from the military-industry partnership approach developed under the nearly thirty-year-old U.S. offensive biological warfare program to industry-university-government partnerships emphasizing the commercial potential of applied biological research. At the same time, such research was also defined as "defensive," obscuring its dual-use potential for developing biological weapons in order to protect against them.

Central to this conversion process was the reformation of government–business relations, away from publicly sponsored research and toward (re)privatization (an approach also characteristic of the interwar period; see Kay 1993). These privatization efforts "consisted of tax incentives; technology transfer between universities, government laboratories and industry; government procurement policies; liberalized anti-trust laws; and relaxation of government-owned patent licenses" (Hurt 2011). As Hurt argues (2011), "these [reprivatization] ideas were not simply about returning to an era of unregulated capitalism; rather they were about creating a new type of entity, such as a hybrid, between the public and private sectors." The result was a large government-sponsored infrastructure of laboratories, test facilities, and production plants committed to biological warfare "defense," spread through contractors at approximately 300 universities, research institutes and corporations (Gould and Connell 2008: 105). An additional effect was the rebranding of biological research as an economic rather than a political endeavor. This was aided by Nixon's "War on Cancer," an initiative designed to channel public fears away from military concerns and toward public health while demonstrating the administration's "total commitment" to the well-being of the population.[4] As Hurt (2011) shows, specific decisions to reprivatize made during the 1960s and 1970s opened the door to the legislative changes of the 1980s, including the Bayh-Dole Act that effectively allowed universities to patent research results that had been publicly financed. This vital piece of legislation was followed six months later by the precedent-setting *Diamond v. Chakrabarty* case, which allowed the patenting of new life forms (a decision more recently diminished by the U.S. Supreme Court in *Association for Molecular Pathology et al. v. United States Patent and Trademark Office et al.*). As a result of these cases, long-standing desires for understanding and controlling human biology were married to the ownership of and profit from biological material, opening the possibility that "living organisms and their DNA could be privately owned—allowing the extraction of monopoly rents" (Kenney 1988: 191) while furthering the political goals of the administration.

Hybrid rule from a molecular perspective

The conjoining during the 1980s of the political and the economic around biological research is best exhibited by the case of John Moore, whose spleen, blood, tissues, sperm, and bone marrow were extracted by a physician at the UCLA Medical Center as part of the "treatment" for hairy-cell leukemia, and which, it turned out, were studied and patented for commercial use. Moore's cell line was patented without his knowledge, while profits from the patent were divided between the UC Regents, the UCLA physician and the Genetics Institute, as a result of a California court ruling on *Moore v. Regents of California* in 1991.[5] Court documents reveal two broad concerns in this ruling. The first was whether Moore owned his cells once they had been extracted, a concern nullified by the fact that Moore had consented to the extraction of his body parts. The second concern is revealing, however, and worthy of lengthy citation:

> The second important policy consideration is that we not threaten with disabling civil liability innocent parties who are engaged in socially useful activities, such as researchers who have no reason to believe that their use

of a particular cell sample is, or may be, against a donor's wishes. To reach an appropriate balance of these policy considerations is extremely important. In its report to Congress, the Office of Technology Assessment emphasized that "[u]ncertainty about how courts will resolve disputes between specimen sources and specimen users could be detrimental to both academic researchers and the infant biotechnology industry, particularly when the rights are asserted long after the specimen was obtained. The assertion of rights by sources would affect not only the researcher who obtained the original specimen, but perhaps other researchers as well. Biological materials are routinely distributed to other researchers for experimental purposes, and scientists who obtain cell lines or other specimen-derived products, such as gene clones, from the original researcher could also be sued under certain legal theories [such as conversion]. Furthermore, the uncertainty could affect product developments as well as research. Since inventions containing human tissues and cells may be patented and licensed for commercial use, companies are unlikely to invest heavily in developing, manufacturing, or marketing a product when uncertainty about clear title exists."[6]

This judicial decision shows clearly how the state has protected and fostered the combination of private companies, private bodies, and academic researchers in order to spur the "infant biotechnology industry" and to control the distribution and use of biological material. The argument that cell extraction is "socially useful" is reminiscent of the old Science of Man program, in which scientists, "unwittingly" participating in ethically questionable endeavors, should nonetheless not be impeded in their endeavors. Indeed, there is a pervasive belief that "public science" and, by extension, scientific entrepreneurs and their patrons should not be politically obstructed because of the potential for progress and profit promised by their research. This judgment decision also reflects some of the dynamics apparent in the Tuskegee experiments, whereby biological material was extracted from research subjects under false pretenses, leaving the subjects no rights to the profit or power gained from their bodies. Given the fact that scientific progress, industrial advancement, and private property regimes trumped Moore's rights to his "own" biological material, it is unsurprising that he felt he had been raped (cited in Andrews and Nelkin 1998).

While Moore's case is important, it illuminates only one of the myriad other uses that the state, via private industry, would put human biology to since the 1980s. For example, recent decades have witnessed the emergence of biometrics coupled with a growing reliance on DNA for biosurveillance, in which "a wad of spit, a spot of blood, a semen stain, or a single hair is all that is necessary to create a DNA 'fingerprint'" (Andrews and Nelkin 2001: 103). Subsequently, such "body data" (Lyon 2001) have been used both to imprison and liberate. On the one hand, in numerous instances it has been possible to extract DNA samples from old crime evidence that, when compared to rapidly expanding databases being compiled by both public authorities and private concerns, permit the reopening of dormant criminal cases and the identification of suspicious people. On the other hand, recovery of such samples has exonerated people accused of committing crimes as well as some individuals long imprisoned for crimes that they did not commit (www.innocenceproject.org/). It is very difficult, it would seem, to argue with genes, blood, and cells. As Franko Aas argues, these technologies work from the premise that "the body does not lie" (2006).

Recent suggestions that DNA is not quite so unique to individuals as has been claimed and assumed for many decades (Macrae 2010), or that biometrics is a "politically successful policy failure" (Andreas and Bierstekar 2003, cited in Magnet 2011) has not stopped the state from enrolling private companies and private citizens into its attempts at achieving total biological surveillance and security, however. The attempt at comprehensive state control over biology not only uses a variety of technologies but also draws from a variety of logics, as Shoshana Magnet argues in her book *When Biometrics Fail*:

> Studying biometric technologies offers a window into State-making in the age of security, including the symbiotic relationship between private enterprise and the State, the increase in information sharing and surveillance, the resurgence of biological racialism, the rise of the prison-industrial complex, the criminalization of poverty, and the mutually constitutive relationship between science fiction and real life.
>
> (Magnet 2011: 155)

While these logics seem unique to the United States, in his study on biosurveillance Bronwyn Parry argues that surveillance systems in the United States and United Kingdom are "now being brought into the same frame of reference to create new, ever more robust and finely calibrated systems of biological surveillance" (2012: 718).

Julian Reid and Michael Dillon (2009) draw out further implications of this ever-expanding and converging biosurveillance network. In their book *The Liberal Way of War: Killing to Make Life Live,* Reid and Dillon argue that the life sciences have been influenced by the growth of information sciences, computing, digitalization, and the so-called sciences of complexity to such an extent that "we have entered the age of life as information" (2009: 21). Within this age, the nature of life is re-problematized by the confluence of the digital and molecular revolutions and biological existence, which is converted into "code," becomes the foundation of political existence (2009: 53). Consequently:

> When life is thus reduced informationally to a coded structure, the key to which is said to have been found and then re-applied to the material world, materiality as such goes live. What was therefore once thought to

be securely biological—life—is no longer so simply understood, or secured biologically either.

(Reid and Dillon 2009: 22)

The effect of living in such a biologically insecure world is that the U.S. state is perpetually trying to secure itself and its populations against biological insecurity. To put it more succinctly, it is now engaged in a war against life on behalf of life. It has enrolled both private institutions and private citizens in this biological war. Two initiatives being promoted by the Obama administration demonstrate the point.

First, the recently inaugurated Global Health Security Initiative (GHSA) aspires to "accelerate progress toward a world safe and secure from infectious disease threats and to take action to promote global health security as an international priority."[7] The GHSA's motto is "the need to prevent, detect, and respond to biological threats."[8] This initiative brings into fruition an appeal that President Obama made in a speech he delivered to the United Nations on September 21, 2011. In his speech, which focused on the pursuit of peace in an imperfect world, Obama (2011) urged the international body to "come together to prevent, and detect, and fight every kind of biological danger—whether it's a pandemic like H1N1, or a terrorist threat, or a treatable disease." The GHSA aims to achieve this goal by launching, strengthening, and linking global networks for real-time biosurveillance and training and deploying an effective biosurveillance workforce, among other things. This global biosurveillance network will include partnerships with at least thirty countries and a host of institutional partners "through multiple platforms, programs, and partnerships," as well as a host of private stakeholders.[9] In a telling op-ed piece co-authored by Secretary of State John Kerry, Secretary of Health and Human Services Kathleen Sebelius, and Lisa Monaco, a senior White House Homeland Security and counterterrorism official, the U.S. state's role in managing and mitigating biological insecurity is evidenced by their assertion that the need to "prevent, detect, and respond" to new biological threats is "not just a health challenge; it's a security challenge as well."[10]

A second example of attempts to address biological insecurity is found in President Obama's Brain Research through Advancing Innovative Neurotechnologies (BRAIN) Initiative. Touted by the White House as "a bold new research effort to revolutionize our understanding of the human mind and uncover new ways to treat, prevent, and cure brain disorders like Alzheimer's, schizophrenia, autism, epilepsy and traumatic brain injury," the BRAIN Initiative aspires to understand how information is stored and processed in neural networks leading to perception, decision-making and, ultimately, human action.[11] Funded by both private organizations (such as the Salk Institute for Biological Studies, the Allen Institute for Brain Science, Howard Hughes Medical Institute, and the Kavli Foundation) and federal agencies, (including the National Science Foundation, the National Institutes of Health, and the Defense Advanced Research Projects Agency), the Initiative's proponents have compared it with the Apollo Program and the human genome project.[12] Among the many outcomes projected for the BRAIN Initiative are better interfaces between computers and human thought, high-tech jobs for Americans in cutting-edge industries of the future, and a sophisticated understanding of the brain, from individual genes to neuronal circuits to behavior.[13]

If we take both of these initiatives together then we can see how the U.S. state continues to exploit biology as a political and economic opportunity. These "big biology" initiatives are not driven by venture capitalists, although they draw from private funds, rather they are state-driven security strategies which take the contingency and mutability of life as both the source of insecurity and the reason to exponentially increase biosurveillance at the global and molecular levels. Private stakeholders are often a more convenient and expeditious mechanism for achieving these goals. In an effort to predict, prevent, and pre-empt any and every kind of biological threat, it is no surprise that the BRAIN Initiative seeks to understand human behavior and the Global Health Security Agenda aspires to understand biological mutability and mobility. "In a molecular world filled with emergent yet unspecifiable risks, biopolitics has merged with geopolitics, and the government of 'life' has revealed itself to be intimately related to the exercise of sovereign power" (2007: 8). Insofar as the U.S. state co-opts the forces of the private sector (including the bodies of private citizens) to address biological insecurity in a global context, then hybridization is increasingly focused on insuring and ensuring security.

Conclusion

Today, "big biology" projects have replaced the "big science" projects of the atomic era, leading some observers to claim that "the grand narratives of the biological sciences are taking the place of the grand narratives of western civilization" (Goodman, Heath, and Lindee 2003: 15). These narratives involve a sense of urgency that seems to be increasing by the day and expanding the domains that molecular biology is asked to improve. Such big projects not only allow the U.S. state to remain competitive in a global political economy, they also contribute to human domination through scientific and commercial enterprise, an enterprise that leads to epistemological, ontological, and instrumental control over every aspect of biological life.

The American state plays a significant role in incentivizing both private investors and public scientists to invest in and profit from biotechnology, biometrics, and biosurveillance. For example, today there are a host of capital formation initiatives directed toward expanding state and regional research and investment in the life sciences. These include research and development tax credits, net operating loss (NOL) carry-forwards, tax credit transferability, sales and use tax exemption, creation of capital access funds, state pension fund investment, capital gains tax reductions, investment tax credit, developing incubator/shared research and manufacturing facilities, and workforce development programs (BIO 2013).

In addition, changes in legislation governing life sciences research, particularly regarding technology transfer, and the blurring of industry and academia have led to a more competitive research environment focused on privatizing the intellectual efforts of life scientists and enhancing the commercial value of life sciences research. The state has made a deep investment in knowing who and what you are, who and what you were, who and what you will become, through predictive analytics, biometric surveillance, and dataveillance. That some biotechnology companies have become rich by helping the United States achieve this goal, even as individual entrepreneurs contribute to the GDP through their efforts, is not only a bonus, it is an incentive for these actors to remain involved and invested. As biotechnology profits wax and wane, however, and given the fact that so many start-up biotech firms fail, it is hard to conclude that the state's investment in biotechnology is simply or primarily about the industry's contribution to GDP. "Security" is as much at issue as health; indeed, the two seem to have become the same.

Finally, paranoia about rogue states with biological weapons of mass destruction, lone wolf terrorists, do-it-yourself biologists, as well as emerging pandemics and natural disasters, has served to increase direct funding for biological research and expand the web of institutions, investigators and actors invested in the study of molecular biology, genetic engineering, and living systems. This reconfigured web not only includes fields as disparate as agriculture, public health, criminal justice, human resources, transportation, information security, disaster studies, medicine, engineering, and urban planning, it also involves every citizen in the seemingly urgent projects of biosecurity, biodefense, and biological optimization. Barriers to this project are addressed through permissive policies that not only allow but promote surveillance (such as those revealed by Edward Snowden) and through program objectives that are obsessed with interoperability (such as those promoted by the Department of Homeland Security and embodied in their Fusion Centers). The end result is hybrid rule in which the public and the private are so thoroughly intertwined in the name of protecting national health and security that disentangling their relationships and identifying their specific roles seems increasingly impossible.

In this environment, it becomes more and more difficult to identify a responsible entity when the lines between institutions and actors are as blurred as they have become. As R. Alta Charo explains, "State laws vary, federal regulations do not apply to all privately funded research, and a patchwork of rules cover the myriad laboratories and biobanks in the United States" (2006: 1517–1519). Questions regarding accountability for the uses to which these commercialized inventions are put, or responsibility for the harmful consequences of hurriedly commercialized processes and products, are increasingly foreclosed. Further, it becomes increasingly difficult to question the myriad social and political uses to which our biology is put and for which it is extracted, studied and sold, when we are repeatedly told that these uses are for our own health and security.

In this chapter, I have argued that, in response to the criticism launched against the "Big" and small science projects of the 1950s and 1960s, the 1970s were characterized by the American state's eager partnership with a willing private sector, seeking to advance biotechnology and genetic engineering while obscuring its own role in the development and growth of this industry. During this period, as a result, the state gained legitimacy as a benevolent, caring peacekeeper even as the funding and protection provided to universities, medical research centers, and industry facilitated a new mechanism of political control over biological research, human bodies, and a burgeoning biotechnology industry. The 1980s and 1990s saw an increasing interest in the biosciences as molecular science replaced atomic science and biology replaced chemistry as primary national research focuses. This interest was obscured and strengthened by the focus on the commercial potential of biotechnology. In the 1990s, the hybrid relationships that were initiated around biotechnology in the 1970s were solidified, as courts actively protected scientific and industrial enterprise over the concerns of sick and vulnerable individuals, while growing biosecurity surveillance concerns colonized and reshaped disparate fields, institutions, and actors.

Hybrid rule challenges the optimistic assumption that we can resist the extensive reach of the state into our bodies, or that there is an outside to this reach. As institutional and individual bodies become hybridized, the reach of the state extends into every aspect of the human body and society under the guise of health, security, democracy and freedom of choice and in line with commercial purposes. The effects of hybridization are both depoliticizing and ontologically destabilizing. These effects are accompanied by a reduction rather than an expansion in embodied rights and choices as body parts are extracted and patented and vital systems are owned, banked, and manipulated.

To conclude, if we fail to attend to the social and political investments in molecular technologies going back to the 1930s, we risk being analytically hamstrung by an economic narrative about biotechnology that begins with the discovery of DNA and largely focuses on venture capital and industrial revolution. Further, as the causes of disease are increasingly sought at the genetic level, the social, economic and political determinants of health cease to be subjects for debate and research, leading "to the depoliticization of the etiology of disease" as apparently insoluble social causes of illness and early death are ignored (Kenney 1988: 17). In depoliticizing the etiology of disease, we also acquiesce to the re-politicization of life wherein global war is waged on biological danger in the name of human health and security.

Notes

1 Rose (2006) Will biomedicine transform society? The political, economic, social and personal impact of medical advances in the twenty-first century, *BIOS*

Working Papers No.1, BIOS, London School of Economics and Political Science, (www.lse.ac.uk/collections/BIOS/workingpapers/001.pdf).
2 Private organizations with eugenic leanings such as the Milbank Fund supported these endeavors on ideological grounds and contributed money toward the autopsies and burials of study participants (Washington 2006: 165).
3 The Tuskegee experiments led to Public Law 93–348 which established the National Commission for the Protection of Human Subjects of Biomedical and Behavioral Research. This Commission published recommendations in the 1979 Belmont Report that established federal recommendations for the protection of human subjects. The guiding principles of the Belmont Report are Beneficence, Respect, and Justice. These U.S.-based efforts were preceded by the creation of the Nurenberg Code of 1945 and the 1964 Declaration of Helsinki, both of which attempted to establish universally applicable ethical guidelines for biomedical research involving human subjects.
4 At the signing of the National Cancer Act, President Nixon described the investment of the government in making a "total national commitment" to the conquest of cancer. See www.presidency.ucsb.edu/ws/?pid=3275 for a copy of the transcript.
5 Moore v. Regents, www.kentlaw.edu/perritt/courses/property/moore-v-regents-excerpts2.htm.
6 Moore v. Regents, www.kentlaw.edu/perritt/courses/property/moore-v-regents-excerpts2.htm.
7 www.cdc.gov/globalhealth/security/pdf/ghs_us_commitment.pdf.
8 guardianlv.com/2014/global-health-security-obamas-initiative-is-the—tip-of-the-global-iceberg/.
9 www.cdc.gov/globalhealth/security/pdf/ghs_us_commitment.pdf.
10 www.cnn.com/2014/02/12/opinion/kerry-sebelius-health-security/.
11 www.whitehouse.gov/share/brain-initiative.
12 www.livescience.com/41413-momentum-builds-for-obama-s-brain-initiative.html.
13 www.nature.com/news/neurotechnology-brain-storm-1.14105; www.whitehouse.gov/share.

Part III
Reflections

10 Hybrid rule and state formation
Some preliminary thoughts, arguments and research items

Shelley L. Hurt and Ronnie D. Lipschutz

When we began this investigation five years ago, we did not envision that two of the biggest stories in the first months of 2014 would center on the Pulitzer Prize going to the intrepid reporters who broke the story about Edward Snowden, the National Security Agency (NSA) contractor or about Thomas Piketty's surprise best seller on wealth inequality, *Capital in the Twenty-First Century.* While these two stories might seem on the surface to be unrelated, we suggest that their common thread is a concern about the future of democracy. Indeed, both ground-breaking stories suggest that the relationship between the private sector and democracy has never been greater. These contemporary concerns in the popular media are also of major concern to scholars throughout the world, as the threats to democracy seem to multiply with every technological breakthrough and with the inexorable march of the private sector's seeming encroachment into the lives of citizens. While these causes point toward democracy's peril, this book suggests that a serious reconsideration of state power, particularly American state power, requires sustained and detailed analysis.

Hybrid Rule and State Formation has pursued three ambitious goals of resetting the clock anew to account for the rise of privatization (periodization), bringing politics back in through a re-examination of the state, and suggesting that the emergence of hybrid rule in the West represents a global shift toward convergence of a more politically authoritative form of economic capitalism in the 21st century that portends the diminution of democracy. In pursuing these three goals, we challenged the dominant explanatory framework of neoliberalism as the catchall for understanding the rise and consequences of privatization during the past thirty-plus years. While we acknowledged that our brief sketch of the copious scholarship on neoliberalism's explanation for the rise of privatization is beyond the scope of this project, we also recognized that important scholarship falls outside of this dominant narrative and argues that privatization has not enervated state power, authority or even autonomy (Hirst and Thompson 1999; Krasner 1999; Weiss 1998; Hibou 1999). For skeptics of the neoliberal explanatory framework, the economic sphere is not in command and never has been. But a clear view of neoliberalism as a *political* tactic and privatization policies as a means toward political ends has not been forthcoming in the scholarship to date. Hence, the empirical puzzle of fully explaining privatization remains unsolved, demanding further investigation into the discrepancy between theory and real-world evidence. We hope this book opens the floodgates for a new rigorous and thorough research agenda that spurs a lively debate into this important topic.

Hybrid rule as an inflection point of state formation

What does the emergence and solidification of *hybrid rule* mean for world politics in the 21st century? We submit that the implications involve a substantive diminution of democracy worldwide both in practice and as an ideal. In many respects, this phenomenon is already rearing its ugly head in many regions of the globe with the troubles experienced after the Arab Spring, the Asian retreat from liberal political reforms, Brazilian and Turkish protests, and the persistent stalemate of democracy in the European Union and the U.S. Congress. The combined socioeconomic forces of the Great Recession of 2008, draconian austerity policies, and the utter failure of political elites to confront middle-class decline is running up against the enduring voraciousness of global capitalism coupled with the militarization and securitization of physical, cyber, and genetic space like never before.

One of the concerns raised by these intertwined developments is that capitalism and the state no longer require democracy or liberal political forms to operate and prosper. Thus, disparate voices such as Slavoj Zizek and James Mann can arrive at similar conclusions when observing the disembedding of capitalism from any semblance of democratic accountability and control (Zizek 2009; Mann 2007). Both Zizek and Mann caution that authoritarian capitalism appears to be gaining steam unabated. For instance, Zizek asked upon the twentieth anniversary of communism's collapse in 2009, "what if this strain of authoritarian capitalism proves itself to be more efficient, more profitable, than our liberal capitalism? What if democracy is no longer the necessary and natural accompaniment of economic development, but its impediment?" (2009: A23). And Mann warned about China's demonstration "that a regime can suppress organized opposition and need not establish legitimacy through elections. It shows that a ruling party can maintain considerable control over information and the Internet without slowing economic growth. And it indicates that a nation's elite can be bought off" (2007: B01). These two lessons of the current historical era suggest that privatization in the form of *hybrid rule* will advance for the foreseeable future, most likely reshaping peoples' fundamental notions of the scope of politics.

The dangers posed by democracy's peril were recently analyzed in comparative detail in a 2013 German Marshal Fund report entitled, *The Democratic Disconnect: Citizenship and Accountability in the Transatlantic Community,* with leading authors such as Seyla Benhabib, Gunther Hellmann, and Richard Youngs, among others. The report asserts, "democracy is in trouble," and "the collective engagement of a concerned citizenry for the public good—the bedrock of a healthy democracy—is eroding."[1] With the world experiencing an evident decline in democratic support and practice, a growing "gap between citizens and those institutions at the national, regional, and transnational levels tasked to answer to the challenges of governance" is emerging to undermine "democratic legitimacy." While the authors lay considerable blame for democracy's decay on the economic forces behind globalization, they also highlight the enduring problem posed by "sovereigntists" and "power politics" on the world stage, which contributes to hyper militarization, skewed priorities, and cynicism. Even though these challenges appear sharpest through a contemporary lens, it remains important to historicize the decline of democracy and the rise of new state forms in an earlier epoch—the 1960s and 1970s—for the purposes of capturing the full panoply of causes.[2] More importantly, this global phenomenon suggests that the fragile democratic victories that emerged in the wake of the political battles of the 20th century are now in jeopardy from the changing 21st-century state.

Our goal in this study is less a focus on the specifics of political struggles— who fights with whom, what is the "correct" account of the state—than in the *what, how* and *why* of the more general phenomenon of *hybrid rule* as a political project, one that works through privatization, seeking pacification and depoliticization to enhance state power. We want, therefore, to "bring politics back in" in order to restore the role of power to its proper place in accounts of the state and government for illuminating the ways in which privatization shifts the apparent locus of decision making out of the public view and toward *hybrid rule*. We aim, therefore, to historicize and problematize *hybrid rule* as the latest manifestation of long-running political struggles to control state institutions so as to shape and manage social order. By bringing politics back in and drawing particular attention to new forms of political power, our research agenda seeks to understand and argue that *hybrid rule* is the manifestation of the *radicalization of politics from above*.

By *radicalization of politics from above* we mean to borrow from C. Wright Mill's observations of "the power elite" and Harold Lasswell's warnings of "the specialists of violence." In so doing, we want to theorize about agency and structure in fomenting change pre-emptively rather than reactively from the top down.[3] Hence, there are several elements of our analysis that must be considered in relation to this perspective. First, as noted above, *hybrid rule* tends to converge on a semi-authoritarian, minimally democratic system while retaining a robust capitalist system. These trade-offs are deemed necessary in protecting national security and the homeland. Contrary to the mistaken prognostications of Francis Fukuyama's *End of History* tale, we now know that the gravitational pull was away from liberal capitalism rather than toward it. The irony of President Obama's meeting in Sunnylands, CA in June 2013 with Xi Jinping, president of China, just as Edward Snowden of Booz Allen Hamilton took protective cover in Hong Kong while he alleged massive National Security Agency data collection and surveillance violations, was not lost on many observers. Both countries now rest on hybrid modalities with the boundaries between the public and private sectors having little distinct meaning. Who is accountable in this system of absent checks and balances? What does representative democracy mean in such a system? For most consumer-citizens, the politics of fear has induced compliant behavior as Americans' concern about terrorism, identity theft, and random crime (even though national crime statistics are at historic lows) prompt "proper" behaviors of individual conformity while exercising "good judgment" in the name of public safety.[4] In this way, a docile and obedient population is created, one that gladly cooperates and collaborates with the hybridized authorities that protect them.[5]

Significantly, this embrace of the private sector by the U.S. government to shield the operations of the national security state helps to facilitate the militarization of American and democratic societies.[6] Jon D. Michaels, Professor at UCLA, has pointed out the consequences for democratic accountability and oversight in light of the tremendous expansion of privatization policies in executing the War on Terror:

> To date, the Executive's apparent practice of identifying and then courting private actors, persuading, coaxing, and sometimes deceiving them to enter into "informal" intelligence-gathering partnerships that often are inscrutable to Congress and the courts, has gone largely unexamined by policymakers and scholars alike. These "handshake agreements," which spawned the now notorious National Security Agency (NSA) warrantless eavesdropping and call data programs, as well as a range of lesser-known collaborations with the likes of FedEx and Western Union, have enabled the Executive to operate outside of the congressionally imposed framework of court orders and subpoenas, and also outside of the ambit of inter-branch oversight. In the process, these informal collaborations may unduly threaten privacy rights, separation of powers, the rule of law, and the legitimacy and vitality of bypassed government institutions. In addition, these private-public partnerships may undermine the integrity of the marketplace and weaken consumer trust in key industries.
> (Michaels 2008: 904)

This thesis has been developed in more detail elsewhere (Lipschutz 2009) and in this volume (see Lipschutz chapter), but it rests on the state's growing, yet invisible, reach in two directions. First, the enhancement of surveillance and intelligence-gathering capabilities, along with the deployment of "danger-at-a-distance" technologies, such as armed drones, frequently takes place in collaboration with the private sector. Second, in order to identify, surveil and apprehend individuals whom the government fears might act against its security interests, the state is harnessing and penetrating myriad commercial enterprises, such as telecoms and banks. Therefore, the common definition of "national security" has been expanded to encompass virtually all walks of life with an accompanying increase in budget allocations and responsibilities.[7]

Pulitzer Prize-winning reporter, Dana Priest, and her colleague, William Arkin, of *The Washington Post* dub this development, *Top Secret America*, wherein hundreds of thousands of Americans are granted security clearances and tens of thousands of companies carry out the national security responsibilities that were once reserved, mostly, for the public sector.[8]

As Michaels suggests, social securitization is most easily accomplished through the electronic communications' infrastructures that became so integral to 21st-century capitalist life once information emerged as a major currency. We noted earlier that privatization increases secrecy by making information proprietary, and thus, not subject to public disclosure. At the same time, the state can use its power over notionally private networks to collect information about individual and group behaviors because it has been collected "privately." This innovative state capacity provides law enforcement officials and intelligence agencies with the ability to obtain information lawfully without violating the Privacy Act of 1974, among many other statutes. This runaround of privacy law protections that emerged in the wake of notorious abuses by the FBI, CIA, and local law enforcement agencies in the 1960s demonstrates a subversion of the democratic expansion that took place in the latter half of the 20th century. Furthermore, as James Risen, Pulitzer Prize-winning reporter from *The New York Times* recently noted in an appearance on *Meet the Press*:

> One of the things that really I think concerns people is that you've created something that never existed in American history before, and that is a surveillance state. The infrastructure that I'm basically using software technology and data mining and eavesdropping, very sophisticated technology to create an infrastructure that a police state would love. And that's what really should concern Americans, is because we haven't had a full national debate about the creation of a massive surveillance state and surveillance infrastructure, that if we had some radical change in our politics could lead to a police state.[9]

This palpable risk should not be underestimated. As Hannah Arendt noted in *The Origins of Totalitarianism*, democratic movements and politics can easily be subverted once governing authority transforms into an unrecognizable guise.

These risks emerge within an ostensibly apolitical context, which leads to the second aspect of *hybrid rule* representing an inflection point in state formation. This aspect deals with the rise of expert authority, which becomes more powerful once shrouded in layers of impenetrable secrecy. This lack of transparency represents a hallmark of *hybrid rule* due to the premise that the private sector commands more authority and respect within American society.[10] Without overstating the case, national political systems are characterized by an unwavering commitment to markets and capitalism, a focus on problem solving by experts, and suppression of political challenges that might undermine these arrangements. Thus, the state takes police actions, from the counter-globalization movement in 1999 to the draconian response to whistleblowers such as Thomas Drake and Edward Snowden, with the spectacle of President Barack Obama's Democratic administration charging and prosecuting more whistleblowers than all other previous administrations combined. Secrecy then represents a constitutive feature of *hybrid rule* assisting us with highlighting the national security rationale behind privatization. Historian Peter Galison has provocatively asserted that those who live in the unclassified universe are unknowingly subsumed within a classification system several times larger:

> Whether one figures by acquisition rate, by holding size, or by contributors, the classified universe is, as best I can estimate, on the order of five to ten times larger than the open literature that finds its way to our libraries. Our commonsense picture may well be far too sanguine, even inverted. The closed world is not a small strongbox in the corner of our collective house of codified and stored knowledge. It is we in the open world—we who study the world lodged in our libraries, from aardvarks to zymurgy, *we* who are living in a modest information booth facing outwards, our unseeing backs to a vast and classified empire we barely know.
> (Galison 2004: 231)

This classified empire becomes ever more distant from democratic accountability and control when it is buttressed with the private sector, whose disclosure laws are virtually non-existent in comparison to the public sector. Hints of this new reality sporadically emerge. For instance, General Michael Hayden, former National Security Agency Director, remarked at an Aspen Institute Security Forum on Cybersecurity in 2011 that private companies would be authorized to carry out activities in cyberspace that would be impossible in physical space.[11] Hayden referred to these new arrangements as "digital Blackwaters." Hence, the combination of technocratic expertise with systemic secrecy breeds a new apolitical reality at home and abroad.

The final inflection point of state formation for understanding *hybrid rule* is that it neither represents a purely American phenomenon nor is it limited to purely national contexts; it has become a fully globalized phenomenon propagated through various mechanisms and institutions of global influence and action, yet, fundamentally premised on the internationalization of the American state (Strange 1989: 161–176; Panitch 2000: 5–20). What is quite evident as the world enters the second decade of the 21st century is that *hybrid rule* is neither "privatization of authority" or a "new medievalism" but, rather, an institutional development whose effect is the re-centering of power and authority in "the state," one in which the United States is central—even as it is possibly in relative decline—but which many other countries are participants.[12] That this process is neither smooth nor even should come as no surprise; there has never been a clearly defined plan or strategy leading to the emergence of *hybrid rule*. Rather, its emergence has followed from various tactics, policies and experiments whose objective is social and political pacification, whose purpose is the restoration of legitimacy and prevention of new shocks to the system, and whose means is a mix of sovereignty and discipline. Lasswell presciently captured these fraught dynamics when writing almost seventy years ago:

> With the socialization of danger as a permanent characteristic of modern violence the nation becomes one unified technical enterprise. Those who direct violence operations are compelled to consider the entire gamut of problems that arise in living together under modern conditions.
> (Lasswell 1941: 459)

We note that the language of risk and danger as well as the extension of "security" to the practices of everyday life only serve to further militarize "the entire gamut of problems that arise in living together under modern conditions." Not surprisingly, since 2001, *hybrid rule* has become globalized as the American state globalizes its authority in international institutions and laws while delegating authority to myriad intermediaries through outright conquest or more subtle levels of domination and control. This process has given rise to new social relations between citizens and the state, public and private, and local and global.

To what and where does *hybrid rule* lead? Or, to put the question another way: What is the future of political power? Notwithstanding some forty years of privatization and hybridization, the legitimacy crisis of the 1960s has not been resolved and political authority continues to be challenged. In the United States and elsewhere, the external challenge was framed as "terrorism," while internal challenges come from left, right, and "home-grown extremists." The response has been a growing militarization of everyday life, featuring the longest wars on record, military spending at an all-time high, citizens designated as enemy combatants, surveillance more intrusive than ever, and a gradual merging of civilian police and armed forces. These collective developments normalize the expansion of government power even while its extended reach becomes harder to detect, in what Mary Dudziak refers to as the new permanency of exceptional politics in "wartime" (2012). Surprisingly, there have been no protests or social movements to challenge these developments. Legitimacy has come to rest on protection against threats and pacification, which has worked impressively as intended in the United States, but less so in Greece, Spain, Egypt, Turkey, Brazil, Argentina and Thailand). All of these examples point toward expanding state efforts to control and shape flows of power for decades to come.

Notes

1 www.gmfus.org/wp-content/blogs.dir/1/files_mf/1366057825TA20123report_May13_complete_web.pdf.

2 Among the myriad causal claims made about these developments, Ian Bremmer, in one among many for instances, argues that "state capitalism began to take shape during the 1973 oil crisis." See Bremmer (2009: 40–55). For a fuller treatment of his argument, see Bremmer (2010). For a much more critical appraisal of similar phenomenon, please see Callinicos (2009: 533–549); Wolin (2010).
3 American Political Development scholars have made major contributions to this line of research in challenging the so-called "bottom up stories" that remain so prevalent in American political history narratives today. For a couple of excellent examples, please see Dudziak (2000); Skowronek (1997); Katznelson (2013).
4 As in Oceania, that which is not explicitly forbidden may, nonetheless, be grounds for arrest, imprisonment, torture and even execution. The end goal is to "love Big Brother," that is, to do nothing of which Big Brother might disapprove. Even more than George Orwell's *1984* parable, Philip K. Dick's sci-fi thriller, *The Minority Report*, seems more fitting today.
5 Indeed, the *Washington Post* and *Pew Center Research* poll, in the wake of Edward Snowden's NSA revelations, surprisingly showed that a majority of Americans wanted the U.S. government to increase data gathering and surveillance even if it meant more reductions in basic liberties. Please see www.washintonpost.com/page/2010-2019/WashingtonPost/2013/06/10/National-Politics/Polling/release_242_xml.
6 We should note here that our reference to militarization does not capture a particular irony, since the military in American society is supposed to be subject to civilian control. A genuine question arises when thinking about a military or paramilitary force that is neither subject to an elected civilian leadership nor to a traditional chain of command. Where does the source of authority for action and judgment arise then?
7 In several respects, these developments harken back to the early days of the Cold War, when McCarthyism and rabid anti-communist hysteria reigned supreme. Louis Hartz noted the dark side of liberalism during wartime as well as many contemporary observers of the Cold War on distorting domestic political culture. For a few notable examples, see Sherry (1997); Grossman (2001); Sparrow (1996).
8 Priest and Arkin provide a wealth of data on the scope of this burgeoning national security state. See Priest and Arkin (2011).
9 See transcript of *Meet the Press* on June 14, 2013 at: www.nbcnews.com/id/52220609/ns/meet_the_press-transcripts/t/june-lindsey-graham-samby-chambliss-mark-udall-bobby-scott-david-ignatius-james-risen-andrea-mitchell/#.UcdjYeDReJU.
In a major development after Risen's television appearance, the United States Court of Appeals for the Fourth Circuit in Richmond, VA, Risen was ordered to testify in a leak investigation. According to Charles Savage of the *New York Times*, the court argued, "The First Amendment does not protect reporters who received unauthorized leaks from being forced to testify against the people suspected of leaking to them." Please see Savage (2013: A1).
10 Even the recent controversy over Kenneth Rogoff and Carmen Reinhart's now notorious article on budget deficits and economic growth demonstrates the authority that experts command in the current economy. Nevertheless, the more important examples are those experts that serve the vast national security state with hundreds of thousands now granted with top-secret security clearances. See Priest and Arkin (2011).
11 The entire presentation is available on *YouTube* at: www.youtube.com/watch?v=yoWkAVXmSsO&feature=youtu.be.
12 For selective representations of this vast literature, please see, respectively, Hall and Biersteker (2003) and Cerny (2010).

Bibliography

Aas, Katja Frank (2006) "'The body does not lie': Identity, risk, and trust in technoculture," *Crime Media Culture*, 2(2): 143–158.
Abbott, Andrew (1995) "Things of boundaries: Defining the boundaries of social inquiry," *Social Research*, 62(4): 857–882.
Abrahamsen, R. and Michael C. Williams (2007) "Selling security: Assessing the impact of military privatization" (book review essay), *Review of International Political Economy*, 15: 131–146.
Abrahamsen, Rita and Michael C. Williams (2010) *Security Beyond the State: Private Security in International Politics*, New York: Cambridge University Press.
Ackerman, Spencer (2013) "NSA illegally collected thousands of emails before FISA court halted program," *The Guardian*, August 21, at: www.theguardian.com/world/2013/aug/21/nsa-illegally-collected-thousands-emails-court.
Adams, James (1998) *The Next World War: Computers are Weapons and the Front Line Is Everywhere*, New York: Simon & Schuster.
Adams, Julia and Mounira M. Charrad (eds) (2011) *Patrimonial Power in the Modern World*, New York: Sage Publications,
Agier, Michel (2008) *Gérer les indésirables. Des camps de réfugiés au gouvernement humanitaire*, Paris: Flammarion.
Aglietta, Michel (1979; re-edited 2000) *A Theory of Capitalist Regulation: The US Experience*, London: Verso.
Aglietta, M. (2000) *Ein neues Akkumulationsregime: Die Regulationstheorie auf dem Prüfstand*, Hamburg: VSA.
Albrecht, U. (2000) "The changing global composition of armed forces and military technology: The trend towards informalization," in M. Kaldor (ed.) *Global Insecurity*, London: Pinter, pp. 120–146.
Allison, Graham (1971) *Essence of Decision: Explaining the Cuban Missile Crisis*, Boston, MA: Little, Brown.
Amsden, Alice H. (1989) *Asia's Next Giant: South Korea and Late Industrialization*, New York: Oxford University Press.
Amsden, Alice H. (2001) *The Rise of the Rest*, New York: Oxford University Press.
Anderson, Curt (2008) "Mistrial in 'Liberty City' terror case," *San Francisco Chronicle*, April 17, online at: http://articles.sfgate.com/2008-04-17/news/17147416_1_m istrial-elie-assad-defense-lawyers.
Anderson, Perry (1974) *Lineages of the Absolutist State*, London: New Left Books.

Bibliography

Andreas, Peter and Thomas J. Biersteker (2003) *The Rebordering of North America: Integration and Exclusion in a New Security Context*, New York: Routledge.

Andrews, Lori and Dorothy Nelkin (2001) *Body Bazaar: The Market for Human Tissue in the BiotechnologyAge*, New York: Crown Publishers.

Andrews, L. and D. Nelkin (1998) "Whose body is it anyway? Disputes over body tissue in a biotechnology age," *The Lancet*, 351 (Jan.): 53–54.

Angell, Marcia (1997) "The ethics of clinical research in the third world," *New England Journal of Medicine*, 337(12): 847–849.

Angwin, Julia (2014) *Dragnet Nation: A Quest for Privacy, Security and Freedom in a World of Relentless Surveillance*, New York: Times Books.

Appadurai, Arjun (1996) *Modernity at Large*, Minneapolis, MI: University of Minnesota Press.

Appel, Toby A. (2000) *Shaping Biology: The National Science Foundation and American Biological Research, 1945–1975*, Baltimore, MD: Johns Hopkins University Press, p. 269.

Arango, Carlos Revillo (1968) "Insurgent counterintelligence," *Studies in Intelligence*, 12(1): 39–53.

Aronowitz, Stanley and Peter Bratsis (eds) (2002) *Paradigm Lost: State Theory Reconsidered*, St. Paul, MN: University of Minnesota Press.

Arrow, Kenneth (1996) "The economics of information: An exposition," *Empirica*, 23(2): 119–128

Atkinson, Richard C. and William A. Blanpied (2008) "Research Universities: Core of the U.S. Science and Technology System," University of California Berkeley, Center for Studies in Higher Education Research and Occasional Paper Series.

Atzmuller, R., J. Becker, U. Brand, L. Oberndorfer, V. Redak and T. Sablowski (eds) (2013) *Fit fur die Krise? Perspektiven der Regulationstheorie*, Münster: Westfälisches Dampfboot.

Avant, Deborah and Lee Siegelman (2012) "Private security and democracy: Lessons from the US in Iraq," *Security Studies*, 19(2): 230–265.

Bamford, James (2009). "Who's in Big Brother's database?" *The New York Review of Books*, Nov. 5, online at: www.nybooks.com/articles/archives/2009/nov/05/whos-in-big-brothers-database/.

Banégas, Richard (1998) "De la guerre au maintien de la paix: Le nouveau business mercenaire," *Critique internationale*, 1 (Oct.): 179–194.

Barfield, Thomas J. (1989) *The Perilous Frontier: Nomadic Empires and China, 221 BC to AD 1757*, Cambridge, MA: Blackwell.

Barrett, Michèle (1985) "Introduction," in F. Engels ([1884]) *The Origin of the Family, Private Property and the State*, Harmondsworth: Penguin, pp. 1–30.

Barry, Andrew, Thomas Osborne and Nikolas Rose (eds) (1996) *Foucault and Political Reason: Liberalism, Neoliberalism and Rationalities of Government*, Chicago, IL: The University of Chicago Press.

Bartley, Tim (2010) "Certification as a Mode of Social Regulation," Jerusalem Papers in Regulation and Governance, Working Paper no. 8.

Bauman, Zygmunt (1992) *Intimations of Postmodernity*, London: Routledge.

Bauman, Z. (1991) *Modernity and the Holocaust*, Cambridge: Polity Press, pp. 100–102.

Beck, Ulrich, Anthony Giddens and Scott Lash (1994) *Reflexive Modernization: Politics, Tradition and Aesthetics in the Modern Social Order*, Palo Alto, CA: Stanford University.

Bell, Daniel (1976) *The Coming of Post-Industrial Society, A Venture in Social Forecasting*, New York: Basic Books, p. 385.
Belorgey, Nicolas (2010) *L'Hôpital sous pression: Enquête sur le 'nouveau management public,'* Paris: La Découverte.
Benamouzig, D. and J. Besançon (2005) "Administrer un monde incertain: Les nouvelles bureaucraties techniques: Le cas des agences sanitaires en France," *Sociologie du travail*, 47(3): 301 and 308.
Berkovitch, Nitza and Adriana Kemp (2012) "Between social movement organizations and social movement corporations: The commercialization of the global project of economic empowerment of women," in D. Bergoffen, P. R. Gilbert, T. Harvey and C. L. McNeely (eds) *Confronting Global Gender Justice. Women's Lives, Human Rights*, London: Routledge.
Bezes, Philippe (2007) "Construire des bureaucraties wébériennes à l'ère du New Public Management," *Critique internationale*, 35 (Feb.): 9–29.
Bezes, P. (2009) *Réinventer l'Etat. Les réformes de l'administration française (1962–2008)*, Paris: PUF.
Biagioli, Mario (2006) "Documents of documents: Scientists' names and scientific claims," in A. Riles (ed.) *Documents*, Ann Arbor, MI: University of Michigan Press, pp. 127–157.
Bierschenk, Thomas, Jean-Pierre Chauveau and Olivier de Sardan (2000) *Courtiers en développement: Les villages africains en quête de projet*, Paris: Karthala.
BIO (2013) Biotechnology Industry Organization, "Bioscience economic development: Legislative priorities, best practices, and return on investment," online at: www.bio.org/sites/default/files/State-Leg-Best-Practices_0.pdf.
Block, Fred (2008) "Swimming against the current: The rise of a hidden developmental state in the United States," *Politics & Society*, 36(2): 169–206.
Block, Fred and Matthew Keller (eds) (2011) *State of Innovation: The U.S. Government's Role in Technology Development*, Boulder, CO: Paradigm Publishers, pp. 31–56.
Blum, Alain and Martine Mespoulet (2003) *L'anarchie bureaucratique. Statistique et pouvoir sous Staline*, Paris: La Découverte.
Boltanski, Luc and Eve Chiapello (2012; tr. from French, 1999) *The New Spirit of Capitalism*, London: Verso.
Bondi, Liz and Nina Laurie (eds) (2005) *Working Spaces of Neoliberalism: Activism, Professionalisation and Incorporation*, Oxford: Blackwell.
Bonelli, Laurent (2010) "Quand les consultants se saisissent de la sécurité urbaine," *Savoir/agir*, 9 (Sept.): 12–28.
Bono, Irene (ed.) (2010a) *In nome della società civile: Un caso di sviluppo participato in Marocco*, Milan: Guerini.
Bono, Irene (ed.) (2010b) "Activisme associatif comme marché du travail à El Hajeb: Normalisation sociale et politique par les 'activités génératrices de revenus'", *Politique africaine*, 120 (Dec.): 25–44.
Boot, M. (2009) "The mercenary debate," *The American Interest*, May/June, online at: www.the-american-interest.com/article-bd.cfm?piece=597.
Borstelmann, Thomas (2013) *The 1970s: A New Global History from Civil Rights to Economic Inequality*, Princeton, NJ: Princeton University Press.
Bortolotti, Bernardo and Enrico Perotti (2007) "From government to regulatory governance: Privatization and the residual role of the state," *The World Bank Research Observer*, 22(1): 53–66.

Bortolotti, Bernardo and Valentina Milella (2007) "Privatization in Western Europe: Stylized facts, outcomes, and open issues," Fondazione Eni Enrico Mattei Working Paper no. 106: Table 1, online at: www.bepress.com/feem/paper106.

Bourdieu, Pierre (1994) *Raisons pratiques: Sur la théorie de l'action*, Paris: Seuil.

Bourdieu, P. (1999) "Rethinking the state: Genesis and structure of the bureaucratic field," in G. Steinmetz (ed.) *State/Culture: State-formation after the Cultural Turn*, Ithaca, NY: Cornell University Press.

Bourdieu, P. (2005) *The Social Structures of the Economy*, Cambridge: Polity Press.

Bovaird, Tony (2004) "Public–private partnerships: From contested concepts to prevalent practice," *International Review of Administrative Sciences*, 70(2): 199–215.

Boyer, Robert (2000) "Is a finance-led growth regime a viable alternative to Fordism? A preliminary analysis," *Economy & Society*, 29(1): 111–145.

Braithwaite, John (2005) "Neoliberalism or Regulatory Capitalism," RegNet Occasional Paper no. 5, Regulatory Institutions Network, Canberra: Australian National University.

Brand, Ulrich (2009) "The internationalized state and its functions and modes in the lobal governance of biodiversity," in Gabriela Kütting and Ronnie D. Lipschutz (eds) *Power, Knowledge and Governance in International Environmental Policy*, London: Routledge, pp. 100–123.

Brand, U. (2013) "State, context and correspondence: Contours of a historical-materialist policy analysis," *Österreichische Zeitschrift für Politikwissenschaft*, 42(4): 425–442

Brand, U. and C. Görg (2008) "Post-Fordist governance of nature: The internationalization of the state and the case of genetic resources—a neo-Poulantzian perspective," *Review of International Political Economy*, 15(4): 567–589

Brand, U., C. Görg, J. Hirsch and M. Wissen (2008) *Conflicts in Environmental Regulation and the Internationalisation of the State: Contested Terrains*, London: Edward Elgar.

Brand, U., C. Görg and M. Wissen (2011) "Second-order condensations of societal power relations," *Antipode*, 43(1): 149–175.

Brand, U. and M. Wissen (2013) "Crisis and continuity of capitalist society–nature relationships: The imperial mode of living and the limits to environmental governance," *Review of International Political Economy*, 20(4): 687–711.

Brand, U. and M. Wissen. (2012) "Global environmental politics and the imperial mode of living: Articulations of state–capital relations in the multiple crisis," *Globalizations*, 9(4): 327–345.

Brand, U. and N. Sekler (eds) (2009) *Postneoliberalism: A Beginning Debate*, Development Dialogue no. 51, Uppsala: Dag-Hammarskjöld-Foundation.

Brandt, Allen M. (1978) "Racism and research: The case of the Tuskegee syphilis study," *Hastings Center Magazine*, December, online at: www.med.navy.mil/bumed/Documents/Healthcare%20Ethics/Racism-And-Research.pdf.

Braudel, Fernand (1974) *Capitalism and material life, 1400–1800*, tr. by Miriam Kochan, London: Fontana.

Braun, Bruce (2007) "Biopolitics and the molecularization of life," *Cultural Geographies*, 14(1): 6–28.

Braun, Stephen (2014) "US network to scan workers with secret clearances," *San Francisco Chronicle*, March 11, online at: www.sfchronicle.com/business/technolo gy/article/US-network-to-scan-workers-with-secret-clearances-5302646.php.

Bremmer, Ian (2010) *The End of the Free Market: Who Wins the War between States and Corporations?*, New York: Portfolio Hardcover.

Bremmer, I. (2009) "State capitalism comes of age," *Foreign Affairs*, 88(3): 44–55.
Brenner, Neil, Jamie Peck and Nik Theodore (2010) "After neoliberalization?" *Globalisation*, 7(3): 327–345.
Brenner, Robert (2003) *The Boom and the Bubble: The US in the World Economy*, New York and London: Verso.
Brie, Michael (2009) "Ways out of the crisis of neoliberalism," *Development Dialogue*, 51: 15–31.
Brooks, Doug (2004) "The challenges of African peacekeeping," Testimony to the House Committee on International Relations, Subcommittee on Africa, online at: www.internationalrelations.house.gov/archives/108/bro100804.htm.
Brooks, D. (2007) "The IPOA perspective on regulation," in Latin America and Caribbean Regional Consultation on the Effects of the Activities of Private Military and Security Companies on the Enjoyment of Human Rights: Regulation and Oversight, The UN Working Group on the use of Mercenaries/Special Procedures assumed by the Office of the High Commissioner on Human Rights, Panama City, 17–18 December.
Brooks, D. (2000) "Messiahs or mercenaries? The future of international private military services," *International Peacekeeping*, 7(4): 129–144.
Brooks, D. (2000) "Write a cheque, end a war: Using private military companies to end African conflicts," *Conflict Trends*, 1 (June): 33–35.
Bruno, Isabelle (2008) *A vos marques, prêts... cherchez! La stratégie européenne de Lisbonne, vers un marché de la recherché*, Paris: Éditions du Croquant.
Brunsson, Nils and Bengt Jacobsson, et al. (2002) *A World of Standards*, Oxford: Oxford University Press.
Brütsch, Christian and Dirk Lehmkulh (2007) "Complex legalization and the many moves to law," in C. Brütsch and D. Lehmkulh (eds) *Law and Legalization in Transnational Relations*, London: Routledge, pp. 9–32.
Brutzkus, Julius (1944) "The Khazar origin of ancient Kiev," *Slavonic And East European Review*. American Series, 3(1): 108–124.
Buckel, Sonja (2011) "The juridical condensation of the relations of forces: Nicos Poulantzas and the law," in Alexander Gallas, Lars Bretthauer, John Kannankulam and Ingo Stüzle (eds) *Reading Poulantzas*, London: Merlin Press, pp. 154–169.
Bugra, Ayse (2007) "Poverty and citizenship: an overview of the social-policy movement in republican Turkey," *International Journal of Middle East Studies*, 39(1): 33–52.
Bugra, Ayse and Kaan Agartan (2007) *Reading Karl Polanyi for the Twenty-First Century: Market Economy as a Political Project*, New York: Palgrave Macmillan.
Burchell, Graham, Colin Gordon and Peter Miller (eds) (1991) *The Foucault Effect: Studies in Governmentality*, Hemel Hempstead: Harvester-Wheatsheaf.
Burchett, Wilfred G. and Derek Roebuck (1977) *The Whores of War: Mercenaries Today*, London: Pelican/Penguin Books.
Burgess, P. (ed.) *Handbook of New Security Studies*, London and New York: Routledge.
Burnham, James (1941) *The Managerial Revolution; What is Happening in the World*, New York: John Day.
Burnham, Walter Dean (1975) "Crisis of American political legitimacy," reprinted in Helen Icken Safa and Gloria Levitas (eds) *Social Problems in Corporate America*, New York: Harper & Row, p. 501.
Bush, George W. (2004) "Executive Order 13328—Commission on the Intelligence Capabilities of the United States Regarding Weapons of Mass Destruction," *The*

American Presidency Project (Gerhard Peters and John T. Woolley), February 6, online at: www.presidency.ucsb.edu/ws/?pid=61423.
Buzan, Barry (1991) *People, States and Fear*, Boulder, CO: Rienner.
Calaguas, Mark J. (2006) "Military privatization: Efficiency or anarchy?" *Chicago-Kent Journal of International and Comparative Law*, 6 (Spring): 58–81.
Callinicos, Alex (2009) "Does capitalism need the state system?" *Cambridge Review of International Affairs*, 11 (Dec.): 533–549.
Callon, Michel, Pierre Lascoumes, and Yannick Barthes (2009) *Acting in an Uncertain World: An Essay on Technical Democracy*, tr. by G. Burchell, Cambridge, MA and London: MIT.
Callon, M. (ed.) (1998) *The Laws of the Market*, Oxford: Blackwell.
Candeias, Mario (2011) "Passive evolutions vs. socialist transformation," background paper for the Commons-Conference in Rome, 28/29 April, Rosa Luxemburg Foundation, Brussels.
Castoriadis, Cornelius (1990) *La société bureaucratique*, new edition of texts written for the review *Socialisme ou Barbarisme*, 1949–65, Paris: Christian Bourgois.
Castree, Noel (2008) "Neoliberalising nature: the logics of deregulation and reregulation," *Environment and Planning A*, 40(2): 131–152.
Central Intelligence Agency (2003) "The darker bioweapons future," November 3, online at: www.fas.org/irp/cia/product/bw1103.pdf.
Cerny, Philip G. (2010) *Rethinking World Politics: A Theory of Transnational Neopluralism*, New York: Oxford University Press.
Chandler, Alfred D. (1977) *The Visible Hand: Managerial Revolution in American Business*, Cambridge, MA: Belknap Press (Harvard University Press).
Charo, R. Alta (2006) "Body of research: Ownership and use of human tissue," *New England Journal of Medicine*, 355(15): 1517–1519.
Chaudhry, Kiren Aziz (1993) "Myths of the market and the common history of late developers," *Politics and Society*, 21(3): 245–274.
Chisholm, Amanda (2013) "Ghurkas in private military and security companies," *International Feminist Journal of Politics*, 16(1): 26–47.
Chorus, Silke (2012) *Care-Ökonomie im Postfordismus*, Münster: Westfälisches Dampfboot.
Christensen, Tom and Per Laegreid (eds) (2006) *Autonomy and Regulation. Coping with Agencies in the Modern State*, Cheltenham: Edward Elgar.
Claessen, Henri J. M. and Petr Skálnik (eds) (1978) *The Early State*, Den Haag: Mouton.
Claessen, Henri J. M. and Pieter van der Velde (eds) (1987) *Early State Dynamics*, Leiden: Brill.
Clark, Gordon (2009) "Temptation and the virtues of long-term commitment: The governance of sovereign wealth fund investment," *Social Science Research Network*, February 25, online at: http://papers.ssrn.com/sol3/papers.cfm?abstract_id=1349123.
Clinton, William J. (1994) "Executive Order 12938—Proliferation of Weapons of Mass Destruction," November 14, *The American Presidency Project* (Gerhard Peters and John T. Woolley), online at: www.presidency.ucsb.edu/ws/?pid=49489.
Clymer, Adam (2002) "Worker corps to be formed to report odd activity," *New York Times*, July 26, online at: www.nytimes.com/2002/07/26/us/traces-terror-security-liberty-worker-corps-be-formed-report-odd-activity.html.
Cochoy, Franck (2007) "La responsabilité sociale de l'entreprise comme 'représentation' de l'économie et du droit,' *Droit et société*, 65: 91–101.

Cockayne, James (2006) "Commercial security in the humanitarian space," New York: International Peace Academy.
Cohen, Abner (1969) *Custom and Politics in Urban Africa: A Study of Hausa Migrants in Yoruba Towns*, London: Routledge & Kegan Paul.
Coker, Christopher (1999) "Outsourcing war," *Cambridge Review of International Affairs*, 13(1): 95–113.
Collins, Francis S. and Victor A. McKusick (2001) "Implications of the Human Genome Project for medical science," *JAMA*, 285(5): 540–544, online at: http://jama.jamanetwork.com/article.aspx?articleid=193524#REF-JSC00413-9.
Collins, Randall (1999) *Macrohistory: Essays in Sociology of the Long Term*, Stanford, CA: Stanford University Press.
Connolly, William (ed.) (1984) *Legitimacy and the State*, New York: New York University.
Cooley, Alexander (2005) *Logics of Hierarchy: The Organization of Empires, States, and Nations in Transit*, Ithaca, NY: Cornell University Press.
Cooper, Melinda (2008) *Biotechnology and Capitalism in the Neoliberal Era*, Seattle: University of Washington Press.
Cowie, Jefferson R. (2012) *Stayin' Alive: The 1970s and the Last Days of the Working Class*, New York: New Press.
Cox, Robert W. (1993) "Gramsci, hegemony, and international relations: An essay in method," in S. Gill (ed.) *Gramsci, Historical Materialism and International Relations*, New York: Cambridge University Press, pp. 49–66.
Cox, Robert W. (1981) "Social forces, states and world orders: Beyond international relations theory," *Millennium: Journal of International Studies*, 10(2): 126–155.
Cox, Robert W. (1986) "Social Forces, States and World Orders: Beyond International Relations Theory," in R. O. Keohane (ed.) *Neorealism and its Critics*, New York: Columbia University Press, pp. 204–254.
Crouch, Colin (2011) *The Strange Non-Death of Neoliberalism*, Malden, MA and Cambridge: Polity Press.
Crozier, Michael J., Samuel P. Huntington and Joji Watanuki (1973) *The Crisis of Democracy: Report on the Governability of Democracies to the Trilateral Commission*, New York: New York University Press.
Culliton, Barbara J. (1977) "Harvard and Monsanto: The $23-million alliance," *Science*, 195(4280): 759–763.
Cutler, C. A. (2003) *Private Power and Global Authority: Transnational Merchant Law in the Global Political Economy*, Cambridge: Cambridge University Press.
Daalder, Ivo H. and I. M. Destler (moderators) (2000) *Arms Control Policy and the National Security State*, Oral History Roundtable, The National Security Council Project, Center for International Security Studies at Maryland, School of Public Affairs, University of Maryland and the Brookings Institution, Washington, DC, March 23: 9.
Dardot, Pierre and Christian Laval (2014; first published in French, 2009) *The New Way of the World: On Neoliberal Society*, London: Verso.
Davies, Margaret (2007) *Property: Meanings, Histories, Theories*, Abingdon: Routledge-Cavendish.
Davies, Margaret and Ngaire Naffine (2001) *Are Persons Property? Legal Debates about Property and Personality*, Aldershot: Ashgate/Dartmouth.
de Certeau, Michel (1984) *The Practice of Everyday Life*, tr. by Steven Randall, Berkeley, CA: University of California Press.

Bibliography

Deleuze, Gilles and Felix Guattari (1987) *A Thousand Plateaus*, Minneapolis, MN: University of Minnesota Press.

Demirović, Alex (1997) *Demokratie und Herrschaft: Aspekte kritischer Gesellschafstheorie*, Münster: Westfälisches Dampfboot.

Demirović, A. (2011) "Materialist state theory and the transnationalization of the capitalist state," *Antipode*, 43(1): 38–59.

Demirović, A., J. Dück, F. Becker and P. Bader (2011) *VielfachKrise im finantzmarktdominierten Kapitalismus*, Hamburg: VSA.

Demirović, A. and N. Poulantzas (2007) *Akualität und Probleme materialisticher*, Münster: Staatsheorie, pp. 226–240.

Demirović, A. and T. Sablowski (2013) *The Finance-dominated Regime of Accumulation and the Crisis in Europe*, Berlin: Rosa Luxemburg Foundation.

Demortain, David (2009) "Rendre transférable plutôt que diffuser: Les experts scientifiques et l'histoire de la norme alimentaire HACCP," in Yves Schemeil and Wolf-Dieter Eberwein, *Normer le monde*, Paris: L'Harmattan, pp. 131–151.

Der Derian, James (1987) "Mediating estrangement: A theory for diplomacy," *Review of International Studies*, 13(2): 91–110.

Derthick, Martha and Paul J. Quirk (1985) *The Politics of Deregulation*, Washington, DC: Brookings Institution.

Destremau, Blandine (2009) *Globalisation de l'intervention sociale, reconfiguration des solidarités*, habilitation thesis, Université Paris I Panthéon-Sorbonne.

de Vries, Michiel S. (2000) "The bureaucratization of participation," *International Review of Administrative Science*, 66(2): 325–342.

Dickson, David and David Noble (1981) "By force of reason: The politics of science and technology policy," in Thomas Ferguson and Joel Rogers (eds) *The Hidden Election: Politics and Economics in the 1980 Presidential Campaign*, New York: Pantheon Books, p. 267.

Diwan, Kirsten (2009) "Sovereign dilemmas: Saudi Arabia and sovereign wealth funds," *Geopolitics*, 14(2): 345–359.

Dombrowski, Peter (ed.) (2005) *Guns and Butter: The Political Economy of International Security*, Boulder, CO and London: Lynne Rienner.

Donnelly, Sally B. (2006) "A new tack for airport screening: Behave yourself," *Time*, May 17, online at: www.time.com/time/nation/article/0,8599,1195330,00.html.

Dorn, Nicholas and Michael Levi (2009) "Private–Public or Public–Private? Strategic dialogue on serious crime and terrorism in the EU," *Security Journal*, 22(4): 302–316.

Dörre, K. and B. Röttger (eds) (2003) *Das neue Marktregime*, Hamburg: VSA.

Drahos, Peter with John Braithwaite (2002) *Information Feudalism: Who Owns the Knowledge Economy*, London: Earthscan.

Drew, S. Nelson (ed.) (1994) *NSC-68: Forging the Strategy of Containment (with Analyses by Paul H. Nitze)*, Washington, DC: National Defense University.

Drucker, Peter (1969) "The sickness of government," *Public Interest*, 14 (Winter): 7.

DuBridge, Lee A. (1980) "Science advice to the president: Important and difficult," in William T. Golden (ed.) *Science Advice to the President*, New York: Pergamon Press, p. 70.

Dudouet, F. X., D. Mercier and A. Vion (2006) 'Politiques internationales de normalisation," *Revue française de science politique*, 56(3): 367–392.

Dudziak, Mary L. (2000) *Cold War Civil Rights: Race and the Image of American Democracy*, Princeton, NJ: Princeton University Press.

Dudziak, Mary L. (2012) *Wartime: An Idea, Its History, Its Consequences*, New York: Oxford University Press.
Duggan, Lisa (2004) *The Twilight of Equality? Neoliberalism, Cultural Politics, and the Attack on Democracy*, Boston, MA: Beacon Press.
Duhigg, Charles (2009) "What does your credit-card company know about you?" *New York Times Magazine*, May 17, online at: www.nytimes.com/2009/05/17/magazine/17credit-t.html.
Duhigg, C. (2012) *The Power of Habit: Why We do What We do in Life and Business*, New York: Random House.
Dunn, Elizabeth C. (2005) "Standards and person-making in East Central Europe," in Aihwa Ong and Stephen J. Collier (eds) *Global Assemblages: Technology, Politics and Ethics as Anthropological Problems*, Oxford: Blackwell, pp. 173–193.
Dupont, Benoit (2005) "Technologie, défense nationale et sécurité intérieure: un ménage à trois dysfonctionnel," in F. Lemieux and B. Dupont (eds) *La militarisation des appareils policiers*, Quebec: Les presses de l'Université de Laval.
Durkheim, Émile (1992) *Professional Ethics and Civic Morals*, London, Routledge.
Earle, Timothy K. (1997) *How Chiefs Come to Power: The Political Economy in Pre-History*, Stanford, CA: Stanford University Press.
Economist (1999) "The mystery of the world's second-richest businessman: Prince Alwaleed is the modern face of Saudi royalty, but his sums don't add up," February 25.
Edmonds, Martin (1998) "Defense privatisation: From state enterprise to commercialism," *Cambridge Review of International Affairs*, 13(1): 114–129.
Egil, Francois (2005) "Les éléphants de papier: Réflexions impies pour le cinquième anniversaire des Objectifs de développement du millénaire," *Politique africaine*, 99 (October): 97–115.
Eisenhower, Dwight D. (1961) "Eisenhower's Farewell Address to the Nation," online at: http://mcadams.posc.mu.edu/ike.htm.
Elliot, Lorraine and Graeme Cheesman (2002) "Cosmopolitan theory, militaries and the deployment of force," *Department of International Relations Working Paper 2002/8*, Canberra: Australian National University, p. 55.
Elyachar, Julia (2005) *Markets of Dispossession. NGOs, Economic Development, and the State in Cairo*, London: Duke University Press.
Engels, Friedrich ([1884] 1985) *The Origin of the Family, Private Property and the State*, Harmondsworth: Penguin.
Eriksen, Stein Sundstøl (2011) "'State failure' in theory and practice: The idea of the state and the contradictions of state formation," *Review of International Studies*, 37 (1): 229–247.
Evans, Peter, B. (1997) "The eclipse of the state? Reflections on stateness in an era of globalization," *World Politics*, 50(1): 62–87.
Ervik, Rune (2005) "Changing normative bases of the Nordic welfare states? The case of pension provision in Norway," in N. Kildal and S. Kuhnle (eds) *Normative Foundations of the Welfare State: the Nordic Experience*, Abingdon: Routledge, pp. 171–190.
Eyraud, Corine (2013) *Le capitalisme au cœur de l'Etat: Comptabilité privée et action publique*, Bellecombe en Bauges: Éditions du Croquant.
Faden, Ruth R. and Tom L. Beauchamp (1986) *A History and Theory of Informed Consent*, New York: Oxford University Press, pp. 151–199.

212 Bibliography

Fainaru, Steve (2008) *Big Boy Rules: In the Company of America's Mercenaries Fighting in Iraq*, Cambridge: Da Capo Press.

Falkenrath, Richard A., Robert D. Newman and Bradley A. Thayer (1998) *America's Achilles' Heel: Nuclear, Biological and Chemical Terrorism and Covert Attack*- Cambridge, MA: MIT Press.

Fassin, Didier (2012) *Humanitarian Reason: A Moral History of the Present Times*, tr. by R. Gomme, Berkeley, CA and London: University of California Press.

Feigenbaum, Harvey and John Henig (1994) "The political underpinnings of privatization: A typology," *World Politics*, 46(1): 186.

Ferguson, James (1994) *The Anti-Politics Machine: 'Development,' Depoliticisation and Bureaucratic Power in Lesotho*, Minneapolis: University of Minneapolis Press.

Ferguson, Yale H. and Richard W. Mansbach (1996) *Polities: Authority, Identities, and Change*, Durham, NC: University of South Carolina Press.

Ferrell, J. E. (1990) "Who Owns John Moore's Spleen?" *Chicago Tribune*, February 18, online at: http://articles.chicagotribune.com/1990-02-18/features/9001140537_1_mo-cell-line-blood-cells-spleen/3.

Finnemore, Martha and Judith Goldstein (eds) (2013) *Back to Basics: State Power in a Contemporary World*, New York: Oxford University Press.

Fligstein, Neil (1990) *The Transformation of Corporate Control*, Cambridge, MA: The University of Harvard Press.

Flinders, Matthew V. and Martin J. Smith (eds) (1999) *Quangos, Accountability and Reform: The Politics of Quasi-Government*, New York: St. Martin's Press.

Foucault, M. (2008) *The Birth of Biopolitics: Lectures at the Collège de France, 1978–79*, ed. by M. Senellart, tr. by G. Burchell, New York: Palgrave Macmillan.

Foucault, M. (2007) *Security, Territory, Population: Lectures at the Collège de France, 1977–78*, ed. by M. Senellart, tr. by G. Burchell, New York: Palgrave Macmillan.

Foucault, M. (2003) "Governmentality," in Paul Rabinow and Nikolas Rose (eds) *The Essential Foucault*, New York: The New Press, pp. 229–245.

Foucault, M. (1978) *The History of Sexuality*, Vol. 1, New York: Pantheon Books.

Fourquet, Francois (1980) *Les Comptes de la puissance: Histoire de la comptabilité nationale et du plan*, Paris: Éditions Encres.

Frank, Forrest Russel (1974) *"US arms control policymaking: The 1972 biological weapons convention case,"* PhD dissertation, unpublished, Stanford University, November, p. 161.

Franklin, Simon and Jonathan Shepard (1996) *The Emergence of Rus 750–1200*, London: Longman.

Franklin, Sarah (2003) "Ethical Biocapital: New Strategies of Cell Culture," in Sarah Franklin and Margaret Locke (eds) *Remaking Life and Death: Toward an Anthropology of the Biosciences*, Santa Fe, NM: School of American Research Press, pp. 97–128.

Fredrickson, D. S. (1974) "A History of the Recombinant DNA Guidelines in the United States," *The Donald S. Fredrickson Papers*: 152, online at: http://profiles.nlm.nih.gov/FF/B/B/K/C.

Fried, Morton (1967) *The Evolution of Political Society*, New York: Random House.

Friedberg, Aaron L. (1996) "Review essay: Science, the Cold War, and the American state," *Diplomatic History*, 20(1): 112.

Friedman, Thomas (2005) *The World Is Flat: A Brief History of the Twenty-First Century*, New York: Farrar, Straus and Giroux.

Frye, Ellen L. (2005) "Private military firms in the new world order: How redefining 'mercenary' can tame the 'dogs of war'," *Fordham Law Review*, 73: 2607–2664.

Galbraith, John K. (1967) *The New Industrial State*, Princeton, NJ: Princeton University Press.
Galison, Peter (2004) "Removing knowledge," *Critical Inquiry*, 31(1): 231.
Gallas, Alexander, Lars Bretthauer, John Kannankulam and Ingo Stützle (eds) (2012) *Reading Poulantzas*, London: Merlin Press.
Gambetta, Diego (1993) *"The Sicilian Mafia: The Business of Private Protection*, Cambridge, MA: Harvard University Press.
Garapon, Antoine (2010) *La raison du moindre Etat: Le néolibéralisme et la justice*, Paris: Odile Jacob.
Gardey, Delphine (2008) *Ecrire, calculer, classer. Comment une révolution de papier a transformé les sociétés contemporaines (1800–1940)*, Paris: La Découverte.
Garthoff, Raymond L. (2000) "Polyakov's run," *Bulletin of Atomic Scientists*, 56(5): 37–40.
Geddes, Barbara (1994) *Politician's Dilemma: Building State Capacity in Latin America*, Berkeley, CA: University of California Press.
Gellman, Barton and Greg Miller (2013) "U.S. spy network's successes, failures and objectives detailed in 'black budget' summary," *The Washington Post*, August 29.
Gerschenkron, Alexander (1966) "Economic backwardness in historical perspective," in A. Gerschenkron (ed.) *Economic Backwardness in Historical Perspective*, Cambridge, MA: Harvard University Press.
Gilardi, Fabrizio (ed.) (2008) *Delegation in the Regulatory State: Independent Regulatory Agencies in Western Europe*, Cheltenham: Edward Elgar.
Gill, Stephen (1990) *American Hegemony and the Trilateral Commission*, New York: Cambridge University Press.
Gill, Stephen (ed.) (1993) *Gramsci, Historical Materialism and International Relations*, New York and London: Cambridge University Press.
Gill, Stephen (1995) "Globalization, market civilization and disciplinary neo-liberalism," *Millennium*, 24(3): 399–424.
Ginzburg, Carlo (2002) "To kill a Chinese Mandarin: The moral implications of distance," in C. Ginzburg, *Wooden Eyes: Nine Reflections on Distance*, tr. by Martin Ryle and Kate Soper, London: Verso, pp. 157–172.
Giovalucchi, Francois and Jean-Pierre Olivier de Sardan (2009) "Planification, gestion et politique dans l'aide au développement: Le cadres logique, outil et miroir des développeurs," *Revue Tiers Monde*, 198 (Feb.): 383–406.
Glaberson, William (2010) "Newburgh terrorism case may set a line for entrapment," *New York Times*, June 15, online at: www.nytimes.com/2010/06/16/nyregion/16terror.html.
Glyn, Andrew (2007) *Capitalism Unleashed: Finance, Globalization, and Welfare*, New York: Oxford University Press.
Gompert, David C. and John Gordon IV (2008) *War by Other Means: Building Complete and Balanced Capabilities for Counterinsurgency*, Santa Monica, CA: RAND.
Goodman, Alan H., Deborah Heath, and M. Susan Lindee (2003) *Genetic Nature/Culture: Anthropology and Science Beyond the Two-Culture Divide*, Berkeley, CA: University of California Press.
Gorman, Siobhan (2008) "NSA's domestic spying grows as agency sweeps up data," *The Wall Street Journal*, March 10, online at: http://homepage.mac.com/imfalse/chapel_annex/NSAs_Domestic_Spying_Grows_As_Agency_Sweeps_Up_Data_WSJ.pdf.

Gould, Robert and Nancy D. Connell (2008) "The public health effects of biological weapons," in Barry S. Levy and Victor W. Sidel (eds) *War and Public Health*, Oxford: Oxford University Press.

Gowan, Peter (1999) *The Global Gamble: Washington's Faustian Bid for World Dominance*, London: Verso Books.

Gramsci, Antonio (1991) *Gefängnishefte* [Prison Notebooks], ed. by K. Bochmann and W. F. Haug, Hamburg: Argument Verlag.

Graz, Jean-Christophe (Winter2001) "Beyond states and markets: Comparative and global political economy in the age of hybrids," *Review of International Political Economy*, 8(4): 739–748.

Graz, J.-C. (2008) "Hybrids and regulation in the global political economy," *Competition and Change*, 10(2): 230–245.

Graz, J. C. (2004) "Quand les normes font la loi: Topologie intégrée et processus différenciés de la normalisation internationale," *Revue internationale*, 35(2): 233–260.

Green, Mark and Ralph Nader (1973) "Economic regulation vs. Competition: Uncle Sam the Monopoly Man," *The Yale Law Journal*, 82(5): 871.

Greenwald, Glenn (2013) "On security and liberty," *The Guardian*, online at: www.theguardian.com/commentisfree/series/glenn-greenwald-security-liberty.

Grossman, Andrew (2001) *Neither Dead Nor Red: Civilian Defense and American Political Development During the Early Cold War*, New York: Routledge.

Gunn, John Alexander Wilson (1969) *Politics and the Public Interest in the Seventeenth Century*, London: Routledge.

Habermas, Jürgen (1970) *Toward a Rational Society: Student Protest, Science, and Politics*, Boston, MA: Beacon Press.

Habermas, Jürgen (1975) *Legitimation Crisis*, Boston, MA, Beacon Press.

Habermas, Jürgen (1989, 1995) *The Structural Transformation of the Public Sphere: An Inquiry into a Category of Bourgeois Society* [original ed. 1962], tr. by Thomas Burger with the assistance of Frederick Lawrence, Cambridge, MA: MIT Press.

Haggerty, Kevin D. and Richard V. Ericson (2000) "The surveillant assemblage," *British Journal of Sociology*, 51(4): 605–622.

Hall, Rodney Bruce and Thomas J. Biersteker (eds) (2003) *The Emergence of Private Authority in Global Governance*, New York: Cambridge University Press.

Hallström, Kristina Tamm (2004) *Organising International Standardisation: ISO and the IASC in Quest of Authority*, Cheltenham: Edward Elgar.

Halperin, Morton H. (1974) *Bureaucratic Politics and Foreign Policy*, Washington, DC: Brookings Institution.

Halperin, Sandra (2004) *War and Social Change in Modern Europe: The Great Transformation Revisited*, Cambridge: Cambridge University Press.

Harper, Richard (1998) *Inside the IMF: An Ethnography of Documents, Technology and Organisational Action*, San Diego, CA: Academic Press.

Hart, Oliver (1995) *Firms, Contracts and Financial Structure*, Oxford: Clarendon Press.

Harvey, D. (1989) *The Condition of Postmodernity*, Oxford: Blackwell Publishing.

Harvey, D. (2007) *A Brief History of Neoliberalism*, New York: Oxford University Press.

Heaton, J. Ricou (2005) "Civilians at war: Re-examining the status of civilians accompanying the armed forces," *Air Force Law Review*, 57: 157–208.

Hély, Matthieu (2009) *Les métamorphoses du monde associative*, Paris: PUF.

Henig, Jeffrey (1989/90) "Privatization in the United States: Theory and practice," *Political Science Quarterly*, 104(4): 649–670.

Hertog, Steffan (2004) "Building the body politic emerging corporatism in Saudi Arabia," *Chroniques yéménites*, 12, online at: http://cy.revues.org/index187.html.
Hertog, S. (2007) "Shaping the Saudi state: Human agency's shifting role in rentier-state formation," *International Journal of Mideast Politics*, 39(4): 539–563.
Hester, Rebecca (2014) "Those against whom society must be defended: Mexican Migrants, Swine Flu, and Bioterrorism" (article in preparation).
Hibou, B. (ed.) (2004; first published in French, 1999) *Privatizing the State*, tr. by Jonathan Derrick, London: Hurst; New York: Columbia University Press.
Hibou, Béatrice (2009) "Bureaucratie néolibérale," intervention at the second European congress of the FASOPO, February 6, online at: www.fasopo.org/reasopo.htm#rencontres.
Hibou, B. (2014) *The Bureaucratization of the World in the Neoliberal Era*, London: Verso.
Hibou, B. (2004) "From privatising the economy to privatising the state: An analysis of the continual formation of the state," in B. Hibou (ed.) *Privatizing the State*, London: Hurst; New York: Columbia University Press.
Hibou, B. (1998) "The Political Economy of the World Bank's Discourse in Africa: From Economic Catechism to Missionary Deeds (and Misdeeds)', tr. by Janet Roitman, Les Etudes du CERI, no. 39, online at: www.ceri-sciences-po.org/publica/etude/etude39a.pdf.
Hibou, B. and O. Vallée. (December2006) "Energy of Mali, or the Paradoxes of a 'Resounding Failure'," AFD working paper, no. 37, online at: www.fasopo.ort/publications.
Higate, Paul (2011) "Cat-food and Clients: Gendering the Politics of Protection in the Private Militarized Security Company," SPAIS working paper, no. 08-11, online at: www.bristol.ac.uk/media-library/sites/spais/migrated/documents/higate-08-11.pdf.
Higate, P. (2012) "'Cowboys and professionals': The politics of identity work in the private and military security company," *Millennium*, 40(2): 321–341.
Hindess, Barry (2000) "Citizenship in the international management of populations," *American Behavioural Scientist*, 43(9): 1486–1497.
Hintze, Otto (1975) "Military organization and the organization of the state," in O. Hintze (ed. F. Gilbert) *The Historical Essays of Otto Hintze*, Oxford: Oxford University Press.
Hirsch, Joachim (2005) *Materialistische Staatstheorie: Transformationsprozesse des kapitalistischen Staatensystems*, Hamburg: VSA.
Hirsch, Michael (2006) "The NSA's overt problem: So many conversations, so few clues to the terrorists' chatter," *The Washington Post*, January 1: B01, online at: www.washingtonpost.com/wp-dyn/content/article/2005/12/30/AR2005123001594.html.
Hirschman, Albert O. (1945) *National Power and the Structure of Foreign Trade*, Berkeley, CA: University of California Press.
Hirschman, A. O. (1977) *The Passion and the Interests. Political Arguments for Capitalism before Its Triumph*, Princeton, NJ: Princeton University Press.
Hirst, Paul and Grahame Thompson (1999) *Globalization in Question*, Cambridge: Polity Press.
Hobson, John M. (2011) "What's at stake in the neo-Trotskyist debate? Towards a non-Eurocentric historical sociology of uneven and combined development," *Millennium*, 40(1): 147–166.

Bibliography

Hodge, Graeme and Carsten Greve (eds) (2005) *The Challenge of Public-Private Partnerships: Learning from International Experience*, Cheltenham and Northampton, MA: Edward Elgar.

Hogan, Michael J. (2000) *A Cross of Iron: Harry S. Truman and the Origins of the National Security State, 1945–1954*, New York: Cambridge University Press.

Hogle, Linda (2003) "Life/Time warranty: Rechargeable cells and extendable lives," in Sarah Franklin and Margaret Locke (eds) *Remaking Life and Death: Toward and Anthropology of the Biosciences*, Santa Fe, NM: School of American Research Press, pp. 61–96.

Hogwood, Brian W. (1995) "The 'growth' of quangos: Evidence and explanations," *Parliamentary Affairs*, 48(2): 207–225.

Honneth, Axel (1991) *The Critique of Power: Reflective Stages in a Critical Social Theory*, Cambridge, MA: MIT Press.

Hood, Christopher (1994) *Explaining Economic Policy Reversals*, Buckingham: Open University Press.

Hood, C. (1991) "A public management for all seasons?" *Public Administration* 69(1): 3–19.

Hood, C., O. James, G. Peters and C. Scott (eds) (2004) *Controlling Modern Government. Variety, Commonality and Change*, Cheltenham: Edward Elgar.

Hook, Gregory (1990) "The rise of the Pentagon and US state building: The defense program as industrial policy," *The American Journal of Sociology*, 96(2): 359.

Horkheimer, Max and Theodor W. Adorno (1991) *Dialectic of Enlightenment*, New York: Continuum.

Houppert, Karen (2008) "Another KBR rape case," *Nation*, 8 April.

Hearings before the Select Committee to Study Governmental Operations with Respect to Intelligence Activities of the United States Senate (1976) *Intelligence Activities, Senate Resolution 21*, Ninety-Fourth Congress, First Session, Vol. 1: Unauthorized Storage of Toxic Agents, September 16, 17, and 18, 1975, Washington, DC: US Government Printing Office.

Huntington, Samuel P. (1996) *The Clash of Civilizations and the Remaking of World Order*, New York: Simon & Schuster.

Hurt, Shelley L. (2011) "The Military's Hidden Hand: Examining the Dual Use Origins of Biotechnology in the American Context, 1969–1972," in Fred Block and Matthew Keller (eds) *State of Innovation: The US Government's Role in Technology Development*, Boulder, CO: Paradigm Publishers, pp. 31–56.

Hurt, Shelley L. (2010) "Science, Power and the State: United States Foreign Policy, Intellectual Property Law, and the Origins of Agricultural Biotechnology, 1969–1994," PhD dissertation, New School for Social Research, New York.

IAO (2003) "Report to Congress Regarding the Terrorism Information Awareness Program" (responding to Consolidated Appropriations Resolution, 2003, no. 108-7, Division M, §111(b), online at: www.globalsecurity.org/security/library/report/2003/tia-di_report_20may2003.pdf.

ICIJ (2002) "Marketing the new 'dogs of war'," Centre for Public Integrity, online at: www.publicintegrity.org.

ICRC (2008) "The Montreux Document: On pertinent international legal obligations and good practices for states related to operations of private military and security companies during armed conflict," Geneva, online at: www.icrc.org/eng/resources/documents/publication/p0996.htm.

Jackson, Patrick Thaddeus and David H. Nexon (1999) "Relations before states: Substance, process and the study of world politics," *European Journal of International Relations*, 5(3): 291–332.
Jacob, Jean-Pierre and Philippe Lavigne-Delville (eds) (1994) *Les Associations paysannes en Afrique: Organisation et dynamiques*, Paris: Karthala.
Jacoby, H. (1973; first published in German, 1969) *The Bureaucratization of the World*, tr. by Eveline L. Kanes, Berkeley, CA: University of California Press.
Janssen, Katleen (2012) "Open government data and the right to information: Opportunities and obstacles," *Journal of Community Informatics*, 8(2): online at: www.ci-journal.net/index.php/ciej/article/view/952/954.
Jayasuriya, Kanishka (2005) "Economic Constitutionalism, Liberalism and the New Welfare Governance," Asia Research Centre working paper no. 121, Perth, Western Australia: Murdoch University.
Jen, Stephen (March 3, 2007) "How big could sovereign wealth funds be by 2015?" briefing note, Morgan Stanley, London: Morgan Stanley Global Research.
Jenkins, H. W., Jr. (2010) "Google and the search for the future," *The Wall Street Journal*, Aug. 14, online at: http://online.wsj.com/article/SB10001424052748704901104575423294099527212.
Jennings, Charles (2006) "Battlefield between the ears," *Nature*, 443 (Oct.): 911.
Jessop, Bob (2014) "Repoliticizing depoliticization: Theoretical preliminaries on some responses to the American fiscal and Eurozone debt crises," *Policy & Politics*, 14(2): 207–223.
Jessop, Bob (2007) *State Power: A Strategic-relational Approach*, New York and London: Cambridge University Press.
Johns, F. (1994) "The invisibility of the transnational corporation: An analysis of international law and legal theory," *Melbourne University Law Review*, 19(4): 893–923.
Johnson, Simon (2007) "The rise of sovereign wealth funds," *Finance & Development*, (IMF), 44(3): 3.
Jones, Daniel Stedman (2012) *Masters of the Universe: Hayek, Friedman, and the Birth of Neoliberal Politics*, Princeton, NJ: Princeton University Press.
Jones, Rhys, Jessica Pykett and Mark Whitehead (2011) "Governing temptation: Changing behavior in an age of libertarian paternalism," *Progress in Human Geography*, 35(4): 483–501.
Kaldor, Mary (1998) *New and Old Wars: Organized Violence in a Global Era*, Cambridge: Polity Press, pp. 3–33.
Kaldor, Mary (ed.) (2000) *Global Insecurity*, London: Pinter.
Kaplan, Frederick I. (1954) "The decline of the Khazars and the rise of the Varangians," *American Slavic and East European Review*, 13(1): 1–10.
Kaplan, Robert D. (1994) "The coming anarchy," *Atlantic Monthly*, February.
Katznelson, I. (2006) "At the court of chaos: Political science in an age of perpetual fear," Presidential Address, Annual American Political Science Association Convention, Columbia University.
Katznelson, I. (2013) *Fear Itself: The New Deal and the Origins of Our Times*, New York: Liverlight Publishing.
Kay, Lily E. (1993) *The Molecular Vision of Life*. New York: Oxford University Press.
Kenney, Martin (1988) *Biotechnology: The University-Industrial Complex*, New Haven, CT: Yale University Press.

Kierpaul, Ian (2008) "The rush to bring private military contractors to justice: The mad scramble of Congress, lawyers, and law students after Abu Ghraib," *University of Toledo Law Review*, 39(2): 407–435.

Kingston-Mann, Esther (2003) "Deconstructing the romance of the bourgeoisie: A Russian Marxist path not taken," *Review of International Political Economy*, 10(1): 93–117.

Kinsey, Christopher (2006) *Corporate Soldiers and International Security: The Rise of Private Military Companies*, London: Routledge.

Kirshner, Jonathan (1998) "Political economy of security studies after the cold war," *Review of International Political Economy*, 5(1): 64–91.

Klare, Michael T. (1996) *Rogue States and Nuclear Outlaws: America's Search for a New Foreign Policy*, New York: Hill and Wang, pp. 39–53.

Kobishchanow, Yurii M. (1987) "The phenomenon of 'gafol' and its transformation," in Claessen and van de Velde (eds) *Early State Dynamics*, Leiden: Brill, pp. 108–128.

Koppell, Jonathan G. S. (2003) *The Politics of Quasi Government. Hybrid Organisations and the Dynamics of Bureaucratic Control*, Cambridge: Cambridge University Press.

Kosar, Kevin R. (2008) "The quasi government: Hybrid organizations with both government and private sector legal characteristics," Congressional Research Services, paper no. 539 (updated January 31), online at: http://digitalcommons.ilr.cornell.edu/key_workplace/539.

Krahmann, Elke (2010) *States, Citizens and the Privatization of Security*, Cambridge: Cambridge University Press.

Krasner, Stephen D. (1984) "Approaches to the state: Alternative conceptions and historical dynamics," *Comparative Politics*, 16(2): 223–246.

Krasner, S. D. (ed.) (1983) *International Regimes*, Ithaca, NY: Cornell University Press.

Krasner, S. D. (1999) *Sovereignty: Organized Hypocrisy*, Princeton, NJ: Princeton University Press.

Krige, John (2006) *American Hegemony and the Postwar Reconstruction of Science in Europe*, Cambridge, MA: MIT Press, pp. 11–12.

Kütting, G. and Ronnie D. Lipschutz (eds) (2009) *Power, Knowledge and Governance in International Environmental Policy*, London: Routledge.

Lakoff, Sanford and W. Erik Bruvold (1990) "Controlling the qualitative arms race: The primacy of politics," *Science, Technology & Human Values*, 15(4): 382–411.

Lanning, M. Lee (2002) *Blood Warriors: American Military Elites*, New York: Presidio Press.

Lanning, M. Lee (2005) *Mercenaries: Soldiers of Fortune from Ancient Greece to Today's Private Military Companies*, New York: Ballantine Books.

Lasswell, Harold (1941) "The garrison state," *The American Journal of Sociology*, 46(4): 455–468.

Latham, Andrew (2002) "Warfare transformed: A Braudelian perspective on the revolution in military affairs," *European Journal of International Relations*, 8(2): 231–266.

Leander, A. (2005) "The power to construct international security: On the significance of private military companies," *Millennium*, 33(3): 803–826.

Leander, A. (2006) "Security as business: Towards a technical, de-politicized use of force," in S. Albrecht, R. Braun and T. Held (eds) *Einstein Weiterdenken: Verantwortung des Wissenschaftlers und Frieden im 21. Jahrhundert* (Thinking Beyond

Einstein Scientific Responsibility and Peace in the 21st Century), Frankfurt: Peter Lang, pp. 333–355.

Leander, A. (2007) "Regulating the role of PMCs in shaping security and politics," in S. Chesterman and C. Lehnardt (eds) *From Mercenaries to Markets: The Rise and Regulation of Private Military Companies*, Oxford: Oxford University Press, pp. 49–64.

Leander, A. (2009a) "Securing sovereignty by governing security through markets," in R. Adler-Nissen and T. Gammeltoft-Hansen (eds) *Sovereignty Games: Instrumentalising State Sovereignty in Europe and Beyond*, London: Palgrave, pp. 151–170.

Leander, A. (2009b) "The privatization of security," in M. Dunn Cabelty and V. Mauer (eds) *The Routledge Handbook of Security Studies*, London and New York: Routledge, pp. 200–210.

Leander, A. (2010a) "Commercial security practices," in P. Burgess (ed.) *Handbook of New Security Studies*, London and New York: Routledge, pp. 208–216.

Leander, A. (2010b) "Practices (re)producing orders: Understanding the role of business in global security governance," in Morten Ougaard and Anna Leander (eds) *Business and Global Governance*, London: Routledge, pp. 57–78.

Leander, A. (2010c) "The paradoxical impunity of private military companies: Authority and the limits to legal accountability," *Security Dialogue*, 41(5): 467–490.

Leander, A. (2011) "Risk and the fabrication of apolitical, unaccountable military markets: The case of the CIA "killing program," *Review of International Studies*, 37 (5): 1–16.

Leander, A. (2012) "What do codes of conduct do? Hybrid constitutionalization and militarization in military markets," *Global Constitutionalism*, 1(1): 91–119.

Leander, A. (ed.) (2013a) *Commercialising Security: Political Consequences for European Peace Operations*, New York: Routledge.

Leander, A. (2013b) "Marketing security matters: Undermining de-securitization through acts of citizenship," in Guillaume and Huysmans (eds) *Security and Citizenship: The Constitution of Political Being*, London and New York: Routledge.

Leander, A. and S. Christopher (2013) "Conclusion," in A. Leander (ed.) *Commercialising Security: Political Consequences for European Peace Operations*, New York: Routledge, pp. 202–218.

Lefort, Claude (1960) "What is bureaucracy?" *Arguments*, no. 17; reprinted in *Eléments d'une critique de la bureaucratie*, 1979, Paris: Gallimard, pp. 271–307 and translated as "What is bureaucracy?" in John B. Thompson (ed./intro.) *The Political Forms of Modern Society: Bureaucracy, Democracy, Totalitarianism*, 1986, Cambridge, MA: MIT Press, pp. 89–121.

Leitenberg, Milton and Raymond A. Zilinskas (2012) *The Soviet Biological Weapons Program: A History*, Cambridge, MA: Harvard University Press.

Lenoir, Tim (2000) "All but war is simulation: The military-entertainment complex," *Configurations*, 8: 289–335.

Lesser, Lenard I., Cara B. Ebbeling, Merrill Goozner, David Wypij and David S. Ludwig (2007) "Relationship between funding source and conclusion among nutrition-related scientific articles," *PLOS Medicine*, 4(1): e5.

Levi-Faur, David (2009) "Regulatory capitalism and the reassertion of the public interest," *Policy and Society*, 27(3): 181–191.

Levi-Faur, D. and Jacint Jordana (eds) (2005) "The rise of regulatory capitalism: The global diffusion of a new order," *Annals of the American Academy of Political and Social Science*, 598 (March): 200–217.

Bibliography

Lewellen, Ted (1992) *Political Anthropology: An Introduction*, 2nd edition, Westport, CT: Bergin & Garvey.

Lichtblau, Eric and James Risen (2005) "Spy agency mined vast data trove, officials report," *New York Times*, December 24, online at: www.nytimes.com/2005/12/24/politics/24spy.html.

Lipietz, Alain (1985) Akkumulation, krisen und auswege aus der krise, *Prokla*, 15(1): 109–137.

Lipschutz, Ronnie D. (2009) *The Constitution of Imperium*, Boulder, CO: Paradigm Publishers.

Lipschutz, Ronnie D. and Heather Turcotte (2005) "Duct tape or plastic? The political economy of threats and the production of fear," in Betsy Hartmann, Banu Subramaniam and Charles Zerner (eds) *Making Threats: Biofears and Environmental Anxieties*, Lanham, MD: Rowman & Littlefield.

Lipschutz, Ronnie D. (2008) "Imperial warfare in the naked city: Sociality as critical infrastructure," *International Political Sociology*, 3(3): 204–218.

Lipschutz, Ronnie D. and Rebecca J. Hester (2014) "We are the Borg! Human assimilation into cellular society," in M.G. Michael and Katina Michael (eds) *Uberveillance and the Social Implications of Microchip Implants: Emerging Technologies*, Hershey, PA: IGI Global.

Lipsky, John (2009) "The global downturn and oil markets," IMF presentation, 18 March, online at: www.imf.org/external/np/speeches/2009/pdf/031809.pdf

Liptak, Adam (2013) "Justices, 9–0, bar patenting human genes," *New York Times*, June 13, online at: www.nytimes.com/2013/06/14/us/supreme-court-rules-human-genes-may-not-be-patented.htm.

Littlewood, Michael (2010) "Pre-funding a government's future financial obligations: The New Zealand superannuation case study," *New Zealand Economic Papers*, 41 (1): 91–111.

Locke, John (1698) "Of Property," *Second Treatise of Government*, Ch. V, §27, London: Awnsham Churchill.

London, J. Phillip (2008) *Our Good Name: A Company's Fight to Defend its Honour and Get the Truth Told About Abu Ghraib*, Washington, DC: Regenery Publishing.

Love, John (1986) "Max Weber and the theory of ancient capitalism," *History and Theory*, 25(2): 152–172.

Lowenthal, Richard (1976) "Social transformation and democratic legitimacy," *Social Research*, 43(2): 246.

Ludwig, Gundula, Birgit Sauer and Stefanie Wöhl (eds) (1985) *Staat und Geschlecht, Grundlagen und aktuelle Herausforderungen feministischer Staatstheorie*, Baden-Baden: Nomos.

Lynch, Tony and A. J. Walsh (2000) "The good mercenary," *Journal of Political Philosophy*, 8(2): 133–153.

Lyon, David (2001) *Surveillance Society: Monitoring Everyday Life*, Buckingham: Open University Press.

Lyons, Richard D. (1970) "Nixon reorganizing vast federal science complex," *New York Times*, November 1: 1.

MacAskill, Ewen (2013) "NSA paid millions to cover PRISM compliance costs for tech companies," *The Guardian*, August 23, online at: www.theguardian.com/world/2013/aug/23/nsa-prism-costs-tech-companies-paid.

Macherey, Pierre (2009) *De Canguilhem à Foucault: La force des normes*, Paris: La Fabrique.

Machiavelli, Niccoló (2004/1532) *The Prince*, London: Penguin, pp. 51.
MacKenzie, Donald (2006) *An Engine, Not a Camera: How Financial Models Shape Markets*, Cambridge, MA: MIT Press.
Macpherson, C. B. (1962) *The Political Theory of Possessive Individualism: Hobbes to Locke*, Oxford: Oxford University Press.
Macpherson, C. B. (1978) *Property: Mainstream and Critical Positions*, Toronto: University of Toronto Press.
Macrae, Fiona (2010) "DNA fingerprinting techniques 'can sometimes give the wrong results'," *Daily Mail*, August 18, online at: www.dailymail.co.uk/sciencetech/article-1302156/DNA-fingerprinting-wrong-results.html.
Magnet, Shashana Amielle (2011) *When Biometrics Fail: Gender, Race and the Technology of Identity*, Durham, NC: Duke University Press.
Maier, Charles S. (2006) *Among Empires: American Ascendancy and Its Predecessors*, Cambridge, MA: Harvard University Press.
Malkki, Liisa H. (1995) *Purity and Exile: Violence, Memory and Cosmology among Hutu Refugees in Tanzania*, Chicago, IL: University of Chicago Press.
Mandel, Robert (2001) "The privatization of security," *Armed Forces and Society*, 28 (1): 129–151.
Mann, James (2004) *Rise of the Vulcans: The History of Bush's War Cabinet*, New York: Penguin Books.
Mann, James (2007) "A shining model of wealth without liberty," *Washington Post*, May 20: B01.
Mann, Michael (1984) "The autonomous power of the state: Its origins, mechanisms and results," *Archives Européennes de Sociologie*, 26(2): 185–213.
Mann, Michael (2012) *The Sources of Social Power, Vol. 2: The Rise of Classes and Nation States, 1760–1914*, 2nd edition, New York: Cambridge University Press.
Markusen, Ann, Sean DiGiovanna and Michael C. Leary (eds) (2003) *From Defense to Development? International Perspectives on Realizing the Peace Dividend*, London and New York: Routledge.
Marshall, Didier (2008) "Justice et LOLF: Quelle compatibilité?," *Revue française de finances publiques*, 103 (Sept.): 25–35.
Marteau, Theresa and Martin Richards (eds) (1999) *The Troubled Helix: Social and Psychological Implications of the New Human Genetics*, Cambridge: Cambridge University Press.
Martin, Janet (2007) *Medieval Russia, 980–1585*, 2nd edition, Cambridge: Cambridge University Press.
Marx, Karl (1981) *Capital: A Critique of Political Economy*, vol. 3, New York: Penguin.
Marx, Karl ([1848] 2004) "The German ideology," in J. Rivkin and M. Ryan (eds) *Literary Theory: An Anthology*, 2nd edition, Cambridge, MA: Blackwell Publishing, pp. 653–658.
Mazzetti, Mark (2014) "Behind clash between CIA and Congress, a secret report on interrogations," *New York Times*, March 7, online at: www.nytimes.com/2014/03/08/us/politics/behind-clash-between-cia-and-congress-a-secret-report-on-interrogations.html.
Mazzetti, M. and Eric Schmitt (2014) "US militant, hidden, spurs drone debate," *New York Times*, February 28, online at: www.nytimes.com/2014/02/28/world/asia/us-militant-hidden-spurs-drone-debate.html.

McAllister, Ian and Donley T. Studlar (1989) "Popular versus elite views of privatization: The case of Britain," *Journal of Public Policy*, 9(2): 157–178.
McConnell, Mike (2007) "Overhauling intelligence," *Foreign Affairs*, 86(4): 49–58.
McNally, David (2009) "From financial crisis to world slump: Accumulation, financialisation, and the global slowdown," *Historical Materialism*, 17(2): 35–83.
McNeil, DonaldG., Jr. (2012) "Bird flu paper is published after debate," *New York Times*, June 21, online at: www.nytimes.com/2012/06/22/health/h5n1-bird-flu-research-that-stoked-fears-is published.html.
Mellanby, Kenneth (1947) "Medical experiments on human beings in concentration camps in Nazi Germany," *British Medical Journal*, 1(4490): 148–150.
Melman, Seymour (1970) *Pentagon Capitalism: The Political Economy of War*, New York: McGraw-Hill.
Mendelsohn, Everett (1993) "The politics of pessimism: Science and technology circa 1968," *Sociology of the Sciences Yearbook*, 17: 151–173.
Boot, M. (2009) "The mercenary debate," *The American Interest*, May/June, online at: www.the-american-interest.com/article-bd.cfm?piece=597.
Merrien, F.-X. (1999) "La nouvelle gestion publique: Un concept mythique," *Lien social et politique*, 41 (Spring): 95–103.
Meselson, Matthew S. and Julian Perry Robinson (2008) "The Yellow Rain Affair: Lessons from a discredited allegation," in Anne L. Clunan, Peter R. Lavoy and Susan B. Martin (eds) *Terrorism, War, or Disease? Unraveling the Use of Biological Weapons*, Stanford, CA: Stanford University Press, pp. 72–96.
Michaels, Jon D. (1999) "Focused logistics in 2010: A civil sector force multiplier for the operational commander," *Air Force Journal of Logistics*, 23(2): 14–17.
Michaels, Jon D. (2008) "All the president's spies: Private–public intelligence partnerships in the War on Terror," *California Law Review*, 96: 904.
Milliard, Todd S. (2003) "Overcoming post-colonial myopia: A call to recognize and regulate private military companies," *Military Law Review*: 1–95.
Mitchell, Dean (2010) *Governmentality: Power and Rule in Modern Society*, London: SAGE Publications.
Mitchell, Timothy (1991) "The limits of the state: Beyond statist approaches and their critics," *American Political Science Review*, 85(1): 77–96.
Moore, Kelly (2008) *Disrupting Science: Social Movements, American Scientists, and the Politics of the Military, 1945–1975*, Princeton, NJ: Princeton University Press.
Morgan, Lewis Henry ([1877] 1963) *Ancient Society, or Researches in the Lines of Human Progress from Savagery through Barbarism to Civilization*, ed. by Eleanor Bruke Leacock, Cleveland, OH: Meridian.
Moskos, Charles C. (2000) "Toward a postmodern military: The United States as a paradigm," in C. Moskos, J. Williams and D. Segal (eds) *The Postmodern Military: Armed Forces After the Cold War*, Oxford: Oxford University Press, pp. 14–31.
Mucchielli, Laurent (2002) *Violences et insécurité. Fantasmes et réalités dans le débat français*, Paris: La Découverte.
Munzer, Stephen R. (1990) *A Theory of Property*, Cambridge: Cambridge University Press.
Murphy, Craig N. and Joanne Yates (2009) *The International Organization for Standardization: Global Governance Through Voluntary Consensus*, London: Routledge.
Naim, Moises (2013) *The End of Power: From Boardrooms to Battlefields and Churches to States—Why Being in Charge isn't What it Used to Be*, New York: Basic Books.

Nakashima, Ellen (2008) "Travelers' laptops may be detained at border," *The Washington Post*, August 1: A01, online at: www.washingtonpost.com/wp.srv/content/article/2008/08/01/laptops.html.
National Research Council, Committee on Mapping and Sequencing the Human Genome (2000) *Mapping and Sequencing the Human Genome*, Washington, DC: National Academy Press.
National Research Council (2008) *Protecting Individual Privacy in the Struggle Against Terrorists: A Framework for Program Assessment*, Washington, DC: National Academies Press, online at: https://epic.org/misc/nrc_rept_100708.pdf.
Neumann, Iver B. (2004) "Beware of organicism: The narrative self of the state," *Review of International Studies*, 30(2): 259–267.
Neumann, I. B. and Ole Jacob Sending (2010) *Governing the Global Polity: Rationality, Governmentality, Practice*, Ann Arbor, MI: University of Michigan Press.
Nightingale, Paul and Paul Martin (2004) "The myth of the biotech revolution," *Trends in Biotechnology*, 22(11): 564–569.
Nixon, Richard M. (1970) "Annual Message to the Congress on the State of the Union," January 22, *The American Presidency Project* (Gerhard Peters and John T. Woolley), online at: www.presidency.ucsb.edu/ws/?pid=2921.
Nixon, Richard M. (1973) "Message to the Congress Transmitting Reorganization Plan 1 of 1973 Restructuring the Executive Office of the President," January 26, *The American Presidency Project* (Gerhard Peters and John T. Woolley), online at: www.presidency.ucsb.edu/ws/index.php?pid=3819.
Noonan, Thomas (2001) "The Khazar Qaghanate and its impact on the early Rus' state: The translation imperii from Itil to Kiev," in Anatoly Mikhailovich Khazanov and Andre Wink (eds) *Nomads in the Sedentary World*, Richmond: Curzon.
Norland, Rod (2012) "Risks of Afghan war shift from soldiers to contractors," *New York Times*, February 11, online at: www.nytimes.com/2012/02/12/world/asiaafghan-war-risks-are-shifting-to-contractors.html.
NOU (Norges offentlige utredninger) (1983) *Petroleumsvirksomhetens framtid* (The petroleum industry's future), Oslo.
NOU (Norges offentlige utredninger) (1988) *Norsk økonomi i forandring: Perspektiver for nasjonalformue og økonomisk politikk i 1990-årene* (The Norwegian economy in transition: Perspectives for national and economic policy in the 1990s), Oslo.
Novoseltsev, Anatoliy P. (1982) "*K voprosu ob odnom iz drevneyshikh titulov russkogo knyazya,*" in Istoriya SSSR, 4th edition.
Nye, Joseph S., Jr. (2011) *The Future of Power*, New York: Public Affairs.
NYPD (New York Police Department) (n.d.) Intelligence Division & Counterterrorism Bureau, online at: www.nypdintelligence.com/.
Obama, Barack (2009) "Executive Order 13526—Classified National Security Information," December 29, *The American Presidency Project* (Gerhard Peters and John T. Woolley), online at: www.presidency.ucsb.edu/ws/?pid=87362.
Obama, Barack (2011) "Remarks by President Obama in Address to United Nations General Assembly," Office of the Press Secretary, September 21, online at: www.whitehouse.gov/the-press-office/2011/09/21/remarks-president-obama-address-united-nations-general-assembly
Obama, Barack (2010) "Remarks by the President at the Opening Plenary Session of the Nuclear Security Summit," April 13, online at: www.whitehouse.gov/the-press-office/remarks-president-opening-plenary-session-nuclear-security-summit.

O'Brien, Kevin (2000) "Private military companies and African security, 1990–1998," in A. Musah and K. J. Fayemi (eds) *Mercenaries: An African Security Dilemma*, London: Pluto Press, pp. 43–75.

O'Connor, James (1986) *Accumulation Crisis*, London: Blackwell Publishing.

Offe, Claus (1987) Die Staatstheorie auf der Suche nach ihrem Gegenstand. Beobachtungen zur aktuellen Diskussion, in *Jahrbuch zur Staats- und Verwaltungswissenschaft*, Baden-Baden: Nomos, pp. 309–320.

Offe, C. (updated edition, ed. by J. Borchert/S. Lessenich,2006) *Strukturprobleme des kapitalistischen Staates: Aufsätze zur politischen Soziologie*, Frankfurt: Campus.

Ogien, Albert (1995) *L'Espirit gestionnaire*, Paris: Éditions de l'EHESS.

Ogien, A. and S. Laugier (2010) *Pourquoi désobéir en démocratie?* Paris: La Découverte.

Olivier de Sardan, Jean-Pierre (2000) "La gestion communautaire sert-elle l'intérêt public?," *Politique africaine*, 80 (Dec.): 153–168.

Osgood, Kenneth A. (2000) "Form before substance: Eisenhower's commitment to psychological warfare and negotiations with the enemy," *Diplomatic History*, 24(3): 405–433.

Osgood, K. (2006) *Total Cold War: Eisenhower's Secret Propaganda Battle at Home and Abroad*, Lawrence: University of Kansas.

Owens, Patricia (2008) "Distinctions, distinctions: 'public' and 'private' force?" *International Affairs*, 84(5): 977–990.

Panitch, Leo and Martijn Konings (eds) (2009) *American Empire and the Political Economy of Global Finance*, Basingstoke and New York: Palgrave.

Panitch, Leo (2000) "The new imperial state," *New Left Review*, 2 (March): 5–20.

Parry, Bronwyn (2012) "Domesticating biosurveillance: 'Containment' and the politics of bioinformation," *Health and Place*, 18(4): 718–725.

Patton, Paul (1994) "MetamorphoLogic: Bodies and powers in a thousand plateaus," *Journal of the British Society for Phenomenology*, 25(2): 157–169.

Pelton, Robert Young (2006) *Licensed to Kill: Hired Guns in the War on Terror*, New York: Crown Publishers.

Peñafiel, Ricardo (2008) *L'événement discursif paupériste, lutte contre la pauvreté et redéfinition du politique en Amérique Latine, Chili, Mexique, Venezuela, 1910–2006*, doctoral thesis in political sciences, Université du Québec, Montréal, online at: www.fasopo.org/reasopo/jr/these_penafiel_vol1etvol2.pdf.

Percy, Sarah (2007) "Mercenaries: Strong norm, weak law," *International Organization*, 61(2): 367–397.

Peregrine, Peter N. (2007) "Archaeology and world-systems theory," *Sociological Inquiry*, 60(1): 486–495.

Perlstein, Rick (2008) *Nixonland: The Rise of a President and the Fracturing of America*, New York: Scribner.

Pierru, Frederic (2007) *Hippocrate malade de ses réformes*, Bellecombe-en-Beauge: Éditions du Croquant.

Polanyi, Karl ([1944, 1957] 2001) *The Great Transformation: The Political and Economic Origins of Our Time*, Boston, MA: Beacon Press and Paperback.

Porphyrigenitus, Constantine ([ca. 950] 1967) *De Administrando Imperio*, Washington, DC: Harvard University Press.

Poulantzas, Nicos ([1978] 2002) (quoted material from orig. German/Hamburg edition, 1978) *State, Power, Socialism*, London and New York: Verso.

President's Review Group on Intelligence and Communications Technologies (2013) "Liberty and Security in a Changing World: Report and Recommendations," Washington, DC: The White House, December 12, online at: www.whitehouse.gov/sites/default/files/docs/2013-12-12_rg_final_report.pdf.
Priest, Dana and William M. Arkin (2011) *Top Secret America: The Rise of the New American Security State*, New York: Little, Brown and Company.
Priest, Dana (2010) "US military teams, intelligence deeply involved in aiding Yemen on strikes," *The Washington Post*, January 27, online at: www.washingtonpost.com/wp-dyn/content/article/2010/01/26/AR2010012604239.html.
Procacci, Giovanna (1996) "La naissance d'une rationalité moderne de la pauvreté," in S. Paugam (ed.) *L'exclusion. L'état des savoirs*, Paris: La Découverte, pp. 405–416.
Pugliese, Joseph (2010) *Biometrics: Bodes, Technologies, Biopolitics*, New York: Routledge.
Pye, Lucian W. (1971) "The legitimacy crisis," in Leonard Binder (ed.) *Crises and Sequences in Political Development*, Princeton, NJ: Princeton University Press.
Pykett, Jessica (2012) "The new maternal state: The gendered politics of governing through behaviour change," *Antipode*, 44(1): 217–238.
Pynchon, Thomas (1973) *Gravity's Rainbow*, New York: Viking.
Radin, Margaret Jane (1996) *Contested Commodities: The Trouble with Trade in Sex, Children, Body Parts and Other Things*, Cambridge, MA: Harvard University Press.
Rakowsky, K. (2006) "Military contractors and civil liability: Use of the government contractor defense to escape allegations of misconduct in Iraq and Afghanistan," *Stanford Journal of Civil Rights & Civil Liberties*, 2(2): 366–397.
Ramo, Simon (1971a) "The coming social-industrial complex," the Third Annual Farfel Lecture, University of Houston, October 21, Houston, TX: University of Houston.
Ramo, Simon (1971b) "Toward a social-industrial complex," *Vital Speeches of the Day*, 38(3): 80–86.
Ramo, Simon (1972) "Technology and resources for business: Government-industry-science," delivered at the White House Conference on the Industrial World Ahead: A Look at Business, Washington, DC, February 7, reprinted in *Vital Speeches of the Day*, 38(10): 313–318.
Reid, Julian and Michael Dillon (2009) *The Liberal Way of War: Killing to Make Life Live*, New York: Routledge.
Relyea, Harold C. (2007) *National Emergency Powers*, Congressional Research Service, updated August 30, online at: http://ftp.fas.org/sgp/crs/natsec/98-505.pdf.
Renfrew, Colin and John Cherry (eds) (1986) *Peer Polity Interaction and Socio-Political Change*, Cambridge: Cambridge University Press.
Report Prepared for the Subcommittee on Science, Research and Technology of the Committee on Science and Technology (1976) *Genetic Engineering, Human Genetics, and Cell Biology: Evolution of a Technological Issue: DNA Recombinant Molecule Research (Supplemental Report II)*, House of Representatives, Ninety-Fourth Congress, Second Session, December 1976, Washington, DC: The US Government Printing Office: 59.
Riles, Annelise (ed.) (2006) *Documents; Artifacts of Modern Knowledge*, Ann Arbor: University of Michigan Press.
Riles, Annelise (2000) *The Network Inside Out*, Ann Arbor: University of Michigan Press.

Rimbert, Pierre (2004) "Les managers de l'insécurité: Production et circulation d'un discours sécuritaire," in L. Bonelli and G. Sainati (eds) *La machine à punir: Pratiques et discours sécuritaires*, Paris: L'Esprit frappeur, pp. 235–276.

Rizzi, Bruno (1985; first published in French, 1939) *The Bureaucratization of the World: The USSR: Bureaucratic Collectivism*, tr. and with an intro. by Adam Westoby, London: Tavistock.

Robinson, William I. (2001) "Social theory and globalization: The rise of a transnational state," *Theory and Society: Renewal and Critique in Social Theory*, 30(2): 157–200.

Roland, Alex (1985) "Science and war," *Osiris*, 2nd series, 1: 247–272.

Roland, Gerard with Foreword by Joseph E. Stiglitz (2008) *Privatization: Successes and Failures*, New York: Columbia University Press.

Rosanvallon, Pierre (1999; 1st edition, 1979) *Le capitalisme utopique: Histoire de l'idée de marché*, Paris: Le Seuil.

Rose, Carol M. (1994) *Property and Persuasion: Essays on the History, Theory, and Rhetoric of Ownership*, Boulder, CO: Westview.

Rose, Nikolas (2006) *The Politics of Life Itself: Biomedicine, Power, and Subjectivity in the Twentieth-First Century*, Princeton, NJ: Princeton University Press.

Rose, Nikolas (1999) *Powers of Freedom: Reframing Political Thought*, Cambridge: Cambridge University Press.

Rosenberg, Justin (2006) "Why is there no international historical sociology?" *European Journal of International Relations*, 12(3): 307–340.

Rosenfeld, Seth (2012) *Subversives: The FBI's War on Student Radicals, and Reagan's Rise to Power*, New York: Farrar, Straus and Giroux.

Roy, Benjamin (1995) "The Tuskegee syphilis experiment: Biotechnology and the administrative state," *Journal of the National Medical Association*, 87(1): 56–67.

Rudra, Sil and Peter J. Katzenstein (2010) "Analytic eclecticism in the study of world politics: Reconfiguring problems and mechanisms across research traditions," *Perspectives on Politics*, 8(20): 411–431.

Ruggie, John Gerard (1982) "International regimes, transactions, and change: Embedded liberalism in the postwar economic order," *International Organization*, 36(2): 379–415.

Russell, Edmund (2001) *War and Nature: Fighting Humans and Insects with Chemicals from World War I to Silent Spring*, New York: Cambridge University Press.

Ruwet, Coline (2011) "Towards a democratization of standards development? Internal dynamics of ISO in the context of globalization," *New Global Studies*, 5(2): online at: www.bepress.com/ngs/vol5/iss2/art1.

Sablowski, Thomas (2009) "Die Ursachen der neuen Weltwirtschaftskrise," *Kritische Justiz*, 42(2): 116–131.

Sahadi, Jeanne (2005) "Your identity…for sale," *CNNMoney.com*, May 9, online at: http://money.cnn.com/2005/05/09/pf/info_profit/index.htm.

Sainati, Gilles and Ulrich Schalchi (2007) *La décadence sécuritaire*, Paris: La Fabrique: 11.

Sales, Nathan Alexander (2010) "Share and share alike: Intelligence agencies and information sharing," *The George Washington Law Review*, 78(2): 279–352.

Samuel, Boris (2009) "Les cadres stratégiques de lutte contre la pauvreté et les trajectoires de la planification au Burkina Faso," *Sociétés politiques comparées*, 16 June, online at: www.fasopo.org/reasopo/n16/article.pdf.

Sassen, Saskia (2008) *Territory, Authority, Rights: From Medieval to Global Assemblages*, 2nd edition, Princeton, NJ: Princeton University Press.

Sauer, Birgit (2013) "'Putting patriarchy in its place': Zur Analysekompetenz der Regulationstheorie für Geschlechterverhältnisse," in Roland Atzmüller, Joachim Becker, Ulrich Brand, Lukas Oberndorfer, Vanessa Redak and Thomas Sablowski (eds) *Fit für die Krise? Perspektiven der Regulationstheorie*, Münster: Westfälisches Dampfboot, pp. 111–131.

Sauer, B. and S. Wöhl (2011) "Feminist perspectives on the internationalization of the state," *Antipode*, 43(1): 108–128.

Savage, Charles (2013) "Court tells reporter to testify in case of CIA date," *New York Times*, July 19: A1.

Savage, Charlie (2013) "NSA chief says surveillance has stopped dozens of plots," *New York Times*, June 18, online at: www.nytimes.com/2013/06/19/us/politics/nsa-chief-says-surveillance-has-stopped-dozens-of-plots.html.

Scahill, Jeremy (2008) *Blackwater: The Rise of the World's Most Powerful Mercenary Army*, New York: Nation Books.

Schemeil, Yves and Wolf-Dieter Eberwein (eds) (2009) *Normer le monde*, Paris: L'Harmattan.

Schméder, Geneviève (1998) "Global trends in military efforts and activities," in Mary Kaldor, Ulrich Albrecht and Geneviève Schméder (eds.) *The End of Military Fordism: Restructuring the Global Military Sector*, London: Bloomsbury Academic, pp. 11–35.

Schneider, Jane (1977) "Was there a pre-capitalist world system?" *Peasant Studies*, 6 (1): 20–29.

Schneiker, Andrea and Jutta Joachim (2012) "Of 'true professionals' and 'ethical hero warriors': A gender-discourse analysis of private military and security companies," *Security Dialogue*, 43(6): 495–512.

Schulman, Bruce J. and Julian E. Zelizer (2008) "The incomplete revolution," *The Chronicle of Higher Education*, March 21.

Schulman, B. J. (2001) *The Seventies: The Great Shift in American Culture, Society, and Politics*, New York: The Free Press.

Schwartz, Herman M. (2007) "Dependency or institutions? Economic geography, causal mechanisms and logic in understanding development," *Studies in Comparative International Development*, 42(1): 115–135.

Schwartz, H. M. (2001) "Round up the usual suspects: Globalization, domestic politics and welfare state change," in Paul Pierson (ed.) *New Politics of the Welfare State*, Oxford: Oxford University Press, pp. 17–44.

Schwartz, H. M. (1994) "Small states in big trouble: The Politics of state reorganization in Australia, Denmark, New Zealand and Sweden in the 1980s," *World Politics*, 46(4): 527–555.

Schwartz, H. M. (2010) *States versus Markets: The Emergence of a Global Economy*, 3rd edition, New York: Palgrave Macmillan.

"Science: Nixon v. the Scientists" (1973) *Time*, February 26, online at: www.time.com/time/magazine/article/0,9171,910590,00.html.

SCOTUSblog (2014) "Association for Molecular Pathology v. Myriad Genetics, Inc.," online at: www.scotusblog.com/case-files/cases/association-for-molecular-pathology-v-myriad-genetics-inc/.

Seaborg, Glenn T. (1960) *Scientific Progress, the Universities, and the Federal Government: Statement by the President's Scientific Advisory Committee*, Washington, DC: US Government Printing Office.

Seifert, Jeffrey W. (2004) "Data mining: An overview," CRS Report for Congress, updated May 3, online at: www.fas.org/irp/crs/RL31798.pdf.

Semple, Robert B., Jr. (1971) "Nixon counts on conversion of military facilities," *New York Times*, October 19: 28.
Servet, Jean-Michel (2006) *Banquiers aux pieds nus: La microfinance*, Paris: Odile Jacob.
Service, Ellman (1975) *Origins of the State and Civilization: The Processes of Cultural Evolution*, New York: Norton.
Setser, Brad (2008) "Good bye, petrodollars ...," December 8, online blog at: http://blogs.cfr.org/setser/2008/12/08/good-bye-petrodollars/.
Shane, Scott (2005) "US germ-research policy is protested by 758 scientists," *New York Times*, March 1.
Shaw, Martin (2000) *Theory of the Global State: Globality as an Unfinished Revolution*, New York: Cambridge University Press.
Shearer, David (1998) "Private military force and challenges for the future," *Cambridge Review of International Affairs*, 13(1): 80–94.
Shepherd, Bob (2008) *The Circuit: An Ex-SAS Soldier's True Account of One of the Most Powerful and Secretive Industries Spawned by the War on Terror*, London: Macmillan.
Sherry, Michael (1997) *In the Shadow of War: The United States since the 1930s*, New Haven, CT: Yale University Press.
Shiva, Vandana (1997) *Biopiracy: The Plunder of Nature and Knowledge*, Cambridge: South End Press Collective.
Sil, Rudra and Peter J. Katzenstein (June 2010) "Analytic eclecticism in the study of world politics: Reconfiguring problems and mechanisms across research traditions," *Perspectives on Politics*, 8(2): 411–431.
Silverstein, Ken (2000) *Private Warriors*, New York and London: Verso.
Singer, P. W. (2007) "Can't Win with 'Em, Can't Go to War without 'Em: Private Military Contractors and Counterinsurgency," Policy Paper no. 4, Foreign Policy at Brookings, Washington, DC: The Brookings Institution.
Singer, P. W. (2001/2) "Corporate warriors: The rise of the privatized military industry and its ramifications for international security," *International Security*, 26(3): 186–220.
Singer, P. W. (2007) *Corporate Warriors: The Rise of Privatized Military Industry*, Ithaca, NY: Cornell University Press.
Skelcher, Christopher (1998) *The Appointed State: Quasi-Governmental Organizations and Democracy*, Buckingham: Open University Press.
Skloot, Rebecca (2010) *The Immortal Life of Henrietta Lacks*, New York: Random House.
Skowronek, Stephen (1997) *The Politics Presidents Make: Leadership from John Adams to Bill Clinton*, Cambridge, MA: Belknap Press.
Slee, Tom (2012) "Seeing like a geek," Out of the Crooked Timber (blog), June 25, online at: http://crookedtimber.org/2012/06/25/seeing-like-a-geek/.
Smith, Bruce L. R. (1990) *American Science Policy Since World War II*, Washington, DC: Brookings Institution, p. 91.
Smith, Henry E. (2008) "Governing water: The semicommons of fluid property rights," *Arizona Law Review*, 50(2): 445–478.
Smith Hughes, Sally (2001) "Making dollars out of DNA: The first major patent in biotechnology and the commercialization of molecular biology, 1974–1980," *Isis*, 92(3): 541–575.

Smith, Merritt Roe (1985) "Introduction," in Merritt Roe Smith (ed.) *Military Enterprise and Technological Change: Perspectives on the American Experience*, Cambridge, MA: MIT Press, pp. 1–37.
Sparrow, Bartholomew H. (1996) *From the Outside In: World War II and the American State*, Princeton, NJ: Princeton University Press.
Spearin, Christopher (2001) "Private security companies and humanitarians: A corporate solution to securing humanitarian spaces?" *International Peacekeeping*, 8(1): 20–43.
Spearin, Christopher (2008) "Private, armed and humanitarian? States, NGOs, international private security companies and shifting humanitarianism," *Security Dialogue*, 39(4): 363–382.
Spicer, Tim (1998) 'Interview with Lt. Col. Tim Spicer," *Cambridge Review of International Affairs*, 13(1): 165–173 .
Spicer, Tim (1999) *An Unorthdox Soldier: Peace and War and the Sandline Affair*: Edinburgh: Mainstream.
Spiro, David (1999) *The Hidden Hand of American Hegemony*, Ithaca, NY: Cornell University Press.
Spruyt, Hendrik (2002) "The origins, development, and possible decline of the modern state," *Annual Review of Political Science*, 5: 142.
Stanger, Allison (2009) *One Nation Under Contract: The Outsourcing of American Power and the Future of Foreign Policy*, New Haven, CT: Yale University Press.
Stanley, Amy Dru (2008) *From Bondage to Contract: Wage, Labor, Marriage and the Market in the Age of Slave Emancipation*, Cambridge: Cambridge University Press.
Starr, Paul (1987) "The limits of privatization," in Steve Hanke (ed.) *Prospects for Privatization*, New York: Academy of Political Science, p. 132.
Starr, Paul (1988) "The meaning of privatization," *Yale Law and Policy Review*, 6(1): 6–41.
Stein, Gil (1999) *Rethinking World Systems: Diasporas, Colonies, and Interaction in Uruk Mesopotamia*, Tucson, AZ: University of Arizona Press.
Stein, Judith (2011) *The Pivotal Decade: How the United States Traded Factories for Finance in the Seventies*, New Haven, CT: Yale University Press.
Stern, Fritz (1977) *Gold and Iron: Bismarck, Bleichroeder, and the Building of the German Empire*, New York: Knopf.
Stever, H. Guyford (1980) "Science advice: Out of and back into the White House," in William T. Golden (ed.) *Science Advice to the President*, New York: Pergamon Press, pp. 71–72.
Steward, Julian H. (1955) *Theory of Culture Change*, Urbana, IL: University of Illinois Press.
Strange, Susan (1998) *States and Markets*, 2nd edition, London: Bloomsbury Academic.
Strange, Susan (1989) "Toward a theory of transnational empire," in Ernst Otto Czempiel and James N. Rosenau (eds) *Global Changes and Theoretical Challenges: Approaches to World Politics for the 1990s*, Lanham, MD: Lexington Books, pp. 161–176.
Sulzberger, A. G. (2010) "Defense cites entrapment in terror case," *New York Times*, March 17, online at: www.nytimes.com/2010/03/18/nyregion/18newburgh.html.
Sum, Ngai-Ling and Bob Jessop (2014) *Towards a Cultural Political Economy*, London: Edward Elgar.
Sunder Rajan, Kaushik (2006) *Biocapital: The Constitution of Postgenomic Life*, Durham, NC: Duke University Press.

Suri, Jeremi (2003) *Power and Protest: Global Revolution and the Rise of Détente*, Cambridge, MA: Harvard University Press.

Suri, Jeremi (2007) *The Global Revolutions of 1968*, New York: W. W. Norton & Company.

Susman, G. I. and S. O"Keefe (eds) (1998) *The Defense Industry in the Post-Cold War Era: Corporate Strategies and Public Policy Perspectives*, Oxford: Pergamon.

Tabarrok, Alex (2007) "The rise, fall and rise again of privateers," *The Independent Review*, 11(4): 565–577.

Taipale, K. A. (2003) "Data mining and domestic security: Connecting the dots to make sense of data," *Columbia Science and Technology Law Review*, 5(2): 1–83, online at: http://ssrn.com/abstract=546782.

Talbot, John (1995) "Regulation of world coffee markets: Tropical commodities and limits to globalization," in P. McMichael *Agrarian and Food Orders in the World Economy*, New York: Praeger.

Taliani, Simona (2011) "A credible past and a shameless body. History, violence and repetition of asylum women in Italy," *Sociétés politiques comparées*, 32, online at: www.fasopo.org/sites/default/files/article_n32.pdf.

Tanner, Ruth (2008) "Mercenary madness: Now muzzle new dogs of war," *Tribune Magazine*, 24 February.

Terrell, Paul (1979) "Private alternatives to public human Services administration," *The Social Service Review*, 53(1): 56–74.

Thaler, Richard and Cass Sunstein (2008) *Nudge: Improving Decisions about Health, Wealth, and Happiness*, New Haven, CT: Yale University Press.

Thatcher, Mark and Alec Stone Sweet (eds) (2003) *The Politics of Delegation*, London: Frank Cass.

Thévenot, Laurent (1997) "Un gouvernement par les norms: Pratiques et politiques des formats d'information," in B. Conein and L. Thévenot (eds) *Cognition et information en société*, Paris: Éditions de l'EHESS, pp. 204–242.

Thomas, Helene (2010) *Les Vulnérables. La démocratie contre les pauvres*, Bellecombes-en-Bauges: Éditions du Croquant.

Thomas, Peter D. (2009) *The Gramscian Moment: Philosophy, Hegemony and Marxism*, London: Brill Academic Publishing.

Thompson, Janice E. (1994) *Mercenaries, Pirates and Sovereigns: State-building and Extraterritorial Violence in Early Modern Europe*, Princeton, NJ: Princeton University Press.

Tiefer, Charles (2007) "The Iraq debacle: The rise and fall of procurement-aided unilateralism as a paradigm of foreign war," *University of Pennsylvania Journal of International Economic Law*, 29 (Fall): 1–56.

Tilly, Charles (1992) *Coercion, Capital and European States, AD 990–1992*, Cambridge, MA: Blackwell.

Tilly, C. (2004) "Social boundary mechanisms," *Philosophy of the Social Sciences*, 34 (2): 211–236.

Time (1973) "Nixon v. the scientists", February 26, online at: www.time.com/time/magazine/article/0,9171,910590,00.html.

Tranøy, Bent Sofus (2009) "Recommodification, residualism and risk: The political economy of housing bubbles in Norway," in H. Schwartz and L. Seabrook (eds) *The Politics of Housing Booms and Busts*, Basingstoke: Palgrave.

Traverso, Enzo (2009) *1914–1945: La guerre civile européenne*, 2nd edition, Paris: Stock.

Trosa, Sylvie (2006) "Vers un management public postbureaucratique," *Sociétal*, 53 (July): 44–49.
Truman, Edwin M. (2008) "A blueprint for sovereign wealth fund best practices," Peterson Institute for International Economics, policy brief no. PB08-3, (April), online at: www.iie.com/publications/pb/pb08-3.pdf.
Truman, Harry S. (1950) "Proclamation 2914—Proclaiming the Existence of a National Emergency," December 16, *The American Presidency Project* (Gerhard Peters and John T. Woolley), online at: www.presidency.ucsb.edu/ws/?pid=13684.
UN (2002) *Report of the Second Meeting of Experts on the Traditional and New Forms of Mercenary Activities (E/CN.4/2003/4)*, New York: UN, online at: www.ohchr.org/EN/Issues/Mercenaries/SRMercenaries/Pages/SRMercenariesIndex.aspx.
US Congress, Committee on Commerce, Science and Transportation (1977) *A Legislative History of the National Science and Technology Policy, Organization and Priorities Act of 1976*, Washington, DC: US Government Printing Office.
US Congress (1986) *A History of Science Policy in the United States, 1940–1985*, Report for the House Committee on Science and Technology Task Force on Science Policy, 99th Cong., 2nd session, Washington, DC: US Government Printing Office.
U.S. Customs and Border Protection Agency (2005) "National targeting center keeps terrorism at bay," *US Customs and Border Protection Today*, March, Washington, DC, online at: www.cbp.gov/xp/CustomsToday/2005/March/ntc.xml.
US Department of Health and Human Services and Department of Energy (1990) *Understanding Our Genetic Inheritance: The US Human Genome Project: The First Five Years*, Washington, DC: US Dept. of Health and Human Services.
US Treasury (June 21, 2007) "Remarks by Acting Under Secretary for International Affairs Clay Lowery on sovereign wealth funds and the international financial system," press release hp-47, online at: www.treasury.gov/press-center/press-releases/Pages/hp471.aspx.
Valcarce Lorenc, Frederico (2011) *La Sécurité privée en Argentine: Entre surveillance et marché*, Paris: Karthala.
van der Pijl, Kees (1984) *The Making of an Atlantic Ruling Class*, London: Verso.
Verkuil, Paul R. (2007) *Outsourcing Sovereignty: Why Privatization of Government Functions Threatens Democracy and What We Can Do About It*, New York: Cambridge University Press.
Vernadsky, George (1943) *Ancient Russia: A History of Russia*, vol. 1. Cambridge, MA: Harvard University Press.
Vernadsky, G. (1959) *The Origins of Russia*, Oxford: Clarendon.
Vettel, Eric J. (2008) *Biotech: The Countercultural Origins of an Industry*, Philadelphia: University of Pennsylvania Press.
Vogel, Steven Kent (1998) *Freer Markets, More Rules: Regulatory Reform in Advanced Industrial Countries*, Ithaca, NY: Cornell University Press.
Vu, Tuong (2010) "Studying the state through state formation," *World Politics*, 62(1): 150.
Wade, Nicholas (1976) "Guidelines extended but EPA balks," *Science*, 194(4262): 304.
Waldby, Catherine. (2002) "Stem cells, tissue cultures and the production of biovalue," *Health*, 6(3): 305–323.
Walker, R. B. J. (1992) *Inside/Outside: International Relations as Political Theory*, Cambridge: Cambridge University Press.
Walzer, Michael (2008) "Mercenary impulse: Is there an ethics that justifies Blackwater?" *The New Republic*, 12 March.

Walzer, M. (1983) *Spheres of Justice: A Defense of Pluralism and* Equality, New York: Basic Books.

Wampler, Robert A. (ed.) (2001) "National Security Decision Memorandum (NSDM) 35, "United States Policy on Chemical Warfare Program and Bacteriological/Biological Research Program, from Kissinger to Vice President, the Secretary of State, the Secretary of Defense, etc.," November 25, 1969, *The September 11th Sourcebooks*, vol. 3: BIOWAR, The Nixon Administration's Decision to End US Biological Warfare Programs, National Security Archive Electronic Briefing Book no. 58, October 25, online at: www2.gwu.edu/~nsarchiv/NSAEBB/NSAEBB58.

Wampler—a, Memorandum: Secretary Laird to Secretary of State, Assistant to the President for National Security Affairs, and Director, Central Intelligence Agency, Chemical Warfare and Biological Research—Terminology, December 9, 1969 "Secret."

Wampler—b, The Joint Chiefs of Staff's Military Services also "propose[d] $14.6 million for defensive equipment in FY 72." See Interdepartmental Political-Military Group, "Annual Review of United States Chemical Warfare and Biological Research Programs—as of November 1970," "SECRET" "GROUP 3, Downgraded at 12-year intervals; not automatically declassified.

Wampler—c, Memorandum: John N. Irwin II, Chairman to The President, Subject: "Annual Review of the US Chemical Warfare and Biological Research Program," February 4, 1971, document 24a.

Wampler—d, Litton received 14 contracts whereas Aerojet-General Corp. received 25 in the 1960s. Appendix I to Appendix C, "Fort Detrick RDTE Type Contracts": 89.

Wang, Jessica (1998) *American Science in and Age of Anxiety: Scientists, Anticommunism, and the Cold War*, Chapel Hill: North Carolina University Press.

Ward, Grace Faulkner (1954) "The English Danegeld and the Russian Dan," *American Slavic and East European Review*, 13(3): 299–318.

Warrick, Joby (2006) "The secretive fight against bioterror," *The Washington Post*, July 30: A1.

Washington, Harriet A. (2006) *Medical Apartheid: The Dark History of Medical Experimentation on Black Americans from Colonial Times to the Present*, New York: Random House.

Watt, Nicholas (2013) "NSA surveillance played little role in foiling terror plots, experts say," *The Guardian*, June 12, online at: www.theguardian.com/world/2013/jun/12/nsa-surveillance-data-terror-attack.

Weaver, Warren, Jr. (1969) "Laird backs Senate curb on chemical war agents," *New York Times*, August 10: A1.

Weber, Max (1978) *Economy and Society*, ed. by G. Roth and C. Wittich, Berkeley, CA: University of California Press.

Weber, M. (2003) *General Economic History*, tr. by F. H. Knight, Mineola, NY: Dover Publications; Newton Abbott: David and Charles; first published as *Wirtschaftsgeschichte* in 1923.

Weber, M. (1994) *Political Writings*, ed. by Peter Lassman and Ronald Speirs, Cambridge: Cambridge Press.

Weiser, Benjamin (2013) "Appeals court upholds convictions of men in Bronx synagogue plot," *New York Times*, August 23, online at: www.nytimes.com/2013/08/24/nyregion/appeals-court-upholds-convictions-of-men-in-bronx-synagogue-plot.html.

Weiss, Linda (1998) *The Myth of the Powerless State*, Cambridge: Polity Press.

Weiss, L. (2003) *States in the Global Econom: Bringing Democratic Institutions Back*, New York: Cambridge University Press.
Wendt, Alexander (2004) "The state as person in international theory," *Review of International Studies*, 30(2): 289–316.
Wendt, Alexander (1999) *Social Theory of International Politics*, Cambridge: Cambridge University Press.
Westwick, Peter J. (2003) *The National Labs: Science in an American System, 1947–1974*, Cambridge, MA: Harvard University Press.
White, Leslie (1949) *The Science of Culture*, New York: Farrar, Strauss and Giroux.
Wichterich, Christa (2013) "Gemeinschaflich Sorge tragen," Impulsreferat fur den politischen Salon der Heinrich-Böll-Stiftung, Donnerstag, March 18, Berlin, online at: http://commondsblog.files.wordpress.com/2008/04/wichterich-praesi-commonssalon.pdf.
Wolin, Sheldon (2010) *Democracy Incorporated: Managed Democracy and the Specter of Inverted Totalitarianism*, Princeton, NJ: Princeton University Press.
Wood, David Murakami (2013) "What is global surveillance? Towards a relational political economy of the global surveillant assemblage," *Geoforum*, 49 (Oct.): 317–326.
Wood, Ellen Meiksins (1995) *Democracy Against Capitalism: Renewing Historical Materialism*, New York: Cambridge University Press, pp. 19–48.
Worth, Robert F. (2005) "New York's hidden team on the trail of terrorism," *New York Times*, February 23, online at: www.nytimes.com/2005/02/23/nyregion/23analyst.htm.
Wright, Susan (1990) "Biotechnology and the military," in Steven M. Gendel, A. David Kline, D. Michael Warren and Faye Yates (eds) *Agricultural Bioethics: Implications of Agricultural Biotechnology*, Ames: Iowa State University Press, pp. 76–96.
Wright, Susan (1994) *Molecular Politics: Developing American and British Regulatory Policy for Genetic Engineering, 1972–1982*, Chicago, IL: University of Chicago Press.
Yankelovich, Daniel (1974) "A crisis of moral legitimacy?" *Dissent*, 21 (Fall), online at: www.danyankelovich.com/acrisis.pdf.
Yoon, Carol Kaesuk (1997) "Families emerge as silent victims of Tuskegee syphilis experiment," *New York Times*, May 12, online at: www.nytimes.com/1997/05/12/us/families-emerge-as-silent-victims-of-tuskegee-syphilis-experiment.html?pagewanted=all&src=pm.
Zamparelli, C. (1999) "Competitive sourcing and privatization: Contractors on the battlefield," *Air Force Journal of Logistics*, 23(3): 1–17.
Zarate, Juan Carlos (1998) "The emergence of a new dog of war: Private international security companies, international law and the new world disorder," *Stanford Journal of International Law*, 34(1): 75–162.
Zedner, Lucia (2006) "Liquid security: Managing the market for crime control," *Criminology and Criminal Justice*, 6(3): 267–288.
Ziemba, Rachel (2008) "Petrodollars: How to spend it," *RGE Monitor*, March 20, online at: www.economonitor.com/analysts/2008/03/20/petrodollars-how-to-spend-it/.
Zimmer, Carl (2013) "A family consents to a medical gift, 62 years later," *New York Times*, August 7, online at: www.nytimes.com/2013/08/08/science/after-decades-of-research-henrietta-lacks-family-is-asked-for-consent.html.
Zizek, Slavoj (2009) "20 years of collapse," *New York Times*, November 9.

Index

"The Circuit" 145

agricultural chemicals 113, 139
Arendt, H. 199
aristocracy 41–2
ArmorGroup 154
Ash Council 111–2
Asilomar Conference 116

Beckerian 126–30
bio-opticon 8, 161–2, 167, 173
biocapital/biovalue 179–80
biodefense 102, 120, 190
bioeconomy 184
Biological Research Program 28, 102, 105, 108–9, 119
biological sciences 8, 102, 106, 108, 112, 115, 179, 187, 189–91
Biological Warfare Program 28, 102, 105, 110–1, 117, 119, 184
Biological Weapons Convention (BWC) 28, 102, 108–9, 114–5, 117
biometrics 186, 189
biopiracy 180
biopolitics 181, 189
biosurveillance 179, 186–9
biotechnology 4, 6, 8,104, 112, 114, 176–81, 184, 186, 189, 190–1
Blackwater 1, 150
Bogota 153–4
Boot, M. 150
Brain Research through Advancing Innovative Neurotechnologies (BRAIN) 188
Bretton Woods 27, 80
bureaucracy 6, 59–62, 67–9, 71–2, 75, 138–9
bureaucratization 59–63, 66, 68–72, 74, 76
Bush, G. W. 29, 101, 160

capitalism 5, 8, 15, 39–40, 59, 63, 67–8, 79–80, 87, 92, 104, 177, 179, 182, 185, 195–7, 199
Carson, R. 184
causality 40, 57
Central Intelligence Agency (CIA) 37, 103, 114, 117, 120, 199
centralization 24, 90, 102, 104, 107, 119
Christianity 55
Church Committee 17, 117
Clinton, W. J. 101
collective investment funds 126
commodification 67, 71, 157
contractors 1, 6–7, 32, 143–5, 151, 185
convergence 3, 8, 60, 76, 195
conversion process 110–2, 114–5, 119, 184
Cox, R.W. 87
cyber-regime 162

data doppelganger (DD) 162, 171
data mining 162, 164; definition 166
decentralization 25, 29
depolitisation 73–4
deregulation 21, 24, 29, 32–3, 102, 140, 177
Détente 26, 28, 102, 108–9, 114
Diamond vs. Chakrabarty 185
DNA 115–8, 178–9, 181, 184–7, 191
Drucker, P. 24
dual-use 28, 112, 147, 178, 184
Dubridge, L. A. 105, 110–1, 113
Durkheim, E. 48–50
Dutch disease 125, 128–9, 138

Eisenhower, D. D. 105–8, 152
Engels, F. 47–9, 82
eugenics 178, 182

federal science policy 103–7, 111–2, 115, 119–20, 177, 181, 183–4
feudalism 41, 43
Ford, G. 6–7, 31–2, 115–9
Fordism 79–80, 83, 89–92, 95, 172
Foreign Service Surveillance Court 165
Fort Detrick 108, 110–2, 120
Foucault, M. 17–8, 59, 67, 72, 140, 172, 181
fragile states 39
Freedom of Information Act (FOIA) 20

genetic engineering 116, 118, 177, 179, 181, 190–1
Global Health Security Initiative (GHSA) 188–9
globalization 1, 34, 41, 56, 200,
Goldberg, L. J. 112–3
Gramsci, A. 6, 82, 86, 89
Green, M. 32–3
Greenwald, G. 164

Habermas, J. 15, 157
Haldeman, H. R. 23
Halperin, M. H. 105
Harvard University 29, 113
historic bloc 83, 87–8
HUMINT (human intelligence) 164
Huntington, S. 29–30
hybrid rule: definition of 2, 3, 4, 5, 6, 7, 8, 13–4, 16–7, 19, 24–5, 29, 31, 33–7, 59–61, 63, 69, 71, 74, 76, 79–81, 87, 102, 104, 106, 119–20, 144, 157–8, 161–2, 168, 172, 176, 190–1, 195–7, 199–201
hybrid security 143–4, 146, 153
hybrid state 7, 94, 123, 139–40, 146
hybrid war 161, 172
hybridity 7, 79–80, 143–46, 153, 155–8
hybridization: definition of 2, 4, 5, 6, 7, 14, 39–41, 45, 56–7, 79–96, 123–4, 126, 128, 133–7, 140, 175, 144, 178, 189, 191, 201

Imperial Presidency 36, 103
Information Awareness Office (IAO) 164
intellectual property rights (IPR) 80, 168
International Organization for Standardization (ISO) 64–6, 70
internationalization 79, 81, 87–8, 92, 95, 200
interventionism 60–3
Invisible Hand 149

Javits, J. J. 116–8
Johnson, L. B. 20

Kaplan, R. 52–3, 147
Katznelson, I. 34–5
Kennedy, E. M. 116–8
Khazars 52–3
Kiev 52–5
Kissinger, H. 20, 26, 105, 108, 112–3

Lacks, H. 177
laissez-faire capitalism 107
Lasswell, H. 34–5, 197, 201
LeFort, C. 59
legitimation crisis 15, 18–9, 90
liberalism 56, 60, 67, 72, 91, 129
Locke, J. 162, 168, 171–2
Lysenko Period 110

Mann, M. 17, 35, 196
Marx, K. 3, 47, 68–9, 82
mercantilism 39, 42
mercenarism 146, 148–53, 156–7
Michaels, J. D. 198
migration 47–8, 79, 88, 90
military markets 7, 144, 146–50, 152–7
military-industrial complex 7, 26, 31, 106, 153
Milliard, Major T. 149
Mills, C. W. 33, 35
molecular biology 8, 28, 102, 108–10, 113, 115–9, 177–8, 180, 182, 184, 189–90
molecular politics 181
Monsanto 113
Moore, J. 177, 185
Morgan, L. H. 46–50
Moyers, B. 20
Moynihan, D. P. 18, 26

Nader, R. 21, 32
National Biodefense Analysis and Countermeasures Center (NBACC) 120
national emergency 101, 103, 120
National Institutes of Health (NIH) 115–9, 184
National Research Council (NRC) 23
National Science Foundation (NSF) 112, 119, 184
national security 2, 5, 13–6, 27–9, 31–2, 34, 102–4, 106–7, 113, 115, 119–20, 176, 197–200
National Security Agency (NSA) 6, 103, 161, 164–5, 171, 195, 198

National Targeting Center of the U.S. Customs and Border Protection Agency 166
neoliberalism 1–2, 13, 15, 40, 56, 59–60, 67, 69, 72, 90, 172, 176–7, 195
New Federalism initiative 23–4
New Public Management 6, 56, 60–1, 63, 68–9, 75
Nixon Doctrine 24, 26
Nixon, R. M. 5–7, 18–9, 23–9, 31–2, 102, 104–12, 114–5, 117, 119, 178, 184–5
nomadic polities 45–7, 51, 54
Norway 7, 125–6, 128–32

Obama, B. 101, 160, 165–6, 188, 197, 200
offshore assets 132
ownership (land) 41–2, 44, 46, 55, 63, 71, 73; (state) 106, 113, 123–4, 136; (personal data) 162, 168–9, 170–1; (biology) 176, 185

patents 4, 113
patrimonial rule 40
PAYGO 124
peace dividend 146–7, 156
pension 7, 124–6, 129–32, 134, 136–7, 140, 189
People's Action Party (PAP) 135–6
periodization 3, 40, 57, 103
Pine Bluff Arsenal 110
pocket litter 8, 161–2, 166–9, 171
Polanyi, K. 67, 146
political capitalism 124, 126, 137–8, 140
political elites 2–3, 5, 14–7, 20–1, 23, 27–9, 36, 90, 120, 128
post-Fordist 6, 79–80, 90, 92, 94–6
Poulantzas, N. 6, 84–5
poverty 72–3
Powell, Jr., L. F. 29
power bloc 84, 86–7, 89, 92
Prince Sviatoslav 55
private military company 151, 154
private power 104
private property 43, 80, 91, 138, 162, 169, 171, 184, 186
privatisation 17, 60–1, 66, 71
privatization 1–7, 13–19, 24–33, 79, 90, 102, 104, 106–7, 115, 119, 124, 132, 140, 144, 176, 183–5, 195–201
Project Bioshield 102
property rights 44, 49, 51, 80, 91, 93, 125, 163, 168–9, 171–2, 186
psychological warfare campaigns 105

Public Health Service (PHS) 175, 179
public military 151, 157
public power 17, 40
public relations campaigns 105–6
public-private partnerships 2, 106
Pynchon, T. 124

quangos 41

Ramo, S. 13, 29, 31–2
Reagan, R. 20, 29
regulatory capitalism 161
Reorganization Plan No. 1112
reprivatization 25, 107
revolution in military affairs (RMA) 147
Risen, J. 199
Rockefeller Foundation 182
Roosevelt, F. D. R. 183
Russia (Russian state) 5, 40, 42–5, 51, 56, 128, 134, 141, 147, 161

Saudi Arabia 138–9
Science and Technology Exchange Program 114
secrecy 7, 28, 104–7, 115, 119–20, 123, 125, 199–200
security market 145, 153
security politics/security contracting 143
sedentary polities 45–7, 51–2, 54
Service, E. 50
Sierra Leone 144, 150
Singapore 7, 125, 128, 133, 134–6, 139
Smirnov, Colonel General Y. I. 114
Snowden, E. 161, 164, 173, 190, 195, 197, 200
SOBEL 144
social securitization 161, 199
social-industrial complex 31–2
sovereign wealth funds (SWFs) 7, 123–5, 131, 133, 137–8, 140–1
sovereignty 5, 41–2, 60, 69, 81, 89, 180–1, 201
Soviet Union 6, 20, 26, 28, 108–10, 113–4, 118, 147
Spicer, Lt. Colonel T. 150
Spruyt, H. 35–6
Starr, P. 16
state capitalism 94, 123, 140–1
Stein, G. 51
Stever, H. G. 112, 114–5
Strange, S. 17, 35

Temasek 133–4, 136
thalidomide scare 183

Thatcher, M. 1, 17, 19
Tilly, C. 40, 49–50
Total Information Awareness (TIA) 164
Tuskegee experiments 8, 175, 177–9

Utah facility 164

Vikings 52–3
Vu, Tuong 36

War on Cancer 108, 111, 185
Warrick, J. 120
weapons of mass destruction (WMDs) 101–2, 120, 169, 190

Weber, M. 6, 36, 48–9, 59, 67–9, 72, 124, 126, 137, 140
Weberian ethic 141
Weberian state 15, 39
Weberian value rationality 137
weberianism 62
World Trade Organization (WTO) 64, 93
World War Infinity (WWInf) 8, 161–2, 172

yoking 43, 172

zero tolerance 69–70

eBooks
from Taylor & Francis
Helping you to choose the right eBooks for your Library

Add to your library's digital collection today with Taylor & Francis eBooks. We have over 50,000 eBooks in the Humanities, Social Sciences, Behavioural Sciences, Built Environment and Law, from leading imprints, including Routledge, Focal Press and Psychology Press.

Choose from a range of subject packages or create your own!

Benefits for you
- Free MARC records
- COUNTER-compliant usage statistics
- Flexible purchase and pricing options
- 70% approx of our eBooks are now DRM-free.

Benefits for your user
- Off-site, anytime access via Athens or referring URL
- Print or copy pages or chapters
- Full content search
- Bookmark, highlight and annotate text
- Access to thousands of pages of quality research at the click of a button.

Free Trials Available

We offer free trials to qualifying academic, corporate and government customers.

eCollections
Choose from 20 different subject eCollections, including:

- Asian Studies
- Economics
- Health Studies
- Law
- Middle East Studies

eFocus
We have 16 cutting-edge interdisciplinary collections, including:

- Development Studies
- The Environment
- Islam
- Korea
- Urban Studies

For more information, pricing enquiries or to order a free trial, please contact your local sales team:

UK/Rest of World: **online.sales@tandf.co.uk**
USA/Canada/Latin America: **e-reference@taylorandfrancis.com**
East/Southeast Asia: **martin.jack@tandf.com.sg**
India: **journalsales@tandfindia.com**

www.tandfebooks.com